A THEATER OF OUR OWN

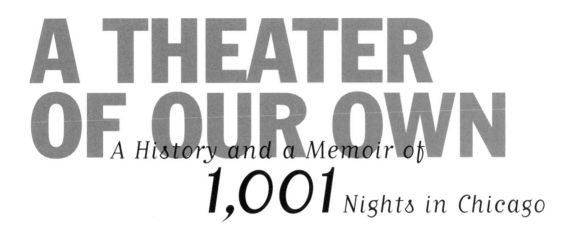

A THEATER OF OUR OWN

A History and a Memoir of
1,001 *Nights in Chicago*

RICHARD CHRISTIANSEN

Foreword by Brian Dennehy

NORTHWESTERN UNIVERSITY PRESS
EVANSTON, ILLINOIS

Northwestern University Press
Evanston, IL 60208-4170

Printed in Canada

10 9 8 7 6 5 4 3 2 1

ISBN 0-8101-2041-0

Library of Congress Cataloging-in-Publication Data
Christiansen, Richard.
    A theater of our own : a history and a memoir of 1,001 nights in
Chicago / Richard Christiansen ; foreword by Brian Dennehy.
      p. cm.
    Includes bibliographical references and index.
    ISBN 0-8101-2041-0 (alk. paper)
    1. Theater—Illinois—Chicago—History—19th century.
    2. Theater—Illinois—Chicago—History—20th century. I. Title.
PN2277.C4C57 2004
792'.09773'1109034—dc22
                                                          2004020389

Book design by Kim Bartko

PROGRAMS PICTURED ON THE ENDSHEETS ARE FROM THE COLLECTIONS OF ELAYNE LETRAUNIK, JAY MARSHALL, PATRICIA
MOORE, AND THE AUTHOR AND ARE USED BY PERMISSION OF *PLAYBILL*, THE LEAGUE OF CHICAGO THEATRES, AND THE
INDIVIDUAL THEATERS.

FOR MY PARENTS,

WHO WENT TO CHURCH AND TO THE THEATER

AND TOOK ME WITH THEM

CONTENTS

William Farnum and Neva Boyd,
Billy Murray and Mina Kolb.

Menasha Skulnik, Eubie Blake,
Noble Sissle, and Carol Burnett.

Richard Mansfield, Adelina Patti,
Minnie Maddern Fiske, and Molly Picon.

Sam Wanamaker and Eddie Foy,
Fay Templeton and Lorado Taft.

Viola Spolin, Tracy Letts,
Dankmar Adler, and *Bleacher Bums*.

Goodman, Woodman,
Reich, and Mosher.

Nussbaum, Mamet,
Maggio, and Falls.

Merritt and Franz and Joe Mantegna,
Frank Galati and Severn Darden.

Ramis and Radner and Oscar Brown,
Tom O'Horgan and Forrest Arden.

Belushi, Aykroyd, and Kazurinsky,
Danny Newman and William Pullinsi.

Lady Gregory and Percy Hammond,
Mummy Wrappings and Kingsley Day.

W. H. Macy, Meshach Taylor,
Jacobs and Casey and Ronna Kaye.

Rokko Jans, Linda Kimbrough,
Studs Terkel, and Whitford Kane.

Bella Itkin, James McVicker,
Dan Marble, and Nathan Lane.

Stuart Oken, Ron Dean,
Dennis Farina, and Elizabeth Rich.

Tom Aldredge and wife Theoni,
Joyce Piven and husband Byrne.

Billy Petersen, Zohra Lampert,
Jose Quintero, and Glenna Syse.

Malkovich, Metcalf, Sinise, and Cole,
Kinney, Landau, and Hedy Weiss.

Joan Allen and Lillian Russell,
Robert Motts and Maurice Browne.

Ivan Lazareff, Helena Modjeska,
Mia McCullough, and Arie Crown.

Hinky Dink Kenna, Bathhouse Coughlin,
Laura Dainty Pelham, and Esther Rolle.

The Booths, the Barrymores, the Belushis,
Beulah Bondi, and *American Buffalo*.

Okay, I'll stop now.

H. L. Mencken wrote in 1917, "I give you Chicago. It is not London and Harvard. It is not Paris-and-buttermilk. It is American in every chitling and sparerib, and it is alive from snout to tail." Chicago has changed in the last ninety years, of course, but it is still a riotous bouillabaisse of talent, hustle, and hard work. This restless, seeking joie de vivre has always been most apparent in Chicago theater, that rock-'em, sock-'em, in-your-face explosion of energy and brains.

My friend Richard Christiansen has written a loving and joyous celebration of one hundred seventy-five years of Chicago theater. As head critic for both the *Chicago Daily News* and the *Chicago Tribune,* he has had a front-row seat, literally and figuratively, for more than forty of those years, and his honest and insightful reporting has made a significant contribution to the development of modern Chicago theater. David Mamet, John Malkovich, Gary Sinise, Joan Allen, Laurie Metcalf, Bob Falls, Bill Petersen, and Aidan Quinn are only a few of the individuals who were encouraged by Christiansen early in their careers.

There was no group so small, no venue so forbidding, that he would not find himself climbing flights of stairs or descending into damp cellars to see what delights or disasters the latest group of young thespians would deliver. His enthusiasm for Steppenwolf Theatre a quarter century ago, for example, was in no small way responsible for that group's enormous success and the considerable impact it has had on the English-speaking theater.

When young people ask me how they can "break into" this business, and the phrase "break in" is all too appropriate, I always tell them to go to Chicago. Besides being a great place to live, there is a lot of theater going on, and if you can't get a job, you can always start your own theater. Everyone else does.

And if you're a really lucky young actor, or even an old one like me, there will be someone like Richard Christiansen sitting out there in the dark, his eyes twinkling with joy, ready to help you on your way. Even if he has to give you a little push in the right direction.

BRIAN DENNEHY

BRIAN DENNEHY *has been associated with theater in Chicago since 1985, when he played the old Wisdom Bridge Theatre in Ron Hutchinson's* Rat in the Skull. *Since then, he has appeared at Goodman Theatre, under Robert Falls's direction, in* Galileo, *by Bertolt Brecht (1986), Arthur Miller's* Death of a Salesman *(1998), and the Eugene O'Neill dramas* The Iceman Cometh *(1990),* A Touch of the Poet *(1996),* Long Day's Journey into Night *(2002), and* Hughie *(2004).*

WRITING ABOUT THEATER, YOU QUICKLY come to realize that the experience you're trying to describe already has vanished. In the living theater, the actors will never again give quite the same performance you saw, and the audiences will always be different. Once the present moment arrives, it zips into the past, unrepeatable.

That rare, precious, and frustrating quality sets the performing arts apart from movies, TV shows, recordings, and the printed word, where, though the viewers may change, the subject matter stays exactly the way it was, is, and ever will be. In the theater, you're sitting through a once-in-a-lifetime experience.

In a review, especially in the immediacy of a daily newspaper review, the goal is to capture this moment, at least to some degree, by giving the reader a sense of what it was like when you were there—and over the years, as the shows accumulate, to put those individual moments into the perspective of a larger time frame.

As time goes by, however, the sharp memory of a show fades, and the specific content of those reviews is forgotten, like yesterday's newspaper. Living in the moment, and concerned with the work just ahead, people in the theater often don't have time to have a sense of their past. And audiences, too, become hazy in recollecting the plays and the players that once were so fresh for them.

This book is an attempt to capture at least a little of the lightning in a bottle by setting down between covers the stories of some of the many people, events, and details that fit into the large picture of a rich history.

The story starts in 1837, a date I chose because it is the year in which Chicago was incorporated as a city and the year in which a troupe of

Backstage in 1982 at the Theatre Building, 1225 W. Belmont Avenue, as the Remains
Theatre actors prepare to go onstage for their production of Sam Shepard's *The Tooth
of Crime:* William L. Petersen (standing) with (seated from right to left) Alan Novak,
Natalie West, Amy Morton, and, getting his hair fixed, Gary Cole. More than twenty
years after this picture was taken, the cramped dressing room area in this classic off-
Loop theater space had changed not a whit.
RON BAILEY

traveling actors staged the first legitimate theater performance in the new city. From there, it moves on more or less chronologically to the present, with the first-person singular popping up in the early 1960s, when I began attending and reviewing the performing arts in Chicago on a professional basis.

All my life I've been eager to go to the theater, seeing it as neither an expendable entertainment nor a boring necessity. I've liked everything about it: the lobby talk and the intermission coffee and the buzz after the show. It is a communal experience without peer, something that unites you with your fellow audience members as you sit there and watch the story in front of you unfold.

It is my good fortune to be working in Chicago when the theater is telling a lot of terrific stories. My reward, in writing this book, came not only in retracing the territory I had covered in the *Chicago Daily News* and the *Chicago Tribune* for many years but in finding my way through areas that I had not previously explored. Digging into the immediate past of my first-hand knowledge and into a long ago past I had not known, I was struck again with the singular nature of theater in my sweet home Chicago, and it gave me great pleasure to learn so much more about it.

Chicago has been an important theater center for more than a century, and in the last few decades it has become a central, influential force in American drama, sending out significant plays and players into the great world. Writing about it now is more than a case of parochial pride. This is an essential (and fascinating) story of American theater.

My goal here has been to present an accurate account of that story, and to make the account a good read. Accuracy, particularly in relating the early years of theater, is a chancy business, and in cases where there is a question of different versions of a name or date, I've followed the journalism practice of relying on three confirming sources. Sometimes, my memory has not gibed with that of others. Carolyn Gordon, who was in the original cast of David Mamet's *Sexual Perversity in Chicago* in 1974, and who has an excellent memory, has a different recollection of the play's last scene than I do. But I treasure my remembrance, and I'll stick by it.

The problem with writing about theater in Chicago is that it resists comprehensiveness. There's so much of it, and there's no end to it. In

Front of house in 1984 at Steppenwolf Theatre, 2851 N. Halsted Street: off-Loop
audience members gather around the refreshment stand at intermission for a
performance of *Fool for Love,* by Sam Shepard.
LISA EBRIGHT, SPECIAL COLLECTIONS AND PRESERVATION DIVISION, CHICAGO PUBLIC LIBRARY

the 1970s, it was possible for one hyperactive person to pretty much
cover the beat. That's impossible now. There are too many people, too
many theaters, too many shows; and they all make up a jumble-tumble
of a living history, without a finish.

I've tried to make this a history that hits the big moments and the necessary data but does not read like a family newsletter or a "Principal
Products of Brazil" term paper. It is not the final word, but it's a start
on investigating a vast subject, a first word that I hope will lead to more
and more discussion by more and more people. I trust it has enough pertinent information and good storytelling to be enjoyed by both the
hometown folks who know it well and general readers with no connec-

tion to Chicago but with an interest in learning what happened to create such a teeming theater scene in this extraordinary city.

I've tried also to describe the big, essential characters and events of Chicago theater as I've seen them. What I cannot detail is the regular, ongoing reward of getting to know this theater community. I can sketch the highlights, but I cannot do justice to the 1,001 (and more) nights of surprise and pleasure in Chicago theaters.

I think of that shoebox of a storefront at 3450 N. Halsted Street where Philip LaZebnik and Kingsley Day, two recent graduates of Harvard University, put on six original musicals in their Chicago Premiere Society's season of 1977–78, including my favorite, *The Joy of Socks.* For *Mummy Wrappings,* when one scene called for a spooky lighting effect, Day and LaZebnik went to the back of the theater and turned flashlights on their actors.

I remember two Chicago actors, Guy Van Swearingen and Roslyn Alexander, giving a strong, humble beauty to their roles of damaged son and troubled mother in *Taking Care,* by Chicago playwright Mia McCullough, which Tim Hopper so sensitively directed in a production in 2003 at the Steppenwolf Garage.

I'm still shaken by the shock of pleasure I felt on a spring evening in 2003 in a second-floor church auditorium, watching TimeLine Theatre Company's premiere of *Hannah and Martin,* a complex, engrossing, world-class first play by Kate Fodor, with a stunning portrayal by the actress Elizabeth Rich of the philosopher Hannah Arendt as she grappled with her feelings toward Martin Heidegger, her mentor and lover and a Nazi sympathizer.

And I smile, automatically, when I recall Dale Benson, an actor I've watched since he was a juvenile, pulling so much heart and soul and hysterical laughter out of the character of the beleaguered widower in Gary Griffin's buoyant staging of *Loot,* by Joe Orton, at Writers' Theatre in 2000.

Just another night in the theater in Chicago.

RICHARD CHRISTIANSEN

A THEATER OF OUR OWN

From the earliest days of Chicago theater: two handbills for programs of drama, comedy, and variety at Rice's Theatre. Note the ticket prices.

Chapter 1

"A Thrilling Little Place"

IN 1838, WHEN HE WAS NINE, Joseph Jefferson III gave the first of what would be his hundreds of performances in the city of Chicago. The young actor and his parents had traveled to the city with a group of itinerant players who wanted to present a brief season of drama in a small theater space, the Rialto, set up on an upper floor of a former auction house at 8 S. Dearborn Street. The auditorium, thirty feet by eighty feet, was a crude affair; one customer called it "a den of a place, looking more like a dismantled gristmill than the temple of anybody." Most of the seats consisted of wooden planks, and a few freshly painted bits of canvas served as scenery and a curtain.

Moreover, the arrival of a band of theater folk in Chicago was viewed by some individuals as a blow to the community. One solid citizen, Grant Goodrich, a member of the Common Council, proclaimed theater "a menace to the moral welfare of the city." Benjamin Taylor, an early Chicagoan who attended performances in the new theater, wrote that its patrons consisted of "a small handful of half-breeds, a sprinkling of lieutenants from the army, one or two worn-out paymasters. The pit was full of sailors, with occasionally a wharf rat." And

Joseph Jefferson, about 1888

when these customers lustily applauded the action, or shouted crude remarks at the actors, "the spiders swung in their webs and the mice in walls were whist." However, Taylor noted, "For all that, those dingy old walls used to ring sometimes with readings fine enough to grace Thespis' temple, though there was a farce now and then somewhat broader than it was long."

For Jefferson, who recounted the occasion in his autobiography of 1889, it was a thrilling time, and the little theater, he believed, was "quite the pride of the city." He reveled in the furnishings of the new theater, which had a drop curtain showing "a medallion of Shakespeare, suffering from a severe pain in his stomach, over the center, with ONE TOUCH OF NATURE MAKES THE WHOLE WORLD KIN written under him," and "traps under the stage so convenient that Ophelia could walk from her grave to her dressing-room with perfect ease."

His troupe, he wrote, had left the East by boat on the Erie Canal and "turned our faces to the setting sun," counting themselves "among the first dramatic immigrants to the far West." When they finally arrived at their destination, "there in the morning light stands the little town of Chicago, containing two thousand inhabitants." (Actually, the city's population at that time had topped four thousand.)

Chicago, Jefferson found,

> had just turned from an Indian village into a thriving little place . . . people hurrying to and fro, frame buildings going up, board sidewalks going down, new hotels, new churches, new theatres, everything new . . . bright and muddy streets,—gaudy colored calicos,—blue and red flannel and striped ticking hanging outside the dry goods stores,—barrooms,—real estate offices,—attorneys-at-law,—oceans of them.
>
> With what delight the actors looked forward to the opening of a new theatre in a new town, where dramatic entertainments were still unknown—repairing their wardrobes, studying their new parts, and speculating on the laurels that were to be won!

The prose style here is somewhat inflated, but the pioneer spirit is genuine, and its unquenchable enthusiasm foreshadows the zest of discovery that, more than one hundred years later, was to fill the young artists who came to Chicago to open their own new frontiers and, in so doing, give the city an exciting jolt of theater life.

Jefferson himself returned to Chicago many times in his long career. Onstage since he was four, he played small parts in his first visit to Chicago. "I was the comic singer of this party," he wrote, "and 'small first villager,' now and then doing duty as a Roman senator at the back, wrapped in a clean hotel sheet with my head peering over the profile banquet tables."

For all of his career, he was a touring actor, affectionately known in Chicago as "Our Joe." He introduced his enduring stage vehicle *Rip Van Winkle* to the city in 1867, and in 1903, when at seventy-four he gave his final Chicago performance of that warhorse in Powers' Theatre on Randolph Street, he stepped to the front of the stage at play's close and proudly told the audience that he had first performed in their city sixty-five years before. He died in 1905, his name gradually edging into obscurity, but in 1968, when a band of theater professionals and enthusiasts wanted to pick a name of symbolism and tradition for the annual awards they planned to give for excellence in Chicago theater, they decided to call their group the Joseph Jefferson Awards Committee.

Joseph Jefferson in the title role of *Rip Van Winkle*
FROM *THE AUTOBIOGRAPHY OF JOSEPH JEFFERSON*

Chicago had seen bits and pieces of live entertainment—hypnotists, illusionists, circus acts, and the like— early in the nineteenth century, but it was not until 1837, a year before Joseph Jefferson's local debut, that the first legitimate theater production

The Sauganash Hotel, where it all began

FROM *HISTORY OF CHICAGO*, BY A. T. ANDREAS

was staged in the newly incorporated city. The producers were Harry Isherwood and Alexander McKenzie, gentlemen from the East, and the site was the dining room of the old Sauganash Hotel, just south of Lake Street near Market Street (later Wacker Drive, where a sidewalk plaque now calls attention to the historic spot). Once a lively community gathering place for singing, dancing, and making general whoopee, the place in 1837 was no longer such a central spot.

Isherwood, arriving in town in a pelting rain, had scouted the territory a few months earlier and wrote, "It was the most God-forsaken looking place it had ever been my misfortune to see. The mud was knee deep. No sidewalks, except here and there a small piece. No hall that could be used to any advantage for theatrical production."

Nevertheless, when the Sauganash owners moved their business to a better location, Isherwood saw an opportunity to set up a stage in the abandoned wood-frame/log-cabin hotel. "It was a queer-looking place," he recalled in his later years. "It had been a rough tavern, with an extension of about fifty feet in length added to it. It stood at some distance out on the prairie, solitary and alone."

In what was to become a great Chicago tradition, McKenzie and Isherwood, who was both his troupe's coproducer and its scenery painter, turned a place that was never intended for use as a playhouse (in this case the hotel's dining room), into a small (two-hundred-seat) theater and put on their show. The stage was a simple platform, the rough board seats were loosely arranged on floor level. It wasn't much, but it was enough to make a theater. "I arranged with the owners," Isherwood said, "and painted several pretty scenes."

Once arrived in the raw new city, one of the company members became so unruly that he was asked to leave the troupe. "Where can I go?" shouted the angry actor ("an Irishman," Isherwood carefully noted). "Here we are, with Lake Michigan roaring on one side and the bloody prairie wolves on the other."

Still, despite a heavy licensing fee of $125 imposed by the city, the producers mounted their short season, changing programs of melodramas, comedies, and musical variety nightly and charging 75 cents admission, before dispersing and bumping

Harry Isherwood, pioneer producer
FROM *HISTORY OF CHICAGO*, BY A. T. ANDREAS

on by prairie wagons to Galena and other sites farther west. The next spring, in 1838, they were back in Chicago, playing in the new Rialto, with the flaxen-haired little Joe Jefferson among their actors.

Gradually, as Chicago expanded, so did its theatrical activity. In 1839, the city directory listed eleven actors as residents. That same year, a touring company staged the first Chicago *Hamlet,* and theater reviews (and ads) appeared in the newspapers for the first time.

A cholera epidemic, quick to spread in those times of open sewage, and a national economic depression had severely reduced theater attendance through much of the 1840s, but on June 28, 1847, a premiere event in the city's history came with the opening of the first building specifically designed to house a real theater. Rice's Theatre, a two-story wooden

John B. Rice, actor-producer-mayor

FROM *HISTORY OF CHICAGO,* BY A. T. ANDREAS

structure measuring forty feet by eighty feet was built at 33 W. Randolph Street for four thousand dollars by John Blake Rice, a thirty-eight-year-old theater manager and former actor from upstate New York who, like so many other easterners coming into the young city on Lake Michigan, saw a potential for greatness in its unpaved streets.

Chicago now had almost seventeen thousand residents, and Rice, industrious and inventive in his marketing, touted his theater as a place of luxury and high-tone entertainment. No one would call his playhouse "that dirty old rat trap," as one disgruntled customer had labeled the makeshift old Rialto. By building his theater on Randolph, Rice established that street as the city's primary thoroughfare for downtown entertainment. And, despite belief among some solid citizens that theater was a tool of the devil and its customers were lowlifes, Rice heralded his playhouse as a home for the city's growing population of cultivated gentlemen and proper ladies, as well as the thousands of delegates from eighteen states who journeyed to Chicago to boost the commerce of the West at the expansionist River and Harbor convention of 1847. The high-priced boxes (each seat costing fifty cents) were carpeted and furnished with settees, and a report in the *Chicago Democrat,* the city's first newspaper, stated that a full view of the stage could be had from any seat in the house.

Rice's first, well-received twenty-two week season—staged in the summer and fall, when streets were less likely to be muddy—offered Chicago's first opera *(La Sonnambula),* as well as Shakespeare and popular plays of the period, presented by a resident company and visiting stars. Occasionally, when an actor was ill or detained, Rice himself would take the stage to fill in for the absent player.

James H. McVicker, who worked as Rice's stage manager, wrote of his employer, "He would act two or three important characters in a play, and if numbers were wanted he would throw a black cloak over his other dress and act the mob with a spirit that would appall the villain of the play." One night, McVicker recalled, when the actor portraying the title role in *Othello* failed to show up for curtain time, Rice took over the part and played it until the leading man finally arrived at the theater and finished the performance. That way, McVicker said, the audience got two Othellos for their money, one at 240 pounds (Rice) and the other at 150 pounds (the tardy actor).

In subsequent seasons, Rice's productions offered several heralded stars of the period, including Shakespearean specialists such as Edwin Forrest and Junius Brutus Booth, the comedian Dan Marble in his folksy perennial *Black-Eyed Susan,* and the blackface actor T. D. Rice (no relation to John) in *Jim Crow.* Standard fare for an evening's entertainment was a drama or melodrama, preferably with some special effects, such as a snow flurry, supplied by a stagehand who tossed down the fake flakes from above. This was followed by a farce and a selection of songs and comedy bits by members of the company. (Jefferson had excelled in these afterpieces when he first played Chicago. He sang well, and with members of the audience throwing coins at him, he sang many choruses.)

For his work in the pioneer city, John Rice was hailed as a civic leader, and his theater was established as a continuing point of civic pride. When it burned down in 1850, Rice built a bigger, better 1,300-seat, $11,000 brick building, with its entrance around the corner on Dearborn Street.

Rice—"this wise and honorable man," as Jefferson called him—retired from the theater in 1857 and successfully turned his energy to Republican politics. He was twice elected mayor of Chicago, serving from 1865 to 1869, thereby becoming the first and, so far, the only professional actor to hold the city's highest office. (His second inaugural address is notable for its blunt warning that, if the government wanted to improve its services, higher taxes would be necessary.) In 1873, he was elected representative from the First Congressional District in Illinois, an office he held when he died in 1874. Rice Street, just north of Chicago Avenue on the West Side, is named for him.

"Our city," said the *Chicago Democrat* when his theater opened, "is under great obligation to Mr. Rice for his enterprise. . . . In time, Chicago can boast of being ahead of any city twice its size in the theatrical line."

Rice's Theatre, the modest building in the middle, on Randolph Street

FROM *HISTORY OF CHICAGO,* BY A. T ANDREAS

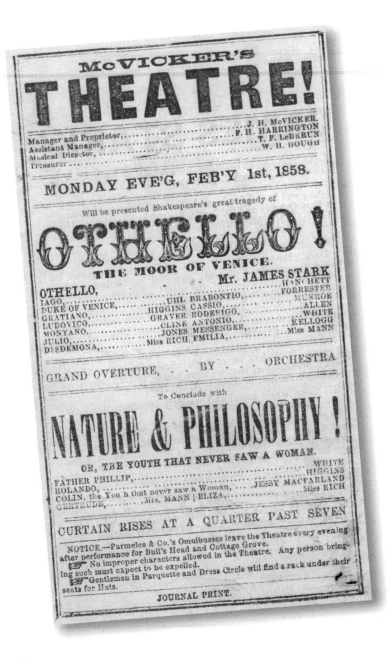

Handbill for an 1858 attraction at the McVicker's Theatre, featuring Shakespeare, a "grand overture," and a light comedy. At bottom, a stern warning against bringing "improper characters" into the theater.

Chapter 2

"Something Attractive at the McVicker's"

WITH THE COMING OF THE RAILROADS in the early 1850s, the people and the raw materials that were needed to construct a great city poured into Chicago; and, as the city expanded, as its dealing in grain and lumber and livestock turned it into a center of wealth and influence, it provided a home for places of arts and entertainment on a grand scale.

Near the end of 1857, with John B. Rice withdrawn from show business, James H. McVicker, who had gone from acting comic roles and stage managing in Rice's stock company to a career in theater management, opened his $85,000, 2,500-seat McVicker's Theatre at 25 W. Madison Street. It was an immediate success. After the November 5 premiere performance of the double bill *The Honeymoon* and *Rough Diamond*, with McVicker in the cast, the *Chicago Tribune* trumpeted, "For the first time since Chicago took rank as one of the first cities of the Union, she has a theater worthy of her citizens who patronize the drama."

McVicker himself was a passionate advocate for the glories of the theater. In "The Press, the Pulpit, and the Stage," an 1881 lecture delivered at the Central Music Hall, he went on the offensive against the onslaughts of criticism by members of the clergy and the newspapers.

McVicker's Theatre, opened in 1857
FROM *HISTORY OF CHICAGO*, BY A. T. ANDREAS

"Those of you who have read the carping criticism of the press or listened to the scathing anathemas of the pulpit," he said, "may be astonished when I tell you, without contradiction, that at no previous period in the history of the world has the stage ranked so high as it does at the present day. No one of the arts had made more progress. Today the public has established a severer regime of good taste and decorum, and the theater keeps pace with civilization, society, and government. There may be much to deplore now in it as in all other matters, but there is certainly comfort in the reflection that the conditions are infinitely better than ever before."

For years, the name McVicker's was synony-
mous with high-class theater in Chicago, a place
established as a magnet for the major stars and
shows of its time. "Would you like to go to the theater this evening?" asked a friend of the young hero
of Horatio Alger's *The Errand Boy*. "There is generally something attractive at the McVicker's."

The four-act, five-and-one-half-hour slapdash
musical extravaganza *The Black Crook* had its first
Chicago performance there in 1866. Sarah Bernhardt, who endeared herself to her audiences when
she called their city "the pulse of America," made
her Chicago debut there in 1881. Edwin Booth, who
later married McVicker's daughter Mary, and his
younger brother John Wilkes Booth both played
Richard III there (before the junior Booth was for-

James H. McVicker, actor-
manager-advocate

FROM *HISTORY OF CHICAGO*, BY A. T. ANDREAS

ever identified as a greater real-life villain). The young James O'Neill
from 1872 to 1874 was a member of the stock company there and played
opposite Edwin Booth in *Othello* and *Julius Caesar,* a famous pairing
that Eugene O'Neill, his son, much later recounted in the supreme autobiographical drama *Long Day's Journey into Night.*

For those who enjoyed "histrionics of local appeal" and "local talent" (as Bessie Louise Pierce noted in her *A History of Chicago*), there
were the successes of *The Chicago Fireman, 180 Monroe Street, Our
Eastern Cousin in Chicago*, and, in 1859, *Speculation,* written by a local
journalist, about the adventures of a wheeling-dealing real estate developer deliciously named Calderon Cornerlotte. Another popular show,
The Three Fast Men, featured scenery depicting the Illinois Central Rail-
road depot, views of Wells and Madison streets, and the Tremont House,
Chicago's leading hotel at the time.

McVicker, who occasionally returned to comic acting as the grave
digger in productions of *Hamlet,* managed his theater for thirty years,
rebuilding it after it was destroyed in the Great Chicago Fire of 1871
and remodeling it in 1885 under the direction of Dankmar Adler and
Louis Sullivan. After a fire ravaged it in 1890, the same architectural
team restructured the theater in their own mold, with Sullivan adding
beautiful decorative walls throughout the house. Replaced in 1922 by a

A FIELD TRIP TO THE THEATER

Eugene Field is best remembered today as the author of the beloved, sentimental poems "Wynken, Blynken, and Nod" and "Little Boy Blue," but in his popular "Sharps and Flats" column in the *Chicago Daily News* in the 1880s, he chatted about adult, urban matters, including the stage and the stage folk of the city.

The poet Harriet Monroe aptly called Field "an odd mixture of fineness and grossness," a man with a sense of humor that "went down to Rabelaisian depths." The gross aspect of his good humor is illustrated in the following story, from the January 14, 1886, edition of the *News,* in which the "colyumist," as he called himself, wrote of a night at the theater in a style that was then intended to be smart and satirical, but which now comes across as an incorrect and unforgivable put-down.

Field wrote about a friend, Dennis Malley, who had been to the McVicker's Theatre to see a production of *Othello,* with the Italian actor Salvini in the title role. "Well, Oi'll be dommed," Field had Malley say in a heavy Irish accent, "if that isn't the quarest piece Oi've iver sane. The dommed naygur is the bist one in the hull crowd." Moving on, Field, who

Eugene Field
S. L. STEIN, CHICAGO HISTORICAL SOCIETY (ICHI-36573)

also had attended the performance, noted that Salvini was indeed a fine actor but spoke his lines in Italian while the supporting cast all spoke English. He poked great fun at this hybrid "Dago drama," and he mocked its audience too: "We noted that a good many of the ladies present carried bouquets that looked like young asparagus beds, and that quite a number of the gentlemen were rigged out with spike-tail coats, and collars that chafed their jaws; we noticed that these persons applauded vociferously whenever the Dagos in the gallery gave the cue—that they smiled approvingly at one another and bore an expression of comfort and self-congratulation, as if, forsooth, they were mighty glad they could afford to patronize an entertainment which called for two dollars a seat."

Crosby's Opera House, 1865 to 1871
FROM *HISTORY OF CHICAGO*, BY A. T. ANDREAS

movie theater on the same site, its name finally vanished when the building was razed in 1984.

Quickly now, the power and prestige of the rising American city was reinforced by the splendor of its theaters, none of them more splendiferous than Crosby's Opera House, a six-hundred-thousand-dollar edifice at 10 W. Washington Street that was conceived by Uranus H. Crosby, a liquor distiller who, having made a fortune in the Civil War, turned his thoughts to giving Chicago a temple of the arts like no other. It was quite a sight, containing a three-thousand-seat auditorium, an art gallery, and several artists' studios, and its programming included everything from grand opera to high drama to low vaudeville. However, from its start in 1865, its aesthetics were overshadowed by its economics.

With no permanent company to keep the building always engaged, Crosby's relied for its income on touring troupes, and only those of the most expensive kind. The opening attraction, for example, was a season of Italian opera, led off by *Il Trovatore*. This was not enough to

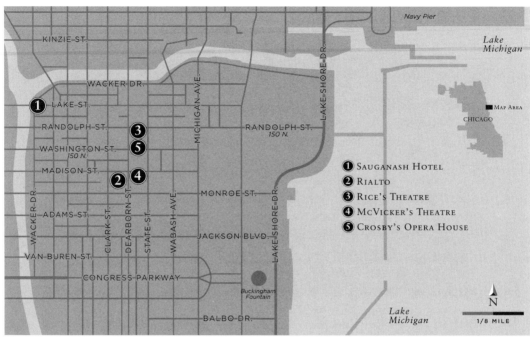

Early Chicago theaters
STEVE RAVENSCRAFT

keep the huge house solvent, so in 1866 Crosby sought to stave off financial failure with a unique scheme. He proposed to raffle off the opera house and its contents, at five dollars a share, with the top prize being the building itself. After much hoopla, 210,000 certificates were issued, all being sold except for 25,593 kept by Crosby, and the grand raffle was held on the stage of the Opera House. After minor doodads and several paintings from the art gallery had been awarded, ticket number 58,600 hit the jackpot. Winner of the Opera House was one A. H. Lee, an out-of-town mystery man who never appeared but who finally stated, through a letter to the *Chicago Republican* newspaper, that the illness of his wife had prevented him from coming to Chicago sooner. Once arrived, he added, he had decided to sell the Opera House back to Crosby for two hundred thousand dollars.

With this incredible and suspicious deal, Crosby made a nifty six-figure profit and retained his temple of the arts. The shows that went on there after the raffle included such varied events as an 1867 gala reception for Edward Payson Weston, a "walkist" who had bet (and won) ten thousand dollars on a wager that he could walk from Portland, Maine, to Chicago in twenty-six days, and the 1869 Republican National Convention that nominated Ulysses S. Grant for president of the United States.

In 1870, a touring visit from the buxom Lydia Thompson and Her British Blondes provoked the first (though certainly not the last) instance in Chicago history of an outraged performer going hell bent for revenge after a newspaper writer who had slammed the actor's work. Thompson, furious with an editorial in the *Chicago Times* that had proclaimed "Bawds at the Opera House! Where's the Police?" sought out *Times* editor Wilbur F. Storey and went at him with a riding whip, an act that cost her and three companions one hundred dollars in fines (later suspended).

More refined attractions of opera *(The Magic Flute),* drama *(Mary Stuart, Jane Eyre),* and even a local comedy (*Young Chicago,* which featured velocipede riding) continued to appear at Crosby's. Especially promising was the program announced for October 9, 1871. The auditorium, redecorated for eighty thousand dollars that summer, was to hold a concert by conductor Theodore Thomas, an orchestra of sixty musicians, and four soloists.

But it never happened. The Great Fire took care of that. The McVicker's, as well as Woods' Museum, Hooley's Opera House, the Dearborn Theater, and other prominent downtown houses, were destroyed by flames on October 9. Some, like the McVicker's, would rise again, and even grander new theaters would be built; but it was all over for Crosby's Opera House. "Its end," wrote the historian A. T. Andreas, "was absolute, for among the institutions obliterated from the earth forever by the fire was Crosby's Opera House."

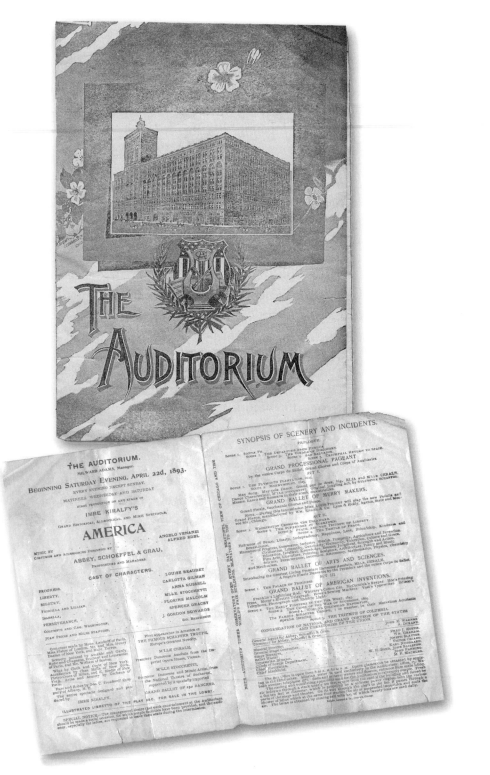

An 1893 Auditorium Theatre program for *America,* a spectacle presented during the period of the World's Columbian Exposition in Chicago. The mammoth production featured, among other highlights, a "grand processional pageant" and "grand ballets" of arts, sciences, and American inventions.

Chapter 3

"The City Assumed a Metropolitan Air"

IN CHICAGO, WROTE THE ENGLISH AUTHOR Sara Clarke Jane Lippin-
cott, "there is no such thing as stagnation and rest." Before the Great
Fire, the Yankee capitalists and the immigrant laborers who planted roots
in the city had combined to build vast industries in wheat, meat, lumber,
and machinery, and during the Civil War, Chicago, firmly on the winning side, prospered mightily in trade. After the fire, amazingly, the pace
quickened. The stockyards, which were out of the flames' way, remained
a powerful presence in American commerce. Many homes and businesses
that had been leveled were rebuilt, and many more institutions were
erected on an even grander scale: world-class hotels, luxurious restaurants, huge stadiums, extravagant mansions, office buildings so tall that
they were called skyscrapers—and theaters so magnificent that they drew
the finest players and offered the most elaborate spectacles.

Thirteen days after the Great Fire, a makeshift theater, plunked in
the shell of an older house and called the Globe, opened on Des Plaines
Street. But its mix of ramshackle structure and nondescript programming was quickly overshadowed by much larger, much more prestigious,
and much more lavishly appointed downtown buildings.

The Auditorium Theatre, Adler and Sullivan's surviving masterpiece
COURTESY OF AUDITORIUM THEATRE OF ROOSEVELT UNIVERSITY

The McVicker's, grandly rebuilt in 1872 on its original Madison Street site, reopened, appropriately, with the comedy *Time Works Wonders*. The fifty-five-thousand-dollar Grand Opera House at 119 N. Clark Street came along in 1880, and the 2,300-seat Chicago Opera House at Clark and Washington streets made its debut in 1885. Hooley's (later rechristened Powers') Theatre, rebuilt after its destruction in the Great Fire, opened on Randolph Street near LaSalle Street in 1872 in a style that was, according to the *Chicago Tribune,* "brilliant in every respect," with a grand foyer lined with paintings that ladies were urged to view at intermission as "relief from the fatigue of long sitting." Hooley's customers paid a dollar for main floor seats and, if they liked, they could have pretheater dinner at the elegant, nearby Henrici's Restaurant on Randolph Street for fifty cents.

In 1879, architect Dankmar Adler and his newly hired assistant Louis Sullivan completed their first multipurpose building, on the southeast corner of State and Randolph streets. Along with offices and shops it contained the Chicago Musical College and the 1,900-seat Central Music Hall. (It was razed in 1900 and replaced by an expansion of Marshall Field's department store.)

Adler and Sullivan became equal partners in 1883, beginning a decade of extraordinary creativity. Their surviving masterpiece, the Auditorium Building, erected with funds gathered by financier Ferdinand W. Peck, housed a hotel fronting on Michigan Avenue (now the downtown home of Roosevelt University), more than a hundred offices in a section facing west on Wabash Avenue, and the great Auditorium Theatre, with its entrance on Congress Street. The largest theater in the country at the time (4,237 seats), it remains to this day a marvel of acoustical engineering (Adler) and decorative splendor (Sullivan). It was dedicated on December 9, 1889, with President Benjamin Harrison in the audience and a program that included a festival ode by the poet Harriet Monroe set to the music of a symphonic cantata by Frederick Grant Gleason and sung by the Apollo Club. For a climax, the sublime soprano Adelina Patti sang "Home, Sweet Home."

In its size and richness, the Auditorium seemed to embody the power and energy that many observers saw in Chicago. In 1890, the historian J. C. Ridpath went to the top of the Auditorium's tower, then the highest point in the city, and, after viewing the city below him, wrote, "Even from the dome of St. Peter's the landscape is by no means so fine, so extended, so full of life and progress and enthusiasm."

The final Adler-Sullivan theater masterpiece was the Schiller, at 64 W. Randolph Street, which began life in 1892 as a home for German-language productions but was later renamed the Garrick when its management was taken over early in the twentieth century by the Shubert Organization. In its superb acoustics and in the vaulting ceiling arcs of its interior design, the 1,300-seat Garrick was a worthy companion to the larger, landmark Auditorium, but it did not last. In 1933, it was converted to a movie theater, and a garish new marquee hid much of the Sullivan ground floor. In 1961, after it had dwindled into disuse, having briefly served as a television studio, and during a sad period of downtown depression, it was razed, despite the pleas of preservationists. Restoration would have preserved a great and valuable performing arts theater for the Loop, but in the shortsighted vision of the time, it was expend-

A Chicago tragedy, the Garrick Theatre in its death throes, 1961

able. "Tear it down!" proclaimed Alderman Mathias "Paddy" Bauler (Forty-third Ward), expressing the dominant belief that the theater was old, ugly, and of no use. It was replaced by a parking garage, which, in a foolish gesture, had copies of some of Sullivan's elegant terra-cotta panels poked into the boxlike shape of its otherwise ugly concrete exterior. (There was a bit of poetic justice ahead. The garage was razed in 1998 to make way for the new Goodman Theatre complex.) A small part of the Garrick's façade—a series of three graceful arches framed and embellished with Sullivan's geometric and floral decorations and topped by the sculpted heads of four German cultural heroes—was saved and was

The Schiller (later Garrick) Theater of 1892
COURTESY OF THEATRE HISTORICAL SOCIETY OF AMERICA

safely installed as the façade of The Second City theater, first in 1961 at 1846 N. Wells Street and in 1967 in the cabaret theater's new home at 1616 N. Wells Street. Walk past that site today and say a little prayer, rejoicing that at least some fragments of the great seventeen-story building were preserved and mourning that all but a small fraction of its urban grace was demolished.

⌒

At the turn of the century, with these imposing playhouses in place and with an affluent audience filling their seats, Chicago was second only to New York as a theater center in the United States. It was often said that if a show had floundered on Broadway, it would most likely make its money back in the Loop. George M. Cohan, who through his vaudeville and musical productions knew all about business possibilities in the cross-country stops for touring shows, made up a little alphabet poem about the road in which Chicago's stature as a theater town is neatly summarized:

Maude Adams
JAY MARSHALL COLLECTION

A stands for Albany, good for one night.
B stands for Boston, for two weeks, all right.
C for Chicago, big money, no yaps.
D stands for Denver, break even, perhaps . . .

All the American and European stars of the stage, many of them bringing their own acting companies, played Chicago: Mrs. Patrick Campbell in *Pygmalion,* Anna Held in *The Little Duchess,* William Farnum in *Ben Hur,* Ethel Barrymore in *Captain Jinks of the Horse Marines,* George M. Cohan in *Little Johnny Jones,* Minnie Maddern Fiske in *Becky Sharp,* Herbert Beerbohm Tree and his Royal Haymarket troupe of London in repertory, Richard Mansfield in *Dr. Jekyll and Mr. Hyde,* Maude Adams in *The Little Minister,* Helena Modjeska in *Camille,* Thomas W. Keene in *Hamlet* and *Richard III,* and of course, Joseph Jefferson in *Rip Van Winkle.*

Anna Morgan, a literary lioness who staged all-female versions of *Hamlet* and George Bernard Shaw's *Caesar and Cleopatra* and who had presented the American premiere of Henrik Ibsen's *The Master Builder* in Chicago, captured some of the starstruck excitement that those engagements produced for Chicago audiences when she wrote of seeing Henry Irving and Ellen Terry perform at the two-thousand-seat Columbia Theatre at 57 W. Monroe Street, in 1885:

> What charming entertainments these great artists and the supporting members of their company gave at that time, what an event it was in Chicago! Nothing approaching it in importance and interest has occurred during my remembrance. The city seemed changed, in some way, assumed a metropolitan air. I remember the closing performance, the play was *Much Ado about Nothing.* The house was packed, many persons, including myself, sitting on the steps leading from the boxes to the parquet. Marshall Field, whom I saw for the first time, sitting with his young son Marshall Field Jr., was in one of the very front seats.

The stars, in turn, loved to play Chicago. What if Rudyard Kipling, after a tour of the United States in the 1880s, had damned this "most

Sarah Bernhardt: they loved her in Chicago

American of American cities" as being so ugly and so "inhabited by savages" that "I earnestly desire never to see it again"? Sarah Bernhardt, the Divine One, played to adoring Chicago audiences in all six of her American tours, commanding an unprecedented top ticket price of $3 for her performances (in French) of such dramas as Alexandre Dumas *fils*'s *Camille* and Racine's *Phedre*. During her first visit, a two-week run at the McVicker's in 1881, her theatrical wiles were denounced with such vigor from the pulpit by the Roman Catholic bishop of Chicago that Bernhardt's press agent sent him a donation of $250 and a letter (with copies to the Chicago newspapers) thanking him for the generous free publicity. It must have worked, because the actress's shows were packed with fans, most of whom understood not a word that she said.

Bernhardt returned the love to Chicago. She immediately sensed the raw energy that, then as now, fascinated so many visitors. "It is a city," she said, dramatically, "in which men pass each other without ever stopping, with knitted brows, with one thought in mind—the end to attain." Returning from a day tour of the Union Stock Yards, she was so haunted by its "dreadful and magnificent sight" that she collapsed onstage while playing *Phedre* that night. (The curtain was briefly lowered, and when Bernhardt recovered and went back onstage, she found that many customers, not having read the English synopsis and believing the show was over, were heading out the doors.)

With its population now more than a million, making it the second-largest city (after New York) in the country, and with its eminence asserted by the huge success of the World's Columbian Exposition of 1893, Chicago now had enough history behind it to lay claim to the first individuals in a long list of famous show business artists and administrators who had spent at least part of their lives in the city. Lillian Russell, the musical-comedy actress with the famed hourglass figure, a sensation at the Columbia Theatre during the

Lillian Russell, the former Helen Louise Leonard of Chicago

Columbian Exposition, had given a song recital at Kimball Hall when she was still just plain little Helen Louise Leonard. Florenz Ziegfeld Jr., the producer who was to bring many editions of his *Ziegfeld Follies* on tour to Chicago, was the son of Dr. Florenz Ziegfeld, cofounder of Chicago Musical College. Mrs. Leslie Carter, whose juicy divorce from her socially prominent husband had been a Chicago sensation of 1889, went on to become an actress protégée of producer David Belasco, starring in his productions of *The Heart of Maryland, Zaza,* and *DuBarry.*

The productions in which the touring stars and the stock companies appeared relied heavily on European classics and recent New York and Lon-don successes. Realism and spectacle, strengthened by technical advances, were favored in production values, and farce, musicals, and melodramas were the preferred vehicles. Among the latter were the durable *East Lynne* and *Uncle Tom's Cabin,* which in an 1882 visit advertised

Program for the Chicago Opera House, 1891, when the attraction was *The Patrol,* a melodrama "founded on the incidents of a Famous Murder Case"
JAY MARSHALL COLLECTION

TRAINED SIBERIAN BLOODHOUNDS
The most savage of their species, which will engage in the Realistic Picture
of the terrible SLAVE HUNT

And all this for a fifty-cent top ticket price.

For a while, the flow of productions to commercial theaters was strictly controlled by the Theatrical Syndicate, a New York organization that had a lock on a large majority of the nation's playhouses and was able to dictate what shows would be booked and how long their engagements would last. A monopoly, in other words. In any era, including our own, this is not a healthy situation, and several Chicago theaters and many actors, including Mrs. Fiske, billed as the First Lady of the American Stage, fought for independence, their cause egged on by some press accounts reviling the "Jew Syndicate" of New York. Nevertheless, from 1896 until at least a decade into the twentieth century, when the trust's power was diluted by competition from another group that Mrs.

Fred Stone as the Scarecrow in *The Wizard of Oz*, 1902

Fiske and producer David Belasco had formed with the aid of the ambitious/voracious Shubert brothers/producers, the Theatrical Syndicate virtually ruled the show business world, building and booking theaters across the country. It hung around until 1916, and it left Chicago and the rest of the country with one central heritage that endures to this day: the national touring company. With railroads now reaching to every major city, it became more efficient and more profitable to send out one centrally controlled, Syndicate-authorized version of a hit show than to distribute the rights to scattered resident stock companies. By controlling selection and distribution, the Syndicate, until the Shuberts came along and beat them at their own game by gaining control of even more theaters, froze out local troupes from immediately presenting first-class productions of new and hot commercial properties.

However, amid the round of European and Broadway successes, there were a few successful (and now extinct) local plays too, several of them by Chicago newspaper writers—*All the Rage* by Will Eaton of the *Times,* and *A Mountain Pink* by Elwyn A. Barron of the *Inter Ocean,* among others. George Ade, humorist and columnist of the *Chicago Record* in the 1890s, had the best run of all with such light comedies as *The County Chairman* and *The College Widow,* which in 1917 was transformed into the charming Jerome Kern–Guy Bolton musical, *Leave It to Jane.*

In 1902, a brand-new musical based on *The Wizard of Oz,* by L. Frank Baum, another former Chicago newspaperman, became a great local hit. With the popular comedian Fred Stone starring as the Scarecrow, and with several significant changes from the book—no Wicked Witch of the West and Toto the dog replaced by Imogene the cow—the show featured songs ("Just a Simple Girl from the Prairie," "When You Love, Love, Love") with music by Paul Tietjens and A. Baldwin Sloane and lyrics by Baum. A year after its triumphant premiere on June 16 at the Grand Opera House in Chicago, it opened in New York and became a leading Broadway hit of the decade.

Among Chicago dramatists, however, none was more singular or more colorful than Samuel Eberly Gross, a real estate developer who built thousands of houses in the Chicago area, including those in the landmark Alta Vista Terrace in the city's Wrigleyville neighborhood and in the western suburb of Grossdale, renamed Brookfield by vote of its

CHICAGO ON BROADWAY

Productions of plays and musicals that were initiated, created, and produced by Chicago theaters for Chicago audiences and that later transferred to Broadway with their directors, designers, and most of their casts intact include:

Joan Allen and John Malkovich in *Burn This,* from Steppenwolf Theatre to Plymouth Theatre, 1987–88

COURTESY OF STEPPENWOLF THEATRE

The Wizard of Oz, originally played in the Grand Opera House in Chicago; moved to the Majestic Theatre in New York in 1903

The Swing Mikado, originated by the Federal Theater Project in Chicago; played the New Yorker Theater, 1939

From the Second City; Royale Theatre, 1961

Warp, Organic Theater; Ambassador Theatre, 1973

Status Quo Vadis, Ivanhoe Theatre; Brooks Atkinson Theatre, 1973

A Moon for the Misbegotten (revival), Academy Festival Theatre in Lake Forest; Morosco Theatre, 1973–74

The Freedom of the City, Goodman Theatre; Alvin Theatre, 1974

Sweet Bird of Youth (revival), Academy Festival Theatre; Harkness Theatre, 1975–76

Working, Goodman; 46th Street Theatre, 1978

Bosoms and Neglect, Goodman; Longacre Theatre, 1979

Morning's at Seven (revival), Academy Festival Theatre; Lyceum Theatre, 1980–81

Do Black Patent Leather Shoes Really Reflect Up? Forum Theatre; Alvin, 1982

The Man Who Had Three Arms, Goodman; Lyceum, 1983

Glengarry Glen Ross, Goodman; John Golden Theatre, 1984–85

Hurlyburly, Goodman; Ethel Barrymore Theatre, 1984–85

The Caretaker (revival), Steppenwolf Theatre; Circle in the Square Theatre, 1986

The Grapes of Wrath, Steppenwolf; Cort Theatre, 1990

The Speed of Darkness, Goodman; Belasco Theatre, 1991

The Song of Jacob Zulu, Steppenwolf; Plymouth Theatre, 1992

The Rise and Fall of Little Voice, Steppenwolf; Neil Simon Theatre, 1994

Buried Child (revival), Steppenwolf; Brooks Atkinson, 1996

The Night of the Iguana (revival), Goodman; Criterion Center Stage Right (Roundabout Theatre), 1996

Death of a Salesman (revival), Goodman; Eugene O'Neill Theatre, 1999

A Moon for the Misbegotten (revival), Goodman; Walter Kerr Theatre, 2000

One Flew over the Cuckoo's Nest (revival), Steppenwolf; Royale Theatre, 2001

Metamorphoses, Lookingglass Theatre Company at the Ivanhoe Theatre; Circle in the Square (transferred from Second Stage Theatre), 2002–3

Hollywood Arms, Goodman; Cort, 2002–3

Not included here are such important shows as *Grease* and *American Buffalo,* which, though written and originated in Chicago, were presented on Broadway with substantially different casts and production teams.

citizens in 1905. In addition to being a flamboyant salesman/showman—he brought prospective settlers out to Grossdale by special excursion trains, greeted them in a pavilion where "entertaining speeches are made," and treated them to band music, hot dogs, beer, and lemonade—Gross was a playwright. He said he wrote his four-act comedy *The Merchant Prince of Cornville* in the 1870s simply "as a diversion amidst business pursuits." But in 1897, when Edmond Rostand published his *Cyrano de Bergerac* in France, Gross astounded and amused the theater world by going to court with charges that the French playwright had stolen key plot elements in his famed romance from Gross's earlier and exceedingly eccentric "diversion."

Specifically, Gross stated, there was the scene in which the loutish, business-minded eponymous character, who prefers to be introduced to strangers as "the Honorable Mayor Hercules Whetstone, the merchant prince of Cornville, near the capital of Illinois—called Hercules after his grand-uncle Hercules, who drove the Indians down the Mississippi"—woos a young lady, looking down on him from her balcony, on a moonlit night. All the while, Major Bluegrass, his big-nosed private secretary and editor of the *Cornville Eagle,* stands in the shadows and feeds him comic and poetic lines of love songs.

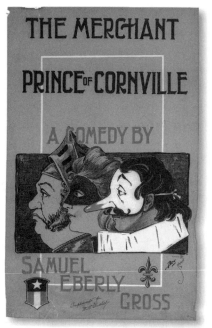

The situation bears some resemblance to the balcony scene in Rostand's drama, in which Cyrano prompts the young, inarticulate suitor Christian with the romantic poetry he mouths to his beloved Roxanne. But the tone and style of the two plays are entirely different. Gross's dialogue ranges from highfalutin verse to crude foreign and yokel accents, while *Cyrano* is consistent in its high romantic poetry.

Rostand, stung by the legal battle, protested, observing that there were "big noses everywhere in the world," but Gross would not be put off. He told the *Chicago Examiner,* "You see, Rostand is trying to

Lithograph for *The Merchant Prince of Cornville,* 1895

make the American people his dupes. He thinks he can do this because he is a Parisian and famous. Perhaps he can, as far as some people are concerned, but I won't sit idly by and let him make the attempt." To show he was dead serious, Gross sent a private detective to France to gather evidence supporting his claim, and, though he did not try to stop a touring French production of the play, he insisted on carrying through his legal fight.

At last, in 1902, U.S. District Court Judge Christian C. Kohlsaat ruled that *Cyrano* was indeed "a piracy upon" the *Merchant Prince* in "plot arrangement, situations, characters, ideas, and language." The judge ordered all profits from *Cyrano* to be awarded to Gross, but Gross, having made his point in a grand and public manner, accepted only damages of a dollar and, better yet, basked in the pride of authorship.

It may have been a victory for "Chicago hustle" over those sneaky Frenchies, as the *Tribune* stated, but it did nothing to advance Chicago playwriting. *Cyrano* endures as a classic, and the *Merchant Prince*

Hooley's Theatre, on Randolph Street east of LaSalle Street

FROM *HISTORY OF CHICAGO*, BY A .T. ANDREAS

exists, if at all, as a curiosity. The critic George Jean Nathan, who knew and liked Gross, said, "I thoroughly believe Rostand swiped my friend's play. But Rostand made it into a beautiful thing, didn't he, so what's the odds?"

Bernhardt, hearing of the judge's decision, remarked that it must have been April Fool's Day in Chicago. Richard Mansfield, the actor whose English version of *Cyrano* on tour had been aborted by Gross's lawsuit, mocked both author and city when he suggested that Gross would be swamped with requests for his plays and that consequently "Chicago may in the future be the center of another new industry."

It would take about seventy-five years before Mansfield's sarcastic

prediction of that "new industry" would truly be ful-
filled; but, in the immediate future, Chicago was building so impressive a theater business that Adelina Patti,
a Chicago favorite since her local debut in 1853,
remarked, "Chicago seems to get everything now. I
wonder what is to become of New York."

There was plenty left in the East, of course, much
of it waiting to be sent out to Chicago, where thirty-
some theaters were waiting. Near the end of the century, a flurry of building saw the opening of the Great
Northern at 20 W. Jackson Boulevard (1896), the
Studebaker in the Fine Arts Building at 410 S. Michigan Avenue (1898), and, most lavish of all, the Illinois,
at 61 E. Jackson Boulevard (1900), created in the
beaux arts mode by the twenty-six-year-old hotshot
architect, Benjamin Marshall.

Richard Mansfield
JAY MARSHALL COLLECTION

Three years later, amid much hyperbole, the theater designed to top
them all, again created by Marshall, opened for business. It was called
the Iroquois.

Program cover and title page for the premiere engagement of *Mr. Blue Beard* at the "absolutely fireproof" Iroquois Theatre, 1903

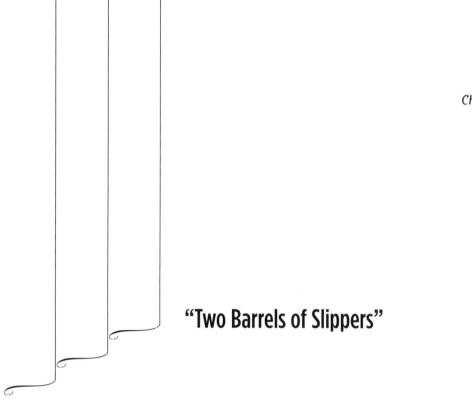

Chapter 4

"Two Barrels of Slippers"

FIRE HAD ALWAYS BEEN A CONCERN for Chicago theaters. Both the early Rice's Theatre and the later, more elaborate McVicker's had gone up in flames but had been rebuilt with happy results. There had been no casualties, and there was even a touch of zaniness in the burning of Rice's house. A nearby stable fire had spread to the theater, but one customer, too drunk to realize that the flames were not part of some extra-special effects, had to be pulled from his seat and lugged to safety.

The danger of fire in crowded theaters was not a joke, however. Writing in his 1886 *History of Chicago,* A. T. Andreas singled out one particular theater, the New Adelphi, later called Haverly's, the largest theater in the city when it opened in 1875 at Dearborn and Monroe streets, as a potential disaster area. Noting that the house's balconies and upper galleries could hold two thousand people, whose only escape route consisted of two exits reached "by crooked staircases scarcely five feet wide," Andreas wrote, "It will be difficult for posterity to believe that their forefathers, and especially their fore-mothers, of Chicago, in the years 1879–80, crowded these dangerous fire-traps over and over again."

Eddie Foy, in costume for the comic "Elephant Walk" number of *Mr. Blue Beard*

The rise of steel and concrete in construction work had eliminated some of the dangers found in the old wood and brick buildings, and, as notice of these advances, some theaters, including the Illinois and the Iroquois, were advertised as "absolutely fireproof."

With the Iroquois, however, the emphasis was on promoting the monumental opulence of the structure. The neoclassic grand entrance, on the north side of Randolph Street, between State and Dearborn streets, was flanked by a pair of two huge stone Ionic columns that framed a three-story archway, within which, supported by two smaller columns, stood a broken pediment nesting the bust of an Iroquois Indian. High above, capping the façade, was a grand pediment containing the masks of comedy and tragedy.

Inside, there were velvet draperies, crystal chandeliers, plush seats, marble columns, wrought-iron balustrades, and, above the auditorium, a dome ringed by a frieze showing the history of theater in Chicago, from Rice's to the Iroquois.

For the theater's premiere attraction, the Theatrical Syndicate producers Marc Klaw and Abraham Lincoln Erlanger imported a musical-comedy spectacle from London, *Mr. Blue Beard,* with a cast of about two hundred people (including supernumeraries) topped by the comedian Eddie Foy, in drag, as a fright-wigged ugly sister to the show's heroine.

The opening was delayed because of inclement weather and nettlesome labor disputes, but finally, in a rush, on November 23, 1903, in time for the peak theatergoing periods around the Thanksgiving and Christmas holidays, the Iroquois welcomed its first customers amid a gale of Windy City superlatives—"the best," "the most beautiful," and the like.

Exterior of the Iroquois Theatre on Randolph Street at the time of the fire, December 30, 1903

CHICAGO DAILY NEWS, CHICAGO HISTORICAL SOCIETY

After the fire, scenes of devastation in the Iroquois auditorium
COURTESY OF *CHICAGO TRIBUNE* NEWS ARCHIVE

In the hurry to get the theater open, however, basic safety consider-
ations were overlooked or ignored, and at about 3:15 P.M., at a packed
family matinee of about 1,900 people on Wednesday, December 30,
1903, shortly before *Mr. Blue Beard* was scheduled to end its Chicago
run, this progression of carelessness, cost cutting, and stupidity came
to a terrible end.

A backstage spotlight that illuminated a "moonlit" song-and-dance
double octet in the second act short-circuited in the overloaded electrical system and sent sparks crackling out to a side curtain, creating a fire
that could not be extinguished with the only materials at hand, a
pathetic few tubes filled with a powdery substance called Kilfyre. The
flames quickly spread to the mass of flammable scenery stored in the fly
lofts above the stage, and in a matter of minutes, the fire was out of con-

Charred remnants of the stage and main-floor seats of the Iroquois
COURTESY OF *CHICAGO TRIBUNE* NEWS ARCHIVE

trol. Foy, running to the stage in costume from his dressing room, tried to calm the crowd, but it was too late. Panic had set in, and there was no stopping the stampede to find the exits.

Complicating matters, the left side of the asbestos curtain that was supposed to shield the audience from the backstage flames got stuck on a lighting fixture on the way down and the curtain never completely closed. When the show's cast and crew members forced open a large freight door at the rear of the stage, the resulting draft of air sent a searing sheet of smoke and flames shooting through the curtain opening into the auditorium and up to the balcony and gallery areas. Some customers were fatally burned before they had a chance to leave their seats. Others were asphyxiated, and many more were trampled to death in the chaotic rush to get out.

Some six hundred persons—two members of the show's company and a little less than one-third of the audience, the majority of which were women and children—died horribly in a space of about twenty minutes, before firemen who had hurried to the theater could help them.

As the *Daily News* extra edition of December 30 rightly bannered it, this was "The Iroquois Fire Horror." One reporter noted, in a bit of poignant detail, that in the wake of the fire, "five bushels of women's purses were picked up, and two barrels of slippers." It was and still is the greatest loss of life by a building fire in our nation's history and the greatest disaster in American theater history. (By comparison, the official body count for the Great Fire of 1871 was three hundred.)

In the days of grief and shock after the fire, clear and stunning reasons for the disaster came to light, all of them stemming from neglect, wishful thinking, hubris, sloth, and greed. The Iroquois obviously had not been ready to open. The ventilators in the rooftop skylights, through which the smoke and flames could have escaped, were inexplicably sealed shut. There was no alarm box, no sprinkler system; there were no water buckets, no hoses, no major fire precautions of any kind in the backstage area. In many cases, the building's fire escapes were incomplete or inoperable. Some exit doors had been locked, and others opened inward, making them all but impossible to open when crowds pressed forward against them. Two stairwells leading from the upper balcony had been sealed off by iron accordion gates, put there by the management to prevent people in the cheaper seats from sneaking down to better seats on the main floor. The carefully wrought exit signs that Benjamin Marshall had ordered had not yet arrived, no temporary signs had been installed, and the crew of young, untrained, unskilled ushers had no idea of how to guide customers to safety.

In spite of all these obvious examples of incompleteness and incompetence, the Iroquois had been given permission by the city to open for business. In the wake of the fire, there were charges that building inspectors had been paid off in order to get the theater up and running for the lucrative holiday business, a reasonable assumption in Chicago's notorious First Ward, where bribery was just another way of doing business and corruption was commonplace. Newspapers were dotted with stories of flagrant payoffs to city workers. An editorial cartoon of the period shows a building inspector rushing to a box office to grab a free

pass, ignoring all the signs of EXIT
LOCKED, INFLAMMABLE SCENERY,
LIGHT NOT PROTECTED, and TISSUE
PAPER FOR SCENERY around him.

There had been warning signals.
A few weeks before the Iroquois
opened, Mayor Carter H. Harrison
Jr. had considered closing all the city's
theaters because an investigation he
ordered had turned up an alarming
lack of safety precautions. But that
prospect was scotched when the City
Council sidetracked the investigation
to its Judiciary Committee.

Soon after the fire, Mayor
Harrison did order every theater in
Chicago closed, but that, as one
newspaper editorial put it, was like
closing the barn door after the steed
had run away. As the days went by,
deep mourning over the disaster was
joined by high outrage, and a bar-
rage of charges was hurled against
the architect, the owners, the producers, and the city officials whose
oversights had led to the inferno.

Black-bordered card printed in memory of the
Iroquois disaster

In the end, after a coroner's jury
submitted its report and after nearly
four years of delays and legal maneuvering, nobody was found guilty.
Levy Mayer, the chief attorney for Will J. Davis, the theater's manager
and co-owner, said, after he had successfully ended the courtroom proceedings, "It was the hand of God that brought about the loss of lives in
the fire and Will J. Davis was no more responsible for their deaths than if
a hurricane had lifted off the roof of the theater." Professor Frederic C.
Woodward of Northwestern University Law School, writing in the *Illinois Law Review,* had a different view. The delays in the trials, he stated,
had sown "the seeds of contempt for law and gives notice to the world of
the inefficiency of our judicial system."

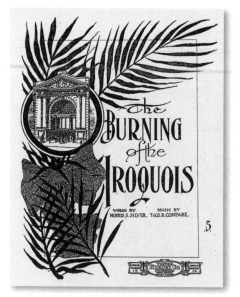

Sheet music issued in the wake of the
Iroquois fire

JOSEPH R. DUCIBELLA COLLECTION

But though Davis and his fellow defendants were freed from legal liability, someone was responsible for the mismanagement, misconceptions, and incredible mistakes that had led to the fire, and the weight of that responsibility certainly did not lie on the men, women, and children whose lives were snuffed out while they were on a holiday outing in the theater.

There were reforms and improvements in safety measures and fire regulations. Lighted exit signs, "panic bars" for exit doors that opened out instead of in, and the use of fireproof materials in scenery all came about as a result of the lessons dearly learned at the Iroquois. And, of course, after the fire, there were plenty of building inspections—conducted, some theater managers complained, with the same old quest for payoffs.

As a sign of the changed times, the 1906 Majestic (later Shubert) Theatre at 22 W. Monroe Street, the first playhouse to be opened after the Iroquois fire, included in its program diagrams and instructions on where to find exits in case of fire. As for the Iroquois, its interior had been ravaged by flames and smoke, but its basic structure had not been significantly damaged, and about nine months after the fire, the building, minus fancy trappings, reopened as Hyde and Behman's Music Hall, a vaudeville house. That lasted about a year, after which the building was sold to Harry J. Powers and Erlanger, rechristened the Colonial, and reopened on October 5, 1904, with George M. Cohan's *Forty-five Minutes from Broadway,* starring Fay Templeton.

In 1924, the theater was torn down to make way for the building that would house the new Oriental Theatre. Posted on the sidewalk near the entrance to what is now the lavishly refurbished Ford Center for the Performing Arts, Oriental Theatre, is a sign briefly noting the Iroquois's history.

A few blocks away, on an interior wall just left of the LaSalle Street entrance to City Hall, there's a sculpture by Lorado Taft that depicts an angelic figure hovering above a grieving mother and other mourners. The

bas-relief, placed in City Hall without any identification of its significance, had once hung in the old
Iroquois Memorial Hospital on
Wacker Drive. The hospital had been
built with money raised by members
of the Iroquois Memorial Association, which also placed a still-stand-
ing memorial tablet in Montrose
Cemetery, on the city's North Side.

Though memories of the Iroquois
disaster faded over time, the building
codes that came about as a result of
the fire remained. Years later, a new
generation of theater artists that had
set up shop in small basements, lofts,
and second-story spaces was faced
with the impossible task of comply-
ing with regulations that had been
written with large auditoriums and

Bas-relief by Lorado Taft in memory of the Iroquois
Theatre fire victims
FREDRIC STEIN

proscenium-arch stages in mind. To avoid being shut down, the management of some of these small theaters did as their predecessors had
done: they put a little money under the cash register when the building
inspector came to call.

Journalists such as Lincoln Steffens and the visiting English editor
William T. Stead in his scathing book *If Christ Came to Chicago* had
written reports about the blatant corruption and grinding poverty
beneath the façade of the glittering city. But the Iroquois disaster, with
its appalling loss of life, dramatized the consequences of graft and indif-
ference to human suffering in a sudden, stark manner. What had started
out as a theater proclaiming the grandeur of Chicago had become instead
a symbol of the most unsavory aspects of Chicago. The Iroquois, meant
to show Chicago at its best, wound up representing Chicago at its worst.

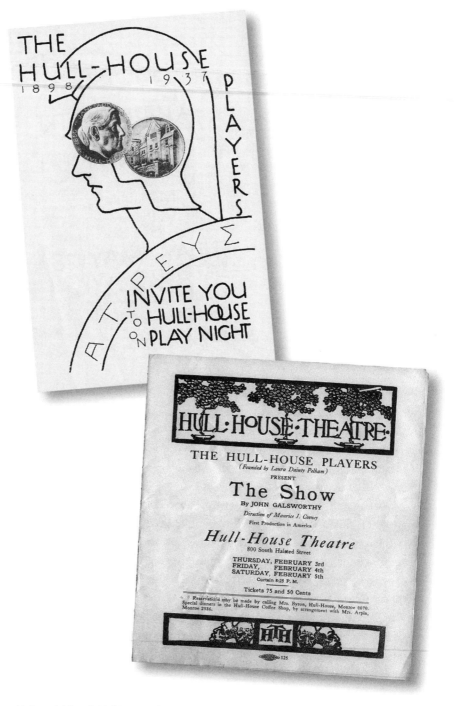

At Jane Addams's Hull-House Theatre, the programs ranged from the Greek classics to contemporary works by John Galsworthy that dealt with social issues of the day.

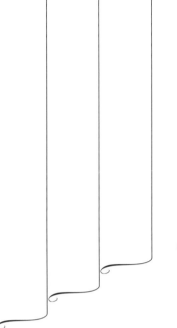

Chapter 5

"A Glimpse of That Order and Beauty"

FOR A BETTER VISION OF CHICAGO'S spirit, you would have to leave the flossy theaters, restaurants, and hotels of the Loop and travel one mile to the slums of the West Side, where the other half lived. Here, on September 18, 1889, in the area that the writer Richard Linberg called "the darkest corner of Chicago," and in an old mansion on Halsted Street that had belonged to the merchant Charles Hull, Jane Addams and her friend Ellen Gates Starr founded Hull House, the settlement house that became a beacon of goodwill for the workers' families who lived in the neighborhood and a symbol of social reform throughout the Western world.

The political boss Michael "Hinky Dink" Kenna, who, with "Bathhouse" John Coughlin, ruled the rowdy First Ward, proudly stated that "Chicago ain't no sissy place," and Jane Addams, though she had been raised far from bare-knuckle ethics, in a respected family in Cedarville, Illinois, about 120 miles northwest of Chicago, was no sissy. She was smart, she was shrewd, she was tough, and, in a city that desperately needed one, she was also considered a saint.

She was twenty-eight when she opened the doors of Hull House to the poor immigrants who had become the core of Chicago's industrial

Jane Addams at her desk, about 1905
CHICAGO HISTORICAL SOCIETY (ICHI-20044)

labor force and who had jammed into that ramshackle area around Halsted and Polk streets. Inspired by the operation of Toynbee Hall, a neighborhood center she had visited in London, Addams turned Hull House into a place that offered a day nursery, health care, and employment services to the people who came there. In less than a decade, the Hull House complex, with twelve new buildings added, covered a city block. Its facilities included an art gallery, a swimming pool, a gymnasium, a circulating library, a book bindery, a public kitchen, and artists' studios.

Under Addams's guidance, Hull House started a kindergarten, opened a public playground, taught English and other subjects in night classes for adults, gave crafts instructions, and set up a music school. (The young Benny Goodman took clarinet lessons there and played in the boys' club band.)

And Addams began a theater program.

The reason for introducing theater to Hull House was, for Addams, a practical one. As she talked to the scores of neighbors who passed through the center every day, Addams learned that theater was an important part of their lives. Years later, in her autobiographical *Twenty Years at Hull House,* she recalled: "Our first Sunday evening in Hull House, when a group of small boys sat on our piazza and told us 'about things around here,' their talk was all of the theater and of the astonishing things they had seen that afternoon."

The theater they talked about was not complex or exalted. It was burlesque and vaudeville and melodrama, in which entertainment was broad and moral values were outlined in crude strokes of villainy and heroism. But it got to these young people as no amount of preaching could, and Addams, smart person and devout social worker that she was, knew that theater, even of this variety, was a liberating force for them.

In a most beautiful passage, one that should be emblazoned in every school in the country, she wrote:

> Nevertheless, the theater, such as it was, appeared to be the one agency which freed the boys and girls from that destructive isolation of those who drag themselves up to maturity by themselves, and it gave them a glimpse of that order and beauty into which even the poorest drama endeavors to restore the bewildering facts of life. The most prosaic young people bear testimony to this overmastering desire.

Theater, Addams believed, had the power to "warm us with a sense of companionship." It was certainly an agent of recreation and education, but she recognized, despite the qualms of some supporters who still viewed the theater as a morally suspect area, that it was also "a vehicle of self-expression for the teeming young life all about us."

And so Hull House put on plays, in the dining room and gymnasium at first, and then in a 230-seat, second-floor theater, complete with small pipe organ. The auditorium was decorated with a mural created by Hull House artists and outfitted with scenery, costumes, and programs created by other residents. The motto for their work, printed in large letters above the stage, was ACT WELL YOUR PART; THERE ALL THE HONOR LIES, an exhortation taken from Alexander Pope's "An Essay on Man."

There were holiday pageants, dramatic readings of poems and stories, children's matinees, melodramas, comedies, and, astonishingly, the *Ajax* of Sophocles, presented by Greek immigrants to show the glory of their homeland. There were plays staged by Russians, Lithuanians, and Poles in their native tongues. An original work about the gulf between Americanized sons and their old-country parents, Addams noted, was depicted so touchingly "that it moved to tears all the older Italians in the audience."

"Act Well Your Part . . .": Shakespeare in an early performance at Hull House
UNIVERSITY OF ILLINOIS AT CHICAGO, UNIVERSITY LIBRARY, JANE ADDAMS COLLECTION

As early as 1893, the Hull-House Players presented an English drama classic, Oliver Goldsmith's *She Stoops to Conquer*. After Laura Dainty Pelham, a no-nonsense actress/manager, came on board in 1900 to guide the Hull-House Dramatic Association, there were productions of new works by Henrik Ibsen, George Bernard Shaw, and John Galsworthy, including the American premieres of Ibsen's *The Pillars of Society* and Galsworthy's *Justice*. These plays, which Addams believed had the power to teach "social righteousness," were surprisingly popular, she said, because they attempted "to expose the shams and pretensions of contemporary life and to penetrate into some of its perplexing social and domestic situations."

The Hull House stage was open to other theater groups, as well. Yiddish troupes occasionally performed there, and one Chicago troupe that was unable to break into a Theatrical Syndicate house presented a winter season of twice weekly performances of Ibsen and French comedies.

Through its pioneering work, theater at Hull House drew reviewers from the city's newspapers who were impressed with the theater's ambitions, if not the professional polish of its amateur actors. Also in the audiences were Addams's moneyed sponsors and a stream of celebrities, from Theodore Roosevelt and the now venerable Joseph Jefferson to Galsworthy and the Irish playwrights William Butler Yeats and Lady Augusta Gregory.

It was Lady Gregory's appearance with Dublin's Abbey Players in Chicago in 1912 that prompted Pelham to plan a trip to Ireland for the Hull-House Players. To raise funds for the trip, she took her group downtown to the Fine Arts Building for a week of repertory. The move irritated at least one local reviewer, James O'Donnell Bennett of the *Record-Herald,* who was unhappy over seeing an amateur group being paid to perform in a downtown house. Nevertheless, the Players did make their trip to Ireland, and Pelham continued her work at Hull House until her death in 1924. Among the dramas she presented were works by such contemporary playwrights as Eugene O'Neill, Gerhart Hauptmann, Arthur Schnitzler, Lennox Robinson, and Stark Young.

Hull House productions continued into the early 1940s. The Northwestern University sociologist Neva L. Boyd and her student Viola Spolin played Boyd's innovative theater games in her Recreational Training School for adults and children in the 1920s, and there was notable work in the thirties from the Russian immigrants Maria and Ivan Lazareff, who taught acting techniques of the Stanislavski method. But it was not until 1963, after most of the original settlement house complex had been razed and replaced by part of the campus of the University of Illinois at Chicago, and headquarters had been moved to 3212 N. Broadway on the city's North Side, that a revived company once more made Hull House a celebrated force in Chicago theater life.

This new Hull House theater took its inspiration from Addams's enduring belief that theater was an essential part of a neighborhood's vitality. Thanks to Addams and Pelham, community theater, as it came to be called, was on its way to glory.

MEDEA

THE CHICAGO LITTLE THEATRE

THE CHICAGO LITTLE THEATRE
434 Fine Arts Building
410 S. Michigan Ave.
Telephone Harrison 5340

Admission, $1.00; members, 50 cents. Season tickets and particulars of membership may be obtained at the box office.

Tea will be served at the conclusion of each performance and from 4 to 6 p. m. on weekdays at a charge of 25 cents, and a light supper from 5 to 7 p. m. on Sundays at a charge of 35 cents, for each person served.

The scenery for THE TROJAN WOMEN has been designed and painted by Bror Nordfelt; the costumes have been designed and executed by Lou Wall Moore. The decorations of THE LITTLE THEATRE have been designed and executed under the supervision of Ernest von Ammon of the Howard D. Wattley Company. The Chinese jars used in the auditorium have been lent by the courtesy of the William H. Hoops Company.

Next production: Strindberg's CREDITORS, translated by Edwin Björkman, and JOINT OWNERS IN SPAIN, by Alice Brown.

The Discussion Circle meets every week on Tuesday at 2:15 p. m., except on the opening Tuesday of each new production, and is open free to members.

Maurice Browne lectures every week on Wednesday at 2:15 p. m. on the plays presented by THE LITTLE THEATRE and cognate subjects. These lectures are open free to members, who are also entitled to bring a guest to one lecture during each season. General admission, $1.00.

Front and back covers for Chicago Little Theatre programs, printed on delicate Japanese rice paper, in the 1912–13 season

Chapter 6

"By All Means Start Your Own Theatre"

THERE WERE MANY COMMUNITIES in the big city of Chicago and surrounding suburbs, each one having a theater that pitched its programming to a specific audience. These ranged from the ornate Timmerman
Opera House, opened in Englewood in 1893, to the humbler Warring-
ton Opera House, in the young suburb of Oak Park, where the Grace
Hayward Stock Company in 1910 advertised "Good, Clean Plays, Well
Presented" at a top ticket price of thirty-five cents.

Cultivated audiences who craved rarer virtues than those found in
the mainstream commercialism of the downtown Theatrical Syndicate
houses patronized little theaters offering noncommercial original
works by local playwrights and the avant-garde of European drama.
At the same time, the European immigrants who came to Chicago
brought with them the varied parts of their culture, including the theater. And in the twentieth century, a new wave of African Americans
put their own stamp on music and theater in the black metropolis of
the South Side.

Hull House had started its little-theater movement with plays staged
in the languages of the immigrant communities it served. And dozens

Helena Modjeska

of other dramatic societies and play-making groups performed in lecture halls and makeshift auditoriums where ethnic theater prospered, sometimes in astonishing ways.

On September 12, 1892, in St. Stanislaus Auditorium, at Noble and Potomac streets, before an overflow audience of more than six thousand members of the city's huge Polish American population, the exalted tragedienne Helena Modjeska starred in a production, in Polish, of the epic historical drama *Jadwiga, Queen of Poland,* by the Chicago playwright Szczesny Zahajkiewicz. A story on the event, printed in the *Chicago Polish Daily,* reported that, after wildly applauded curtain calls, the playwright himself "came upon the stage, with the script in his hand. With great effort he quieted the audience, and finally said, 'After such a magnificent performance no one else should ever portray the heroine of this play. In a tribute to Madame Modjeska, I tear up my script.' And he actually tore it up into shreds and tossed the pieces from left to right over the audience. The standing public in the front rows momentarily disappeared, fishing out from the floor the manuscript pieces to save them as souvenirs of the most bewitching night they ever witnessed."

Henrik Ibsen's landmark drama *Ghosts,* published in 1881, caused such a "violent commotion" (as Ibsen called it) in Europe that it was not produced there until 1883; but on May 20, 1882, it had its world premiere in Chicago—in Norwegian, with a mostly amateur cast—before a Scandinavian American audience. The first recorded production of an Ibsen play in the United States, it later traveled to Minneapolis and other midwestern cities.

Not all productions were so portentous. At the turn of the century, when Chicago was the second-largest Swede city in the world (after Stockholm), the local Scandinavian audiences much preferred the rural comedies, farces, and historic dramas that reminded them of the land they had left behind.

The community of Eastern European Jews that spread around the Maxwell Street area on the Near West Side also favored the folk dramas, melodramas, vaudeville bits, and epics they knew best, peppered with original songs and stories they made up about life in the New World.

Beginning in 1887 and lasting into the 1940s, Yiddish theater and Yiddish players were a constant of Jewish life. The celebrated actor Maurice Schwartz started out as a newsboy in Chicago. In 1909, long before he

Handbill for Glickman's Palace Theatre

became an Oscar-winning (*The Story of Louis Pasteur*) movie actor of the 1930s, Paul Muni was Muni Weisenfreund, a teenager who specialized in playing old men, doing up to ten shows a day with his family in their Weisenfreund's Pavilion Theater on Twelfth Street near Halsted Street. Many years later, an upstart kid from New Jersey, Bernard Schwartz, played in Yiddish theater in Chicago, speaking his lines phonetically. He was billed then as B. White and later, in his movie days, as Tony Curtis. Dina Halpern, a Yiddish star in Eastern Europe, made Chicago her base and performed frequently in such dramas as *Mirele Efros* and *The Witch* after she married publicist Danny Newman.

Touring Yiddish stars appeared in theaters ranging from the downtown Academy of Music to small auditoriums that had been converted into theaters. One story has it that when the actor Boris Thomashefsky hastily outfitted a hall with freshly varnished seats, the varnish, which was still wet, caused major rips in the skirts and trousers of customers when they tried to leave their chairs at intermission, forcing the beleaguered Thomashefsky to pay a huge tailor bill. (This tale is probably too good to be true, but it's also too good not to be repeated.)

From 1919 to 1931, Glickman's Palace Theatre was a major Yiddish playhouse at Twelfth Street and Blue Island Avenue, presenting both local and international touring troupes, such as the Vilna Theatre of Lithuania. Also on Twelfth Street was the People's Music Hall, which featured Yiddish comedies, musicals, melodramas, and variety acts. Yiddish stars such as Molly Picon and Menasha Skulnik played the Douglas Park Auditorium, at the corner of Ogden and Kedzie avenues, which lasted until 1951.

For the Century of Progress Exposition in Chicago in 1933, the Jewish community was able to gather 6,000 singers, dancers, and actors for *Romance of a People,* a mammoth pageant that drew 125,000 people to Soldier Field on the lakefront. A huge production, it was decried by some critics in the Jewish press as a show that drained vitality (and funding) from the smaller Jewish theaters in the city.

From 1922 to 1956, plays related to Jewish life, presented by groups such as the Yiddishe Dramatishe Gezelschaft, were a feature of the bustling Jewish Peoples Institute at Douglas Boulevard and St. Louis Avenue. Here, actor-director Sam Wanamaker, a native Chicagoan, staged some of his first productions. Here, also, the Players' Club of Chicago sometimes presented its productions, offering customers plays in English, with a promise that "dancing will follow the performance." In a very early example of a subscription sales pitch, the Club sold a five-dollar season ticket for eight plays, a savings of three dollars off the regular single ticket price of one dollar. "It is thought," according to a Club statement, "that this issue of season tickets will stimulate interest and be to the advantage of those attending as well as to the Club. If you have hitherto not availed yourself of the opportunity by attending, may we in all earnestness urge you to do so from now on—and by your presence lend encouragement to our organization. Will you help us reach our goal? We count on you! We need you."

The city's large German population attended concerts and plays in neighborhood halls and downtown in the Adler and Sullivan–designed Schiller (later Garrick) Theater, which had been built in large part through the efforts of Anton C. Hesing, newspaper publisher of the Illinois *Staats-Zeitung.*

With the mass arrival of Southern blacks into the city, their music and drama spread over the South Side. One of the landmarks was the Pekin Building, opened in 1904 at 2700 S. State Street as a cabaret and converted into a 1,200-seat theater in 1906 by Robert Motts, a well-connected gambling kingpin and political boss who said he wanted the place to be "a theater for Colored people of this city." The *Broad Ax,* an African American newspaper of the time, called Motts "the new Moses of the Negro race in the theater world." On his deathbed in 1911 he was said to have asked that the Pekin always stay under black ownership. Years later, legend had it that the theater's curtain became stuck

Sheet music for the *Pekin Rag,* showing the theater's interior decked out for a festive occasion

COURTESY OF TIM SAMUELSON

on every opening night, in protest against the fact that white owners now ran the theater.

The Pekin, which boasted of being the finest and largest black-owned theater in the United States, offered musicals, comedies, revues, and dramas in the period 1906 to 1916. Its stock company was an incubator of talent, producing, among others, Charles Gilpin, the actor who in 1921 played the title role on Broadway of Eugene O'Neill's *The Emperor Jones,* and Flournoy Miller and Aubrey Lyles, the comedy team that went on to be featured in *Shuffle Along,* the landmark 1921 black musical on Broadway with songs by two other Pekin alumni, Noble Sissle and Eubie Blake.

Most of these once-vital ethnic and community theaters are gone now, but at 1807 S. Allport Street, in the Pilsen community that in the early twentieth century housed thousands of Czech immigrants, Thalia Hall, a two-thousand-seat theater, still stands. Though battered and boarded up, it retains the impressive Romanesque archway over its main entrance on Allport. It was, up to the 1920s, a handsomely appointed central part of a four-story multiuse building erected in 1892 by John Dusek, a saloon keeper whose business was on the first floor, with an entranceway into the theater space. The theater's principal tenant was the Ludvik Dramatic Players, originally from Prague, who presented plays and operettas in the Czech language.

Community theaters, however, were not confined to ethnic neighborhoods in the city. In Lake Forest, a very prosperous community on the North Shore, Mary (Mrs. Arthur) Aldis presented drama in a theater she had fashioned out of a cottage on the grounds of her family home. Her husband, a philanthropist with cultural leanings, had tried, unsuccessfully, to start the New Theatre as a Chicago home for new plays and playwrights. Mrs. Aldis had better success by planting her little playhouse in her own backyard.

Exterior of the old Thalia Hall
FREDRIC STEIN

Harriet Monroe
CHICAGO HISTORICAL SOCIETY (ICHI-11841)

Her contribution to the theater is charmingly summed up in a *Chicago Tribune* story:

> With leisure, force and originality, and free from all the compulsions that poverty entails, she was, from the first, in the happy position of being able to choose her vocations and amusements. She could, if she liked, coax life along pleasantly by playing golf, going to teas, giving dinners, and sitting in a box at the opera. These diversions proving, upon trial, not particularly satisfying, she paid respectful heed to certain stirrings of talent, commanded a little theater in her garden, and in it gave piquant, grotesquely tragic, or capriciously farcical plays of the most modern type. Her actors were her friends; her small, critical audiences also were her friends. Or interchangeably, her friends were actors and audience. It was immediately interesting, and not infrequently the actors surprised themselves by the excellence of what they did. Ambitious, erratic young playwrights found here an opening for their abilities. Young ladies who had been doomed all their lives to being merely polite and innocuous, seized upon the chance to show that they understood poetry in its most exotic forms, and repeated [the poet Ernest] Dowson in a moonlit garden to the sound of falling waters and the gentle applause of appreciative hands.

Mrs. Aldis's repertory contained works by contemporary Irish and English playwrights, new European works in English translations, and, frequently, a piece by one of her neighbors. For example, she told Harriet Monroe there was a verse fantasy by the poet Frances Shaw. "It was lovely but obscure," Mrs. Aldis said. "The three Dudley sisters gave an eerie mystical presentation, draping the stage with layer upon layer of black net, a few inches apart, through which the ghostly figures appeared as if from another world. The audience was deeply impressed—we had started something."

The actors, Monroe stated, "developed astonishing competence," and when they toured to Boston, the *Transcript*'s theater critic stated, "They act with an ease, freedom and variety rare among amateurs."

Of all these theaters, in all these varied communities, the most famous and most influential was the short-lived Chicago Little Theatre, which ran only five years, 1912 to 1917, in the Fine Arts Building (an 1898 conversion from the Studebaker Building, where the windows had displayed its namesake carriages and wagons) at 410 S. Michigan Avenue.

The Fine Arts was a nest of Chicago cultural activity. At various times it housed the offices of such important literary magazines as *The Dial; The Little Review,* edited by Margaret Anderson; and Monroe's *Poetry: A Magazine of Verse.* Its tenants also included a bookshop with an interior designed by Frank Lloyd Wright and studios for the sculptor Lorado Taft, the artist John T. McCutcheon, the authors George Ade, Hamlin Garland, and Lincoln Steffens, and the formidable drama teacher Anna Morgan.

The Little Theatre, in a rear corridor of the building's fourth floor, was founded by the poet, lecturer, and essayist Maurice Browne, a native of England, and his wife Ellen Van Volkenburg, a Chicago actress and member of a prosperous Chicago family who had met her future husband in Florence on one of her trips to Europe. She was, by all accounts, a woman of strange and unique talents, a gifted impressionist who was able to repeat a play's complete text after sitting through the drama only once, all the while shedding tears in a trancelike state. Browne fancied her right away, and she, in turn, was devoted to him, signing her letters with "I do love you very, very hard, dear," or "IDLYVVHD" for short.

Their professional goal was stated by Browne:

> The Chicago Little Theatre is a repertory and experimental art-theatre, producing classical and modern plays, both tragedy and comedy, at popular prices; preference is given to poetic and imaginative plays, dealing primarily, whether as tragedy or comedy, with characters in action. . . . The Chicago Little Theatre has for its object the creation of a new plastic and rhythmic drama in America.

The *Chicago Tribune,* at the same time, explained to its readers: "The Chicago Little Theatre is an attempt to establish an art theater in Chicago on democratic lines, which shall be as much a civic institution as the Symphony Orchestra or the Art Institute, open to all who are interested in the art of the theater and its development in Chicago."

A program cover from the 1916–17 season suggests the ambience of the Chicago Little Theatre.

When Lady Gregory, the same Irish writer who had encouraged the theater at Hull House, visited Chicago with the Irish Players of Dublin's Abbey Theatre, she gave Browne and Van Volkenburg some advice on starting their own theater: "By all means start your own theatre; but make it in your own image. Don't engage professional players; they have been spoiled for your purpose. Engage and train, as we of the Abbey have done, amateurs: shopgirls, school-teachers, counter-jumpers; cut-throat-thieves rather than professionals.

"And prepare," she counseled the fledgling producers, "to have your hearts broken."

The theater's auditorium seated about ninety people and had a stage fourteen feet wide, twenty feet deep, and only eight feet high. Adjoining it was a screened-off tearoom, where faithful viewers, friends, and guests of honor could enjoy a cup of tea, at twenty-five cents per person, or a light meal of catered chicken salad, while discussing issues of the day. Percy Hammond, the *Tribune*'s theater critic, described this "wee theater" as "rather long, slender and dim and heavily carpeted—comfortable certainly, but not quite cozy." The *Chicago Journal* said it was "a toy theater."

True to their motto—"Create Your Own Theater with the Talent at Hand"—Browne and Nellie Van (as he called her) cast their plays from a devoted band of young little-known actors (although one of them, Chicago-born Beulah Bondi, later became famous for playing mother roles in the movies, particularly as Jimmy Stewart's mom in *It's a Wonderful Life*).

For the rest, Browne and Nellie Van did everything themselves, with a little help from their friends. Browne, who labeled himself "The Autocrat," staged the plays, sometimes acted in them, and ran the primitive switchboard that controlled the stage lights, which were fashioned from

Interior of the Little Theatre
SPECIAL COLLECTIONS LIBRARY, UNIVERSITY OF MICHIGAN

dishpans and tin funnels. Van Volkenburg designed the rice paper programs, founded a children's theater program, and occasionally lent her
gifts as a "puppeteer" (a word she coined) to a production. Her mother,
"Mummy Van," manned the box office and clucked over her children.

The actors and designers had to be versatile. Browne, in his autobiography *Too Late to Lament,* recounts an incident in which the actress
portraying Hecuba in Euripides' *The Trojan Women* also "was arrang-
ing the installation of a fire-escape, demanded at the eleventh hour by
the Chicago Fire Department."

Their repertory, in addition to the classics and dramas by modern
European writers (August Strindberg, Henrik Ibsen, George Bernard
Shaw, William Butler Yeats), contained a few original works by Chicago

Scene from *Grotesques,* by Cloyd Head
SPECIAL COLLECTIONS LIBRARY, UNIVERSITY OF MICHIGAN

authors, including Mrs. Aldis. Reviewing her *Four Plays of Today,* the *Chicago American* stated that if they were "to be taken as signs of the times, then the times are consumed with sex, sex, sex, and sex."

Alice Gerstenberg, daughter of a well-to-do Chicago family and an original member of the Little Theatre Company, became a prolific writer of one-act dramas and had four of her works produced on Broadway. The most original of them, the 1915 *Overtones,* used the inventive device of having four actors portray two envious women, one couple speaking their words and the other speaking their hidden thoughts.

Among the Little Theatre's highly regarded premieres was *Grotesques,* a verse drama subtitled "A Decoration in Black and White," by the Chicago poet Cloyd Head. It was described by Browne as an intense poetic drama, telling its audience that "human beings are puppets manipulated by a god careless of our hopes and fears." It was much praised by Harriet Monroe, who, upon seeing what she described as its "superstylized production" in expressionistic black-and-white scenery and costumes, asked, "Could it be possible that a young poet, here in boiling and bubbling Chicago, was seeing visions and setting them forth in a new strange form too beautiful to die? Was I listening to a bold interpreter of the mystery and poetry of life, one who felt and could suggest its magic and despair?" The answer, for Monroe, was clearly "Yes!" But it is sobering and humbling to read this exultant review many years later, when Cloyd Head is all but forgotten, and his *Grotesques* has long since been out of print and unproduced.

The Little Theatre programming brought out audiences flecked with such Chicago literary dignitaries as Theodore Dreiser, Floyd Dell, and Edgar Lee Masters, as well as visiting celebrities such as John Barrymore and Harley Granville-Barker. "Guest artists" in music and drama who attended frequently were asked to get up onstage after the show to say a few words or play a few notes. The core of the theater's audience, however, consisted of wealthy and middle-class Chicagoans, writers, artists, and intellectuals. Van Volkenburg's friendships with affluent society women resulted in several substantial donations. To make its plays affordable for a wider audience, the management offered coupons, "an economical and convenient method of purchasing tickets," at the rate of twenty-five for twenty dollars or one hundred for sixty-five dollars.

Still, that was not enough to fill the small house. Many times there were fewer people in the audience than onstage. The company toured its production of *The Trojan Women* in thirty-one cities, playing before thirty-three thousand people in fifteen weeks, earning ten thousand dollars, spending twenty-one thousand dollars, and therefore losing eleven thousand dollars, only part of which was made up in donations. At home, when Browne and Van Volkenburg received permission from Shaw to produce his *Mrs. Warren's Profession* and moved the play to a larger theater in the Fine Arts, they lost more money after getting into

Maurice Browne and Ellen Van Volkenburg
SPECIAL COLLECTIONS LIBRARY, UNIVERSITY OF MICHIGAN

a scrape with the landlord over the rental fee. And there were personal problems, including Browne's affair with another woman.

In the end, despite the private funding, and in spite of the praise its work produced, the Little Theatre did not become the home of "popular art" or the powerful factor in "Chicago's surging mental life" that its founders had hoped to create. Deep in debt, and its reputation skewed by its association with the peace movement during World War I, it was evicted from the Fine Arts and went out of business in 1917.

Browne and Nellie Van were divorced but sometimes worked together elsewhere. Discouraged by the failure of their enterprise, she left Chicago and never came back. He continued to direct and write, with great emotion, about the theater, and occasionally he returned to Chicago with a play. In London, in later years, he made a name for himself, and a lot of money, producing R. C. Sheriff's World War I drama *Journey's End* and a *Hamlet* with John Gielgud. For a 1930 *Othello*, with Paul Robeson, Peggy Ashcroft, Sybil Thorndike, and Ralph Richardson, he also played Iago, directed by Van Volkenburg. But George Bernard Shaw said that none of those prestigious London shows "matters a tupenny damn. The work [Browne did] . . . on a fourth-floor-back in Chicago—that is what matters."

Emma "Red Emma" Goldman, the fiery anarchist who frequently visited Chicago on her lecture tours and knew Browne, bluntly gave her explanation for the death of the Little Theatre in her book *Living My Life*:

I was particularly interested in the new dramatic experiment of Mr. Browne. He had talent and sincerity, but he was too dominated by the past to make the Little Theatre an effective audience. The Greek drama and the classics were certainly of great value, I often told him, but thoughtful people were nowadays seeking dramatic expression of the human problems of our own day. As a matter of fact, no one in Chicago outside of Mr. Browne's troupe and their small circle of adherents was aware of the existence of the Little Theatre. Life simply passed it by. The greater the pity, because Maurice Browne was very much in earnest about his efforts.

There's no physical trace of the Little Theatre left. When I roamed around the Fine Arts fourth floor one wintry afternoon, trying to spot a hint of its existence, I found nothing. The whole floor had been radically remodeled several years earlier, erasing any evidence of the shrine I had hoped to find.

Yet the heritage of the Little Theatre, its devotion to promoting and producing contemporary works from near and far, works that attempt to take the theater a step forward in its vision, is still an inspiring force in American theater. And the call to "create your own theater with the talent at hand" is still a battle cry for many young Chicago artists as they set out to conquer the world with their own little theaters. It was a harbinger of things to come. It was small; it was adventuresome; it was motivated by passion; it delighted in turning economic shortcomings into blessings of innovation and experiment.

Browne's essay "The Temple of a Living Art: A Plea for an American Art Theatre" was published in 1914, but its message to theater makers of the future is as urgent today as it was then. He describes, for example, "the thrill that comes from accomplishing one's ends with utterly inadequate materials—the thrill and the soul-sickness of eternally making the best of what one has."

He calls this existence "purgatory," and in florid, fervent prose, he proclaims: "The dilettante and the weakling, the coward and the self-seeker, avert their faces before the fiery breath and are gone, gibbering, into the outer darkness of three meals a day and a regular income."

For the Chicago playgoer, a musical with Al Jolson in the 1920s, and in 1930 an American drama by Paul Green at the Goodman Theatre

Chapter 7

"We Were a Landlocked Town"

ONE OF THE PLAYWRIGHTS SHOWCASED by the Little Theatre was Kenneth Sawyer Goodman, a young businessman and theater devotee whose light one-act plays and masques had also been presented in a season sponsored by the cooperative Chicago Theatre Society, of which he was a founding member. In addition, he had collaborated with the brash Chicago journalist Ben Hecht in several works, including *The Hero of Santa Maria: A Ridiculous Tragedy in One Act* and *The Wonder Hat*, a romantic comedy that gave a breezy contemporary spin to stock characters from the Italian commedia dell'arte.

Though an amateur, Goodman was a serious student of theater. In 1916, he wrote a letter to the Art Institute of Chicago proposing, as part of the museum's mission, a drama department that would mix student artists with professionals in a workshop atmosphere.

While assigned to the Great Lakes Naval Training Station in World War I, Goodman became a victim of the nationwide influenza epidemic and died in 1918. He was thirty-five. In 1922, his parents, guardians of a fortune made in the lumber business, made good on their son's vision and contributed a whopping $350,000 for a theater and drama school

Kenneth Sawyer Goodman
COURTESY OF GOODMAN THEATRE

to be built in the rear of the Art Institute. Its director was Thomas Wood Stevens, who had worked closely with Kenneth Goodman at the Chicago Theatre Society and its allied publishing house, the Stage Guild.

The venerable architect Howard Van Doren Shaw, in his last major work in Chicago, designed the building, giving it a severe, tomblike Greek classic façade, with a carved motto above the entrance taken from Goodman's writings, that stated the theater's goal: TO RESTORE THE OLD VISIONS AND TO WIN THE NEW. (Inside, carved into the wood frame above the stage, was another motto also originally written by Goodman: YOU YOURSELVES MUST SET FLAME TO THE FAGOTS WHICH YOU HAVE BROUGHT. Years later, when a sexual meaning became attached to "fagots," the saying was discreetly covered over. It was briefly undraped in 1982 for the premiere engagement of *The Man Who Had Three Arms,* at the request of the playwright, Edward Albee.)

Because city restrictions on the building's height made it impossible to erect a high fly-space for raising and lowering scenery, the architect compensated by enlarging the wing space at either side of the stage and fashioning a plaster cyclorama at the rear wall of the stage to allow for scenic and lighting effects.

The theater, fronting on Columbus Drive at Monroe Street, opened in 1925, and there it remained, through thick and thin, until 2000, when the Goodman, then the city's oldest and largest resident theater, moved to its new Loop site at 170 N. Dearborn Street.

Goodman's sometime coauthor, Ben Hecht, had come to Chicago from Wisconsin in 1910, when he was still a teenager. By 1921, he had published his first novel, *Erik Dorn,* and was writing his popular "One Thousand and One Afternoons" column for the *Daily News.* Two years later, in 1923, he and the poet Maxwell Bodenheim started their own sassy newspaper, the *Chicago Literary Times,* greeting the world with this salvo: "Chicago, the jazz baby—the reeking, cinder-ridden, joyous

Baptist stronghold; Chicago, the gum-chewing center of the world, the bleating, slat-headed rendezvous of half-witted newspapers, sociopaths and pants maker, in the name of the Seven Holy and Imperishable Arts, Chicago salutes you!"

Looking back on those palmy days in a *Wistfully Yours* piece for an all-Chicago issue of *Theatre Arts* magazine in July 1951, Hecht called the city "a prose town," in which even its many poets wrote in a prose style, albeit a bit "gaudier and more sententious" than was to be found in newspaper columns.

"As for playwrights," Hecht wrote, "they were as rare as rubies. A few of us wrote plays—even 'three acters,' but it was an activity that was looked down on. The first play I wrote was a collaboration with Sherwood Anderson. It was *Benvenuto Cellini,* and we wrote it in secret."

Ben Hecht

Chicago's theater, Hecht stated, "came almost entirely from New York. And, like everything else that came from New York, it had small standing in our eyes. We looked on New York much as New York looks on Hollywood today—as a spawning ground for semiliterate commercialism. Theatrically and journalistically we were a landlocked town no more touched by the glamour of Broadway than the glories of Nineveh."

In his mix of nostalgic and nose-thumbing reminiscence, Hecht found that in those old Chicago days, "oddly enough, we had the finest group of drama critics I have ever known. Ashton Stevens, the Hearst paper's reviewer, had a mysterious virtue, that is—a virtue mysterious for Chicago. This was a love of the theater." Even the worst of them, in Hecht's opinion, the *Daily News*'s Amy Leslie (the pen name of Lillie West Brown)—former actress, former lover of the novelist Stephen Crane, and wife of the big-game hunter Frank "Bring 'Em Back Alive" Buck, whom she had wed when she was in her midthirties and he was a twenty-year-old hotel bellboy—was "a delight to read" in her effusions of "ornate and endless prose." (In her review of *Mr. Blue Beard* at the Iroquois in 1903, Leslie said that the musical "has been rescued from its British stupidity by squandered wealth plain to be seen in the cos-

tumes, the tornadoes of brilliant paint and spangles, the armies of dancing, singing and laughing comedians and a ballet which alone is a delight.")

Other critics of the time included Percy Hammond, who, holding forth at the *Tribune,* came up with the wicked definition of theater criticism as "poison from contented snakes." And at the *Examiner,* there was the reviewer with the fancifully Shakespearean nom de plume of Forrest Arden.

However disdainful Chicagoans may have been about that "semiliterate commercialism" coming to them from New York, it certainly had its flashy moments, and it kept the Loop lights of "that toddlin' town" blazing into the night. There were more than eighty productions in the city's twenty-three theaters in the 1922–23 season, including the cream of the dramas, musicals, and revues of Broadway. Once in a while, there would even be a show that traveled the other way, from Chicago to New York. The musical *No, No, Nanette* played a record-breaking forty-nine weeks in 1924–25 at the Harris Theatre on Dearborn Street before moving on to its London and Broadway engagements.

"I don't believe there are fifty seats [left unsold] in the combined theatres of Chicago," proclaimed Frederick Donaghey in the *Tribune,* with blustering overstatement, "and, unless one be aurally or ocularly infirm, the last row is as good as the first row."

Theatergoers heading downtown in the 1920s could enjoy Al Jolson in *Big Boy* at the Apollo, the *Ziegfeld Follies of 1925* at the Illinois, or director Max Reinhardt's epic *The Miracle,* with a company of six hundred and a symphony orchestra, at the Auditorium. Before the theater, they could dine at Henrici's, Ireland's Oyster House, or the Union Restaurant, and after the show they could go dancing until the early morning hours at the Palmer House on State Street or at Bert Kelly's Stables ("Our waiters sing. Our cook dances") on Rush Street. Chicago was a wide-open town in this time of Al Capone and Prohibition, and it was open all the time.

But there were cracks in the glittering city life. By the late 1920s, most of the vaunted poets and novelists who made up the core of the city's lit-

Entrance to the old Goodman Theatre, 1925 to 2000, with modern panels and screens
added in the 1970s in an effort to enliven the gray severity of the façade

COURTESY OF GOODMAN THEATRE

erary renaissance had moved east. Hecht and his writing partner Charles MacArthur in 1928 set *The Front Page,* their lively American theater classic, in the whirlwind of 1920s Chicago, but by then, both men were long gone from the Chicago action. Another enduring Jazz Age folk tale of sensational crime and the sensation-mongering press, *Chicago* (later triumphantly restaged by ex-Chicagoan Bob Fosse as a 1976 Broadway musical and in 2002 as an Academy Award-winning movie), was written by former *Tribune* reporter Maureen Dallas Watkins and was brought to New York success, after she, too, had left town.

In this, the Chicago emigrants were following the lead of Margaret Anderson, the daring, feisty editor of the *Little Review* who had founded her world-famous literary magazine in Chicago in 1914. In 1917, however, she moved it to New York. In a statement that was echoed through the years by scores of Chicago artists, she set down her reason for the move to the East. She wrote, in her autobiography *My Thirty Years War:*

> Chicago had had all it wanted from us and we had had all that it could give. It was time to touch the greatest city of America. It would then be time for Europe. The only way to make the L.R. [Little Review] the international organ I had planned was to publish it from New York, where our position would be more commanding. . . . I loved Chicago forever, I could never forget it, I would come back to it . . . but I must go on.

And then, in late 1929, the lights of Chicago theaters, of all persuasions, began to waver and go out. The Great Depression and the advent of the movie talkies were devastating to their work.

At the Goodman, the effect of the Depression was immediate. At the end of the 1929–30 season, the theater had a $34,895 deficit, an intolerable amount for the parent Art Institute's board of trustees. Out went Thomas Wood Stevens, who resigned, fearing that the professional theater he had guided would soon be producing what he disdainfully dismissed as "Loop stuff." Instead, after another season that lost $19,000, the professional company was disbanded. The trustees kept the drama school, which had been making money, and the Goodman in 1931 was refashioned as a student theater, a status it maintained for thirty-eight years until, swept along with the tide of a new resident theater movement, it reemerged as a professional organization in 1969.

Downtown, meanwhile, the once-bustling group of big-time theaters dwindled to a handful. By the time of the 1936–37 season, the Loop houses held fewer than half the productions they had housed a decade earlier. The Auditorium, grandest of all, hung on until 1941, but then, deep in debt, it shut down and, narrowly escaping destruction, did not reopen to the public until 1967.

By the mid-1930s, Loop commercialism had been replaced in many instances by federal subsidy, and a major employer of actors in the city was the United States government.

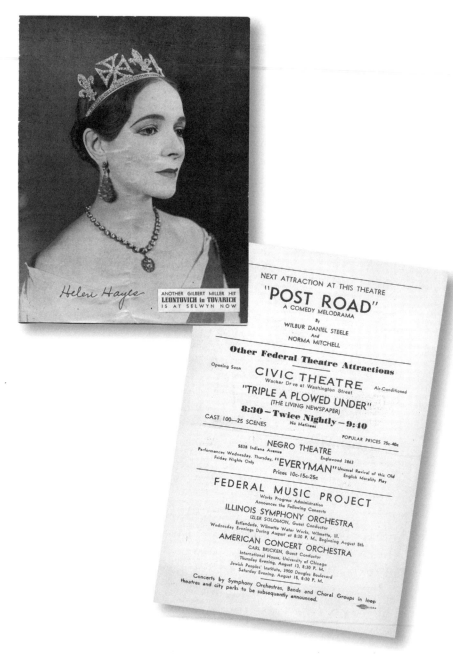

Helen Hayes

ANOTHER GILBERT MILLER HIT
LEONTOVICH in TOVARICH
IS AT SELWYN NOW

NEXT ATTRACTION AT THIS THEATRE
"POST ROAD"
A COMEDY MELODRAMA
By
WILBUR DANIEL STEELE
And
NORMA MITCHELL

Other Federal Theatre Attractions

Opening Soon
CIVIC THEATRE
Wacker Dr ve at Washington Street   Air-Conditioned
"TRIPLE A PLOWED UNDER"
(THE LIVING NEWSPAPER)
8:30 — Twice Nightly — 9:40
CAST 100—25 SCENES   No Matinees

POPULAR PRICES 25c-40c

NEGRO THEATRE
5538 Indiana Avenue
Performances Wednesday, Thursday,   Englewood 3863
Friday Nights Only   "EVERYMAN" Unusual Revival of this Old
Prices 10c-15c-25c   English Morality Play

FEDERAL MUSIC PROJECT
Works Progress Administration
Announces the Following Concerts
ILLINOIS SYMPHONY ORCHESTRA
IZLER SOLOMON, Guest Conductor
Esrlandade, Wilmette Water Works, Wilmette, Ill.
Wednesday Evenings During August at 8:30 P. M. Beginning August 5th
AMERICAN CONCERT ORCHESTRA
CARL BRICKEN, Guest Conductor
International House, University of Chicago
Thursday Evening, August 13, 8:30 P. M.
Jewish Peoples' Institute, 3900 Douglas Boulevard
Saturday Evening, August 15, 8:30 P. M.
Concerts by Symphony Orchestras, Bands and Choral Groups in loop
theatres and city parks to be subsequently announced.

Depression fare: Helen Hayes and her company in 1937 in their touring production of
the cozy history play *Victoria Regina* and a "Living Newspaper" drama from the Federal
Theatre Project

Chapter 8

"There Actually Was a National Theater"

LUCILLE STRAUSS, WHO HAD GROWN UP in the North Shore suburb of Highland Park and had attended a fancy finishing school out east before returning home to attend the University of Chicago, was a member of the first graduating class of the Goodman School of Drama. A lovely young actress, she was getting ready to enter the professional world when the Depression struck. More than sixty years later, when she recalled the impact of that American economic and social disaster for an oral history project for DePaul University, her eyes teared over and her voice trembled when she said, "I can't explain to you how severe the Depression was. It's hard for you who have never lived through it. And you'll never have to again. But I tell you that one would think twice about spending a dime to go downtown."

The bottom had dropped out of the economy in the 1930s, bringing with it a sense of disillusionment and anger at the capitalistic system that had failed so catastrophically.

The theater business, already besieged by the new talking pictures, was hit hard. Some of the big musicals and dramas from Broadway—such as Helen Hayes in *Victoria Regina,* the musicals *Anything Goes*

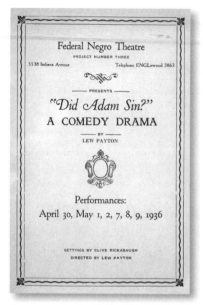

A program for the Federal Negro Theatre

SPECIAL COLLECTIONS AND PRESERVATION DIVISION,
CHICAGO PUBLIC LIBRARY

and *Red, Hot and Blue,* with Ethel Merman, Jimmy Durante, and Bob Hope, and George M. Cohan in Eugene O'Neill's *Ah, Wilderness!*—continued to tour under sponsorship of the Theatre Guild, the Playwrights' Company, and such durable New York producers as Sam H. Harris, Max Gordon, and the brothers Shubert. But the commercial theater, like the other bright pastimes that had buoyed the high times of the 1920s, was deeply in trouble in the tough times of the 1930s, thousands of its artists and craftsmen unemployed.

As a form of white-collar relief, the New Deal administration of President Franklin D. Roosevelt in 1935 created the Federal Theatre Project (FTP), a branch of the Works Progress Administration (WPA), with Hallie Flanagan, head of the Vassar (College) Experimental Theatre, as its national director. The project lasted only until 1939, when Congress, always skittish in dealing with the arts, pulled the plug on the project because of what was perceived to be its left-leaning tendencies. In that brief period, however, the FTP launched scores of original productions, employed thousands of actors, and brought theater to millions of customers.

One of the actors was Strauss. In 1935 she got a call from Whitford Kane, her old director at the Goodman School, who had joined the FTP and was recruiting individuals for it. For their work, actors got about twenty-three dollars a week, and Strauss, eager to supplement her husband's small salary, took the offer.

There were, she estimated, around fifty actors in the Chicago branch of the FTP, plus administrators and business staff, and

Program for the Federal Theatre Project

SPECIAL COLLECTIONS AND PRESERVATION DIVISION,
CHICAGO PUBLIC LIBRARY

The cast of *The Swing Mikado* strutting its stuff
AP/WORLD WIDE PHOTO

within that division were several units—Negro, Yiddish, children's, and experimental arms among others. A touring unit traveled in Illinois, Iowa, and Wisconsin with a repertory of three shows. Alan Peters, who supervised those FTP tours, recalled for the DePaul project that when he sold main-floor tickets to two African Americans in a Peoria theater, he received a call from the district's congressman telling him he could not do that. The congressman was Everett Dirksen, future Republican power broker in the United States Senate, and Peters said he told him, "I will not be countermanded on such a thing as seating a black person on the main floor." The tickets remained valid.

The best known of the FTP's Midwest shows, however, were staged in Chicago, mostly in the downtown Great Northern and Blackstone

MEANWHILE, IN WOODSTOCK . . .

Orson Welles had already completed a successful season as an actor at the Gate Theatre in Dublin and a thirty-four-state American tour of three plays with Katharine Cornell when he produced, directed, and acted in a summer of three plays in the Woodstock (Illinois) Opera House.

It was 1934, and Welles was nineteen.

The Todd Theatre Festival, named for and sponsored by the Woodstock school Welles had attended, and presented in the town's six-hundred-seat Victorian theater, was to be "something of a combination of Bayreuth and a strawberry festival," according to the young producer. To join him and the Todd students in the casts, he engaged Michael (Micheàl) MacLiammoir and Hilton Edwards of the Gate. Their repertoire was *Hamlet,* with MacLiammoir in the title role and Welles as King Claudius; the American premiere of Dimitri Merejkowski's Russian melodrama, *Tsar Paul;* and George Du Maurier's *Trilby,* directed by and starring Welles as Svengali. Whitford Kane, a Dublin native and a mainstay of the old Goodman professional company, had accepted the post of artistic director, but took off for Hollywood in search of a film career and never appeared for the job.

The festival, despite breaking even financially and drawing many "fashionables" from the big city, was rocky artistically in its first and only season. Claudia Cassidy, who had covered the festival for the *Journal of Commerce,* fifty years after the fact still remembered Welles's Claudius as "a mesmerizing creation from this cherubic young man." But Lloyd Lewis's review in the *Daily News,* although recommending the pleasant motor trip to Woodstock, about sixty miles northwest of Chicago, criticized Welles's "eccentric" performance in *Trilby,* stating that the young actor had "made up his face as a sort of satire upon some composite photograph of a hoot owl, Abe Lincoln, Ben Hecht, and John Brown of Osawattomie."

Michael MacLiammoir as Hamlet, Louise Prussing as Gertrude, and Orson Welles as Claudius in *Hamlet* at the Todd Theatre Festival, 1934

COURTESY OF WOODSTOCK OPERA HOUSE

theaters. Beginning in 1936 and continuing through 1939, there were thirty-two of these productions, some, such as Orson Welles's "voodoo" version of *Macbeth*, imported from New York, but most drawn from the Chicago unit. The shows ranged all over the repertory, from a trio of Shakespeare plays featuring the actor Ian Keith ("the poor man's John Barrymore," according to Peters) to the original musical revue *O Say Can You Sing?*

Its biggest hit by far came in 1938 with *The Swing Mikado* in a black "swing" version of the Gilbert and Sullivan operetta devised by Chicago director Harry Minturn. With the scene shifted to the South Sea Islands, and with just a few songs receiving swing arrangements, the show ran for twenty-two weeks, playing to 250,000 customers and clearing $38,000, at a top ticket price of $1.10. It was such a smash that it transferred to Broadway, where, for a while, it played across the street from a competing *Hot Mikado* with tap dancer Bill Robinson, rushed into production by producer Mike Todd after he could not buy the rights to the "swing" version from the FTP. (*The Swing Mikado* inevitably led to a *Tropical Pinafore*, presented by the American Negro Light Opera Association for three weeks at the Great Northern in 1939.)

For Strauss, the most important of all the FTP presentations were the "Living Newspaper" dramas, written about contemporary issues and based on recent news developments. *Spirochete*, which originated in Chicago, tackled the problem of venereal disease. *Power* concerned the government's electrification program through the Tennessee Valley Authority. *Triple A Plowed Under* addressed the desperate poverty of the nation's farmers. *One-Third of a Nation* took its title from President Roosevelt's second inaugural address, in which he stated that he saw "one-third of a nation ill-housed, ill-clad and ill-nourished." When produced in Chicago, it was rewritten to include specific references to the tenements of the city.

Ticket prices as low as fifty-five cents for the main floor and twenty-five cents for the balcony brought in, Strauss believed, "people who had never seen live theater. And I was excited by *Triple A Plowed Under* and *One-Third of a Nation* because they were reflecting the ills of society at that time and they were doing it in a very honest way."

In another expression of socially urgent drama, four years before the advent of the FTP, a core of six nonprofessional Chicago actors in 1931

Epic theater in *Triple A Plowed Under,* produced by the Federal Theatre Project

produced a manifesto stating that to "the thinking theater-goer" it was obvious that "the professional theater and quality of drama it preserves has ceased to satisfy the artistic and intellectual needs of our generation."

Under these circumstances, the actors united to form the Chicago Workers' Theater (CWT), with these goals:

> To crystallize in drama the informed but pressing problems of our times. To present these problems in the most entertaining, stimulating and artistic manner. To mobilize talent and skill in all phases of dramatic activity, which cannot find expression in the ideologically bankrupt commercial theater. To build a permanent theater, technically expert and artistically sound, informed with the vitality and power of this historic movement of the masses.

They would people their shows, they said, echoing the ideals of the Chicago Little Theatre, with "a cast of young actors from the universities, the shops, the factories, the offices of Chicago."

Throughout the 1930s, the Workers' Theatre carried through its mission in contemporary social dramas, in public forums, in acting and playwriting workshops, and in dozens of good, bad, and indifferent original songs, skits, parodies, and plays. If they were a ragtag group of artists, they still were acknowledged as a significant force in theater. In 1937, *Stage Magazine* called the group "the only theater west of Broadway that is carrying out a policy devoted only to plays of social significance." (Danny Newman, many years later an iconic guru of subscription ticket sales in the not-for-profit performing arts movement, was then getting his start in a long show business career with a for-profit group, the Mummers, and he said, jokingly, of the difference between CWT and his troupe, "They did plays of social significance. We did good plays.")

But CWT attracted distinguished allies. Its pro bono lawyer was Arthur Goldberg, future Supreme Court justice and U.S. ambassador to the United Nations. Their sponsors included dancer and choreographer

An Expressionistic lighting and scenic design for *Triple A Plowed Under*

Ruth Page, attorney Clarence Darrow, novelist Meyer Levin, and poet Harriet Monroe.

Their repertoire contained work by such nationally known writers and composers as Langston Hughes, Archibald MacLeish, Paul Green, Norman Corwin, Paddy Chayefsky, John Dos Passos, Irwin Shaw, and Kurt Weill, as well as local writers who turned out their own pageants, sketches, and satires, with titles that clearly demonstrated their political and aesthetic leanings: *Spain, 1937, Peace in Our Time, Pirates of Finance, Election Circus of 1935,* and *An Anti-War Revue.*

They held symposiums on "The Negro in the Theatre." They staged a 1936 celebration for the twelfth anniversary of the *Daily Worker* newspaper. And they put together a mobile theater that sent their productions out to the neighborhoods.

At first, CWT's headquarters was a walk-up studio at 505 S. State Street. Reminiscing for the DePaul project, Peters, a founder of the troupe, remembered that the first two floors of the building were occupied by a bookstore and an art gallery, both managed by the Communist Party. "They let us use the third floor," Peters said. "We built a platform and this was our theater. We had no money so we scrounged ten cents to pay the electric bill every month. We laughed about all that 'Moscow Gold' the Communist Party was supposed to have, and how we weren't getting any of it. All this 'Moscow Gold,' and we couldn't pay the light bill."

In 1935, however, CWT had a solid hit. It got the Chicago rights to Clifford Odets's *Waiting for Lefty,* the short, naturalistic drama about a taxi drivers' strike that had caused a sensation in a New York production by the Group Theatre. Under its new name of Chicago Repertory Group (CRG), it presented the show more than one hundred times in auditoriums all over the city, receiving its first important notices from the city's newspapers. Lloyd Lewis, reviewing the production in the *Chicago Daily News,* called it a "superbly written" drama of "vignettes in vinegar."

Among the *Lefty* cast members joining the group was Louis (later Studs) Terkel, a young writer and former student at the University of Chicago Law School, who was brought into the theater by director Charles De Sheim. "I had never acted before," Terkel remembered. "But he got me to sit in on a rehearsal of *Lefty.* I had never seen anything like it. It was like a war scene. There was such energy. Such passion. Through that experience, and with Charlie De Sheim prodding me, I got involved in this new world.

"For a while," Terkel said, "we were like the farm club of the Group Theatre." This loose alliance paid off, for when the New Yorkers came to town with their productions of Odets's *Golden Boy* and *Awake and Sing,* they gave classes for their friends, providing the Chicagoans with their first taste of the Method in acting.

Moving from one temporary home to the next, the CRG in 1938 had another "success on its hands" (as Claudia Cassidy wrote in the *Journal of Commerce*) with its production of composer Marc Blitzstein's *The Cradle Will Rock,* a musical that had raised a dust storm of controversy on Broadway in a production by Orson Welles. Set in a mythical Steeltown in the middle of a union strike, the show featured a villain named Mr. Mister, who consorted with his fellow corrupt fat cats to squeeze the labor force. Noting its impending arrival in Chicago in the Rep's tiny upper-floor theater at 39 E. Balbo, the *Tribune* headline stated, "Hold Tryouts for Odd Opera Due on Oct. 21."

When *Cradle* did open, with Strauss in a leading role as Moll, a good-hearted and intelligent prostitute, it was warmly welcomed by several reviewers. Carl Harris, in the *Daily Record,* said, "Something besides malted milk runs in the veins of the Chicago stage this week."

The Rep lasted into the 1940s, its antiwar programs giving way to shows that boosted the war effort, but by 1943, with many of its artists dispersed, it ended its spunky history.

For the Federal Theatre Project, the end had come earlier and more abruptly. The final production, Elmer Rice's tenement drama *Street Scene,* finished its run at the Great Northern in late June 1939, and on July 31, members of the Chicago regional office gathered for a farewell party at the 1819 N. Lincoln Park West studios of Pierre Nuyttens, designer of the costumes for *The Swing Mikado.* Friends and neighbors and a German band, along with two kegs of beer, joined the gathering, and there were toasts and tears well into the night. In a memoir of his work at the FTP, Don Farran, who had been in charge of securing original play scripts for the Chicago office, wrote of that final party: "It was the proper end to an era that may not come again, a time when there actually was a national theater in this broad land, and children and even

NATHAN DAVIS, ACTOR: "I HAD NOTHING TO LOSE"

When I was a kid on the West Side of Chicago, I played in the theater program of the Jewish Peoples Institute. I did a Maurice Chevalier imitation in a variety show sponsored by the Young Men's Jewish Charities. [He sings, vivaciously, with a very French accent, "Is it any wonder I'm happy?"]

In 1936, I went down to the University of Illinois at Champaign and joined a Jewish theater troupe there. I became rather political, a premature antifascist. One day I went to Chicago to pick up some pacifist reading materials, and I became interested in the political plays they were doing then. I got involved. I was in *Waiting for Lefty* and *The Cradle Will Rock* and *Bury the Dead*. [He mimes digging a grave, harshly singing, in time with his digging, "I Can't Give You Anything but Love, Baby."] At the time, I was living with my parents, and I went from one little theater to the next. I would play roles like "Joe the Lover," the juvenile lead.

Nathan Davis
FREDRIC STEIN

When the war came, I was drafted. Landed in Normandy and saw service in Europe. Coming home to my wife, Metta, and the first of our three children, I continued my acting. I did some freelance radio work, but then the soap operas moved out of Chicago, and there weren't many outlets for an actor. I had a full-time job with a wholesale drug company, but I managed to do acting work in summer tents and in community theaters all over the city and suburbs. One was the Last Stage, in the Hyde Park neighborhood where I live. It was a little second-floor place on Fifty-first Street, and in that tiny space in the 1960s we did shows like *Ulysses in Night Town* and *Slow Dance on the Killing Ground*.

In 1976, I was fired from my job, but Metta was working as a grade school teacher, and I didn't have to worry about putting bread on the table, so I decided to take a chance on acting for a living. I was turning sixty, and I had nothing to lose. I joined Actors' Equity, and I got a job at Court Theatre at the University of Chicago in a production of *Romeo and Juliet*. Judith Ivey played Juliet. After that, it was three, four, five different shows a year. Pretty steady. Besides that, my son Andrew is a movie director, and when the time comes, he usually casts me in the movie he's making. In 1998, I got a Joseph Jefferson Award for lifetime achievement in the theater community here. That was good.

So I'm still acting. Only now I don't play juveniles.

older children as parents could see and enjoy live actors in live theaters, and the players could eat with regularity and believe in make-believe."

It was not quite the end, however. The FTP had left a legacy. As Terkel has said, "It proved there was a hunger for good, live, pertinent theater in this country, no matter where it's performed."

Many of the artists who had come of age in the 1930s went on to other careers in other theaters. Terkel, Beverly Younger, Gertrude Gunter Soltker, Lucille Strauss, Lester Podewell, Nathan (sometimes billed as Wayne) Davis, and Alan Peters all continued to work in Chicago, bringing with them the political awareness and aesthetic training they had acquired in their work with the FTP and CRG. They acted as a bridge between their turbulent times and the socially conscious times of the sixties.

But first, we had to get through the fifties.

In the 1950s, touring Broadway musicals were standard fare at the downtown Shubert Theatre.

Chapter 9

"Chicago Is Hard Up for Writers"

IN JANUARY 1952, THE *New Yorker* magazine printed a three-part report by A. J. Liebling on Chicago under the general title of "The Second City." The series slyly took its name from the fact that by 1950, with a population of more than 3.5 million, Chicago was indeed second in size to New York, the country's largest city. But Liebling, a journalist with peerless gifts of witty observation, discovered in his visits to 1950s Chicago that behind its façade of a big city lay the soul of a hick town. Outrageous and, in many respects, dead-on accurate, his analysis caused a major cry of the heart from the city's boosters, and it scratched again the ever-festering sore of inferiority that Chicagoans have been picking at for more than a century: We're still not the First City.

Thirty-two years earlier, H. L. Mencken, another journalist of biting abilities, had labeled Chicago "the literary capital of the United States." In this "abattoir on Lake Michigan," Mencken gleefully pointed out, lay the vitality, curiosity, originality, and distinctive style that tired old New York lacked. In every aspect of the arts, including the theater ("The first and best little theater in America was set up in Chicago"), Mencken praised Chicago to New York's disadvantage. Chicago, he wrote, "is overgrown, it is oafish, it shows many of the characters of the upstart and the bounder." For all that, in the works of Sherwood Anderson, Theodore Dreiser, Edgar Lee Masters, and Carl Sandburg, Mencken discovered "a genuine earnestness, a real interest in ideas, a sound curiosity about the prodigal and colorful life of the people of the republic." Above all, he believed, Chicago was full of energy and ambition. As he had written in 1917 in *Civilized Chicago,* another piece exalting the city, "I give you Chicago. It is not London and Harvard. It is not Paris-and-buttermilk. It is American in every chitling and sparerib, and it is alive from snout to tail."

But nine years later, in 1926, when Mencken published an essay on Chicago in his magazine, the *American Mercury,* the headline for Samuel Putnam's piece was "Chicago: An Obituary." It listed thirty-six writers who had left the city, underlining the notion that things weren't what they used to be in that once-vibrant city.

Since then, there had been some further warning signs that the city's reputation for oafishness might be outpacing its inventiveness. In 1935, after Mayor Edward J. Kelly and seven fellow citizens had seen and adjudged a touring production of *Tobacco Road* as "obscene and lascivious," the mayor had effectively shut down that drama about a poor "white trash" family by revoking the license of the Selwyn Theatre, where the play had run for seven weeks. (Kelly remained faithful to his standards. In 1941, he gave the keys to the city to the long-running comedy *Life with Father* and dubbed the cast of the squeaky-clean show First Family of Chicago.)

As evidence of the lack of sophistication in "Porkopolis," critics also pointed to the fact that the play holding the record as the longest running show in Chicago theater history, running for a hundred weeks from 1942 to 1944 at the Blackstone Theatre, was not any of the big Broadway hits of the day, but *Good Night Ladies,* a knockabout sex farce based on the old comedy *Ladies' Night in a Turkish Bath.* (That record, by the way, is still impressive. Many light entertainments, such as *Shear Madness, Pump Boys and Dinettes,* and the Blue Man Group subsequently had longer runs in smaller off-Loop theaters, but *Ladies* still stands as champion in the traditional downtown theaters.)

Liebling, who knew and had lived in Chicago, did not know why the change had come. Friends he asked suggested that Chicago had never really recovered from the blow of the Depression. But he knew something was awry. "For a city, where, I am credibly informed, you couldn't throw an egg in 1925 without braining a great poet," he wrote, "Chicago is hard up for writers."

Claudia Cassidy at her desk, 1944
COURTESY OF *CHICAGO TRIBUNE* NEWS ARCHIVE

As for theater, the *New Yorker* said: "Plays at Chicago theatres, for example, are always locally assumed to be inferior versions of the New York productions, or, if they *are* the New York productions, with original casts intact, the actors are assumed to be giving inferior performances. Chicagoans with the price of airplane tickets do their theatregoing here in New York, where, along with people from Boise, Chillicothe, and Winnemucca, they pay such exorbitant premiums for tickets to hits that most of the natives never see them. . . . Whether this approach to theatregoing originated with the *Tribune,* whose current critic, Claudia Cassidy, is its high priestess; with those producers who have in fact sent out bad shows; or with the airlines' sales-promotion departments, I do not know."

The reference to Claudia (*Tribune* readers always referred to her by her first name) is significant. A native of downstate Shawneetown on the Mississippi River, where she saw her first theater on showboats, she came to Chicago after her graduation from the University of Illinois in 1921 with hopes of becoming a writer. She took courses in typing and shorthand and got a job as a secretary at the *Journal of Commerce* (because, she always insisted, the kind man who gave her the job did so in the belief that, although the rest of the applicants could find work at other places, nobody else would hire her). Pressed into service as a reviewer in 1924, she was soon offered the job of the paper's performing arts critic. "It was," she said, "like being given the keys to the Kingdom of Heaven." She continued to cover theater, dance, and music in Chicago for the next seven decades, the zenith of her influence being from 1942 to 1965, when her "On the Aisle" column was a hugely well-read feature of the *Tribune.*

In the 1950s, although Chicago was generally held in low regard as a theater town, Claudia was held up high as the most powerful critic in the country—outside of New York, of course. There were many names for her—"Medusa of the Midwest," "Acidy Cassidy," and the "Queen of Culture," holding sway in her reign of terror. These sobriquets stemmed from the sharp, stinging way she treated anything she disliked or found mediocre or careless. Reviewing Tennessee Williams's *Summer and Smoke*, she called the leading actress Margaret Phillips "an actress of singularly limited range and almost no perceptible depth." Marie Powers, appearing in Gian Carlo Menotti's *The Medium*, was, for Claudia, a cross between "Hermione Gingold's Brunnhilde with the Three Witches from *Macbeth*," an assessment that sent Powers on an (unsuccessful) mission to the *Tribune* to punch the reviewer in the nose. The actress Cornelia Otis Skinner referred to her style as "pure bitchery," and director Tyrone

"A TOUGH LITTLE PLAY"

The most famous review in Chicago theater history was written, on deadline, by Claudia Cassidy immediately after the pre-Broadway premiere of Tennessee Williams's The Glass Menagerie *on December 26, 1944. Her praise gave a crucial boost to the drama's box office and helped launch a long, illustrious career for Williams, who acknowledged the review's influence and treasured its memory all the rest of his life. Here is the entire notice, as printed in the* Chicago Tribune *for December 27, 1944.*

Too many theatrical bubbles burst in the blowing, but *The Glass Menagerie* holds in its shadowed fragility the stamina of success. This brand new play, which turned the Civic theater into a place of steadily increasing enchantment last night, is still fluid with change, but it is vividly written, and in the main superbly acted. Paradoxically, it is a dream in the dusk and a tough little play that knows people and how they tick. Etched in the shadows of a man's memory, it comes alive in theater terms of words, motion, lighting, and music. If it is your play, as it is mine, it reaches out tentacles, first tentative, then gripping, and you are caught in its spell.

Tennessee Williams, who wrote it, has been unbelievably lucky. His play, which might have been smashed by the insensitive or botched by the fatuous, has fallen into expert hands. He found Eddie Dowling, who liked it enough to fight for it, Jo Mielziner, who devoted his first time out of army service to lighting it magnificently, and Laurette Taylor, who chose it for her return to the stage. He found other people, too, but ah, that Laurette Taylor!

I never saw Miss Taylor as Peg, but if that was the role of her youth, this is the role of her maturity. As a draggled southern belle who married the wrong man, living in a near-tenement, alienating her children by her nagging fight to shove them up to her pathetically remembered gentility, she gives a magnificent performance. The crest of her career in the

Guthrie, who had received lavish praise from Claudia in the past, but who had been slammed in her review of his opening production of *Hamlet* at the Guthrie Theatre in Minneapolis in 1963, called her "that bitch."

But if Claudia took away, she also gave. She could be, and was, generous, gracious, and kind to young writers, as I gratefully discovered; and for all the actors who had felt her scorn, there were an equal number, including Alfred Lunt and Lynn Fontanne, who had been warmed by her praise and adored her. She and Ashton Stevens of the *Chicago American* rescued Williams's *The Glass Menagerie* from oblivion in its premiere at the Civic Theatre in the winter of 1944 and sent it on its way to becoming an American classic; and in 1959, when a frightened Lorraine Hansberry opened her *A Raisin in the Sun* at the Blackstone

delta was the simultaneous arrival of seventeen gentlemen callers, and her pitiful quest in this play—as often funny as sad—is the acquisition of just one gentleman caller for her neurotically shy daughter, the crippled girl played by Julie Haydon. Her preparations for that creature, once she has heckled her son into inviting him, his arrival in the hilarious extrovert played by Anthony Ross, and the aftermath of frustration—these are not things quickly told in their true terms. They are theater, and they take seeing.

Fortunately, I have been able to hang around the Civic at previews and I have seen *The Glass Menagerie* twice. Mr. Dowling was good last night in the double role of the son and narrator (who says the first narrator was the angel of annunciation), but he is twice as good as that when he is relaxed and easy. He had strokes of brilliance last night, but the long easy stride of his earlier performance is on a plane with Miss Taylor's playing and gives the play greater strength.

Laurette Taylor in *The Glass Menagerie*

Mr. Ross enters late, but leaves an impression as unforgettable as his green coat and his face, which is perilously close to being a mug. Late of *Winged Victory,* this stalwart actor does a superb job as the gentleman caller who finds his visit a little more than he bargained for. Which leaves only Julie Haydon and there, frankly, I'm puzzled. At times she has the frailty of the glass animals of the title which are her refuge from reality. But I couldn't quite believe her, and my sympathy went to her nagging mother and her frustrated brother—because whatever the writing, acting is the final word, and they acted circles around her.

ZERO MOSTEL
RALPH MEEKER
RHINOCEROS

Avant-garde fare in a summer tent: program for Eugene Ionesco's *Rhinoceros*, with Zero Mostel and Ralph Meeker, at the Edgewater Beach Playhouse, 1963

PATRICIA MOORE COLLECTION, USED BY PERMISSION OF *PLAYBILL*

Theatre, Claudia's enthusiastic review helped ensure that landmark African American drama's immense success.

As Glenna Syse, theater critic of the *Chicago Sun-Times* during the latter part of Claudia's career, said, "We owe her a lot. She kept plenty of the bad stuff out of town." Danny Newman, the theater press agent who knew her well, said that some producers would hold extra rehearsals before venturing into Chicago and braving Claudia's eye. Claudia herself always said of her vaunted power, "The only 'power' you get comes from the readers who trust what you have to say."

By the 1950–51 season, the downtown scene that Claudia and her fellow critics covered had shrunk to twenty-three shows in seven theaters, down from one hundred three offerings in twenty-three theaters in the 1925–26 season. Still, in the years during and immediately after World War II, the Broadway shows continued to troop into the Loop, and in some years they produced bountiful seasons. You could see *A Streetcar Named Desire* (with Uta Hagen and Anthony Quinn), *Death of a Salesman,* or *Mister Roberts* in productions that rivaled the Broadway originals. In those days, if you said that Chicago had enjoyed a good theater season, you meant that the touring versions of New York shows that came to Chicago had been above average.

In the early 1950s, even as television began to chip away at the size of the audience, downtown was still a lively place for theater and after-theater entertainment. Following a play or musical at the Shubert, Blackstone, Great Northern, Civic, Selwyn, Harris, or Erlanger, one could enjoy supper at Henrici's, Fritzel's, Ireland's, Gibby's Majestic Grill, Alex Sage's, Teddy's L'Aiglon, or Don the Beachcomber or take in a late show at nightclubs and supper clubs like Mister Kelly's, the London House, the Empire Room of the Palmer House, the Boulevard Room of the Conrad Hilton Hotel, or the Chez Paree, where a 10:00 P.M. supper show that gave customers a five-course meal, an after-supper liqueur, and dancing, as well as a show featuring headliners such as comedian Joe E. Lewis, was advertised at $4.95, everything included.

Outside the Loop, there were community theaters, and, late in the 1940s, summer stock began to sprout in the suburbs, spearheaded by a new breed of local producers. Herb Rogers, who affected red socks as part of his persona, set up the first shows under canvas in 1948 with his Tenthouse Theatre in Highland Park, staging a season of two-week runs with a stock company that included Barnard Hughes and Hughes's wife, Helen Stenborg. A few years later, Rogers opened his Music Theatre of Highland Park, for musicals, also in a tent. In the summer of 1949, Marshall Migatz, then only twenty-six, whose subsequent ventures in scattered

Cast list for *Rhinoceros*

Chicago-area venues were to earn him the title of "the Shubert of summer stock," introduced the star system with his Chevy Chase Theatre in a former country club in Wheeling. Resident director there was Richard Barr, who would go on to become Edward Albee's producer.

When the owners of a tent theater in the parking lot of the Martinique restaurant at Ninety-fifth Street and Western Avenue in Evergreen Park went bust, the restaurant's owner, Tony DeSantis, kept the shows going under the banner of Drury Lane Theatre, thus starting a string of Drury Lanes that he operated in Chicago at various times and places for the next fifty years. Early on, DeSan-

Within the program, ads for the many diversions of the Edgewater Beach Hotel

STAGEBILL

DRURY
LANE
THEATRE

GLORIA SWANSON
"*The Inkwell*"   World Comedy Premiere

Gloria Swanson, touring in the "world premiere" of the comedy *The Inkwell*, was the star attraction at Drury Lane Theatre in Evergreen Park in 1962.

PATRICIA MOORE COLLECTION, USED BY PERMISSION OF *PLAYBILL*

tis discovered the benefits in liquor and food sales that came with a popular show, and eventually he moved the theater out of the tent and into much fancier digs within the Martinique, guaranteeing a year-round season for his one-stop dinner-and-show combinations. (This original venue, no longer owned by DeSantis, was sold in 2003 in order to make way for a Wal-Mart store.)

The fare in these summer theaters usually consisted of safe and/or tired warhorses hitched up to the talents of a guest star. But there were some venturesome shows, too. Hughes portrayed Willy Loman in *Death of a Salesman* at Tenthouse; Migatz, in a completely wild-card production, offered guest star Arnold Moss in a severely abridged *Back to Methuselah*, by George Bernard Shaw. And at Drury Lane, where the most popular shows usually involved Pat O'Brien in a family comedy or drama, Katherine Crosby assayed Shaw's *Arms and the Man*, with Chicago actor Tony Mockus as her leading man.

These theaters were valuable workplaces for a couple generations of Chicago actors. Tenthouse was a springboard for Hughes's long Broadway and film career, and local actors such as Mockus, Marrian Walters, George Womack, Sidney Breese, Studs Terkel, and Geraldine Kay all found summer work in the suburbs.

For a while, when the "Chicago style" of live television had its brief moments of fame in the early 1950s, there was some work in the soap opera *Hawkins Falls* and *Studs' Place*. But near the end of the decade, all that employment had gone, never to resurface, and for a young actor just entering the profession, the pickings in Chicago were mighty slim.

The local colleges and universities could boast revered faculty members such as acting coaches Alvina Krause at Northwestern and Bella Itkin at the Goodman School of Drama. And their alumni lists were spotted with a long string of famous theater folk: Charlton Heston,

Cloris Leachman, and Patricia Neal from Northwestern; Mladen Sekulovich (who changed his name to the more manageable Karl Malden), Will Geer, Sam Wanamaker, Geraldine Page, Lee Richardson, Harvey Korman, Shelley Berman, and Tom Aldredge, plus director Jose Quintero and designers Ralph Alswang and Theoni Aldredge, at the Goodman School; and so on. But the great majority of these were theater people who, once out of school, immediately left to start careers far removed from their training grounds. As Maureen Steindler, an actress who graduated from Northwestern in 1948, said, "For an actor in Chicago in the fifties, there was no place to go. There was nothing."

And then, remarkably and suddenly, in the last month of the last year of the 1950s, there was something. And in a brilliant stroke of Chicago sass and irony, its founders took their cue from Liebling and triumphantly called that something The Second City.

No matter what the title or time period, there usually was a future star in the cast of The Second City revues.

COURTESY OF THE SECOND CITY

Chapter 10

"It's a Comedy School"

IN THE PREHOLIDAY WEEK OF December 13, 1959, Chicago's downtown theaters held a total of three shows: *The Music Man,* starring Forrest Tucker, at the Shubert Theatre; *West Side Story* at the Erlanger (both long-running road companies of hit Broadway musicals); plus the Broadway-bound flop comedy *A Mighty Man Is He,* with Nancy Kelly, at the Blackstone. That same week, on Wednesday, December 16, two miles north of the Loop, in the former home of Wong Cleaners and Dyers, at 1842 N. Wells Street, a small cabaret theater that would open the way for a new life in resident theater premiered to an enthusiastic reception by the 120 or so people who had crammed into the space for its debut performance.

It's hard to exaggerate the milestone importance of the opening of The Second City. In years to come, it would evolve into an entertainment juggernaut, its influence on American comedy profound and its roll call of famous actors, directors, and writers incredible. But for the moment, on that midwinter evening in 1959, it was enough to say that in the virtual desert of inventive resident theater, The Second City was an oasis of hometown enterprise, its success based in the wit of its topical com-

Paul Sills, directing at the University of Chicago. Behind him is the actress Joyce Hiller (later Piven).

SPECIAL COLLECTIONS AND PRESERVATION DIVISION, CHICAGO PUBLIC LIBRARY

edy and in the talents of a brash, bright young ensemble that contained not one familiar "star" name. The title of its first show was *Excelsior & Other Outcries*. What was that? The cast consisted of Howard Alk, Severn Darden, Roger Bowen, Eugene Troobnick, Barbara Harris, Mina Kolb, and Andrew Duncan. Who were they?

They were, as audiences quickly found out, a very sharp ensemble of players, performing their revue of fresh, smart material with a brand of comic acting that was unique.

But they did not come from nowhere. Most of them had been working together for years, and their triumph was grounded in a series of short-lived efforts with a roller-coaster history.

Through them all, there was Paul Sills, Second City's cofounder and its first director. Any discussion of the company inevitably focuses on Sills, because he was a prime reason for this band of talented artists coming together. They wanted to work with him. For all his faults, and he could be curt and coarse and cruel in his dealings, he was the great innovator. And before him, as Sills has always insisted, there was "the real genius of the family," his mother Viola Spolin.

Spolin spent much of her professional life in Los Angeles, but she was born in Chicago in 1906 and received her early training from Neva L. Boyd, a Northwestern University sociologist whose use of games as a means of jump-starting imaginative play in children and adults was a great influence. Working at Hull House with Boyd in the 1920s and with the WPA Recreation Project from 1939 to 1941, Spolin developed her own distinctive method of teaching theater, a process in which the games were used to help actors relate to other people and to their surroundings. One basic game, for example, is the "mirror image," in which one actor exactly mirrors the actions of another actor facing him. As Sills says, "It's perfect for developing an ensemble unity."

In combination with internalizing, the digging down into the inner self for inspiration, as filtered through the Method developed by Lee Strasberg at the Actors Studio in New York, Spolin's process of improvisatory games became a bedrock of modern acting techniques, a distinctly American addition to the classic English school of elocution and stage movement.

Spolin codified her technique in *Improvisation for the Theater,* a landmark text published by Northwestern University Press in 1963 that is still used in acting workshops all over the country. Improvisation also was an essential part of Sills's method. He had played Spolin's games from childhood, and he used them throughout his career as a director.

He first came to attention in early 1953, when, as a student at the University of Chicago, he directed the American premiere of Jean Cocteau's *The Typewriter,* with a cast that included himself, Mike Nichols, Joyce Piven (who was then Joyce Hiller), and, as light operator, Sheldon Patinkin, a seventeen-year-old Sills acolyte.

"We rehearsed it for six months," Piven says, "but we spent a lot of that time drink-

Viola Spolin
COURTESY OF PAUL SILLS

ing beer and talking about life." When they finally got it onstage, in an in-the-round production in the Reynolds Club, a small upstairs space in the university's Mandel Hall at Fifty-seventh Street and University Avenue, it drew exceptional notices from the city newspaper reviewers. According to Piven, "It was obvious to them that Paul was an extraordinary talent. He was a visionary." He followed that production with another notable staging, Bertolt Brecht's *The Caucasian Chalk Circle*, presented in its Chicago-area premiere. (The world premiere of *Chalk Circle* had taken place in 1948 at Carleton College in Northfield, Minnesota.)

With these plays demonstrating that Sills and the group of actors who worked with him were capable of remarkable work, and with the addition of David Shepherd, a young man from the East who believed in their cause and had eight thousand dollars to back them, they decided to jump from the campus to the North Side of Chicago with their own company, Playwrights Theatre Club.

In two years, 1953 to 1955, and in two second-floor locations, first at 1560 N. LaSalle Street at North Avenue and then at the corner of Dearborn and Division streets, Playwrights rolled out an impressive list of two dozen productions with a company that contained, in addition to Sills, Edward Asner, Elaine May, Anthony Holland, Mike Nichols, Byrne Piven, Joyce Hiller, Vernon Schwartz, Eugene Troobnick, and two radiant young actresses, Zohra Lampert and Barbara Harris (later married to Sills). Also on hand was Tom O'Horgan, a harpist and composer who in the late sixties and early seventies struck it rich as the director of the musicals *Hair* and *Jesus Christ Superstar* on Broadway.

With them came two newcomers, both of whom were to have a long, substantial influence on their theater. First came Shepherd, a young actor-director-playwright who had met and bonded with Sills at a Steinway drugstore in Hyde Park after arriving in Chicago in 1952. He had a master's degree from Columbia University and a zealot's desire to create a truly popular theater for the proletariat. A New Yorker, he had found nightclub revues in Manhattan too chic and swish and had headed to Gary, Indiana, to set up a cabaret theater. "I hung out with the Communists there," he says, "but they told me the people there wouldn't be interested in what I wanted to do. They just wanted to go home, screw their wives, and watch TV. So I came to Chicago."

Elaine May as Hippolyta and Byrne Piven as Theseus in *A Midsummer Night's Dream* at Playwrights Theatre Club, 1954

COURTESY OF JOYCE PIVEN

Edward Asner as Prospero, with Lee Henry as Caliban, in *The Tempest,* 1954
MORTON SHAPIRO, COURTESY OF JOANN SHAPIRO

A little later, after the first few Playwrights productions, Bernard Sahlins, a theater lover with business experience in his wire-recorder company, came on board as a kind of producer, or, as Sahlins puts it, "a chairman of the board, without the board." He was not an actor, but he was smart, he had business savvy, he had a deep love of theater, and he was not without a sense of humor. Patinkin recalls that when Sahlins met members of the company, he told them he was going to treat them to a meal at "the best restaurant in Chicago." This turned out to be Fluky's, a hot dog stand, which was indeed the best of its kind, but definitely not what the actors had expected.

"We were either brilliant, or we were terrible," Patinkin says of the group's work. And when they were brilliant, as they were in Shakespeare's *Henry IV, Part 1* and *The Tempest,* Ibsen's *Peer Gynt,* and the Bertolt Brecht–Kurt Weill *The Threepenny Opera,* they were unforgettable. Fifty years after seeing it, Sahlins talked about Asner's portrayal of Prospero in *The Tempest* with undiminished awe: "I can see him standing there, near the end of the play, shouting. 'I'll break my staff.' It was wonderful!"

In between acquiring a hatful of glowing reviews, Asner, recently out of the army, supervised the cleanup detail, policing the former Chinese restaurant space on LaSalle Street with a top sergeant's diligence. Several other actors lived in the theater, curtaining off alcoves as bedrooms and sleeping on the floors or on wooden doors that they found slightly more comfortable.

Hiller, who met and married Piven when they worked at Playwrights, says, in a reminiscence that might well apply to scores of youthful companies who came before and after Playwrights, "We were all very close. We had nothing, and we did everything. Costumes, scenery, programs, makeup, cleanup, box office—we worked all of it. We were very young, very sincere, very passionate, arrogant, and innocent, all at the same time. We had big dreams, and we lived on candy bars and macaroni." (Sills smilingly disputes this: "There was a Greek restaurant downstairs that served perfectly decent food.")

They became professionals, members of the Actors' Equity union, but in true tribal spirit, they gave back their salaries to their theater.

Despite this dedicated communal spirit, Piven admits, "We were all divas." When a guest director unfortunately decided to cast *Romeo and Juliet* outside the company with a real teen-aged Juliet, the ensemble was in an uproar.

Sills, who staged most of the shows, was always "very demanding," Joyce Piven says. "He was not very articulate, but he knew what he wanted. He was tough on all of us, and if he didn't believe you were giving 110 percent, brilliant and alive for him, he wouldn't have anything to do with you."

In Elaine May, the ensemble had both a blazing talent and a genuine eccentric. Directing August Strindberg's *Miss Julie*, with Zohra Lampert in the title role, May insisted on closed rehearsals. Since he was assigned to stage-manage the show, Patinkin finally told her he had to see the production in order to do his job. Reluctantly, she said she would let him come to a rehearsal, but only, she cautioned, if he would tell her afterward what the essence of Lampert's portrayal was.

According to Patinkin, May duly asked him after the rehearsal who he thought Lampert was trying to be.

"Bette Davis?" Patinkin ventured.

"She was being a fawn!" May answered, scornfully.

That was the last time Patinkin saw the play before opening night.

However idiosyncratic they were as individuals, and whatever tics and quirks they brought to their work, the Playwrights actors served a rich, challenging program of plays. In the tradition of the Chicago Little Theatre of 1912 to 1917, they presented work outside the mainstream of show business commerce. Dramas by Brecht, Beckett, Schnitzler, Buchner, T. S. Eliot, and Strindberg (as well as original works by Sills and Shepherd) were not favored by commercial theater at that time, and to have them presented in an often inventive, striking manner was manna from heaven for devoted theatergoers. Roger Dettmer, reviewing the troupe in the *Chicago American,* said, "The people who played last night are very new—vigorously, crudely, wonderfully, irrationally new. . . . Their love of the stage is so overwhelming one cannot remain indifferent."

The critics' approval and the two thousand subscribers acquired in the first season were not enough for Shepherd. He had wanted to develop a theater for the masses, and instead he saw Playwrights as just another new haven for the elite. As he wrote in his journal, "In a year and a half, I have helped build a miserable self-centered arts club which talks over the heads of its bourgeois members at the same time it licks their feet for patronage."

His strong feelings, and the conflicting individual ambitions of the ensemble members, might eventually have ended the group's run. But what really shut the place down was the Chicago Fire Department, whose inspectors, acting on the stringent regulations put into effect after the Iroquois Theatre disaster, closed the theater in February 1955. There was no doubt that the two-hundred-seat theater was in violation of rules that had been established for large, proscenium houses. It didn't have a fire curtain, for example. But some Playwrights survivors believe that one of the theater's basic problems had nothing to do with fire codes and a lot to do with the Left-leaning material that the theater was perceived as presenting in this very chilly period of the Cold War.

In any case, Playwrights was over, and its actors scattered. Shepherd, still pursuing his ideal of popular theater, next fastened on a cabaret the-

Early and vintage Second City, from 1960: Mina Kolb and Eugene Troobnick, seated, and Alan Arkin and Paul Sand, standing

MORTON SHAPIRO, COURTESY OF JOANN SHAPIRO

ater that would draw on the news events of the day and on ancient traditions of commedia dell'arte, in which versatile comedians enliven a basic scenario with a clear plot outline but without the use of set, printed dialogue.

After a trial performance at the University of Chicago, with a scenario supplied by Roger Bowen, a former law school student, Sills came into the project and Viola Spolin was imported to conduct a series of workshops for sharpening the cast's improvisation abilities.

On July 5, 1955, the Compass, as Shepherd christened his project, opened in a makeshift theater that had been created by punching a hole in the wall between an empty store and the adjoining Hi-Hat Lounge at 1152 E. Fifty-fifth Street in the familiar U. of C. neighborhood. Entertainment for the ninety or so customers able to squeeze into the cramped cabaret theater consisted of a twenty-minute "Living News" segment, patterned after the "Living Newspaper" plays of the Federal Theatre Project in the 1930s. Mike Nichols, for example, would read a breezy account of a prizefight, as printed in *Sports Illustrated,* after which Mark Gordon would come onstage to read a story in *Ring* magazine of the same fight, reported as a brutal, sweaty affair. Sills once found a particularly heavy-breathing story in *True Confessions* and had the actors read it, word for word in breathless style. "It was hilarious," he says.

After the "News," there was a longer scenario play, usually eight or ten scenes lasting up to an hour, with the actors fleshing out the characters and environment of a bare-bones story they had been handed. The goal was to produce a new scenario every week, with the stories often grounded in actual events in the news. "Elaine May," Shepherd recalls, "wrote six scenarios—two pages single-spaced—in a couple days. She was amazing." One of the best of these scenarios, Sills believes, was "The Liars," based on a short story by Isaac Rosenfeld, about a group of teachers who bait a foreign newcomer, played intensely by a recent arrival to the group, Shelley Berman.

Following the scenario play, the cast then took a break and, after a short huddle together, improvised a scene or sketch based on character and topic suggestions from the audience. Out of such improvisations came *Football at the University of Chicago,* which later evolved into the classic Second City skit about nerdy students trying to grapple with contact sport. After that, the cast improvised scenes based on topic and

Bill Murray, with chairs, about 1973, when he joined The Second City
DICK KLEIN, COURTESY OF THE SECOND CITY

character suggestions tossed out by the enthusiastic audience. The players included May, Shepherd, Bowen, and Robert Coughlan, Loretta Chiljian, and Sid Lazard.

The shows, presented five nights a week, with three shows on Saturdays, proved to be popular, so much so that in October 1955, Shepherd moved the Compass to the Dock, a nightclub at 6473 S. Lake Park Avenue that could hold 140 customers. In spring of 1956, a still-larger home seating 250 persons was found at the Argo Off-Beat Room, 6344 N. Broadway, way up on the city's North Side. "It was the right theater, but the wrong location," Sills believes.

As the Compass grew, and as its performance venue shifted, its strategies and its casts changed substantially. Sills traveled for a while in Europe on a Fulbright grant, his duties taken over by several other directors. In the process, the "Living News" segment ceased publication and the longer scenario plays were replaced by shorter scenes, some featuring Nichols and May in satirical duets and others supplied by Berman, a graduate of the Goodman School whose telephone monologues were precursors of the routines he made famous in his highly successful 1960s career as a solo comedian. Many of the Nichols-May numbers, such as their spoof of the banalities of local radio celebrity interviewer Jack Eigen (called "Jack Ego" in their sketch), were created at this time.

By January 1957, with Shepherd exhausted and with business uncertain on the North Side, the Compass was over. Shepherd, forty-five years later, blamed himself. "I didn't do anything right. I didn't know how to run a business. I f——ed up." For the next few years, the Compass lived on with various casts in various incarnations in various locations, including St. Louis, and Shepherd moved along with it. Late in his seventies, living in Massachusetts, he was still working on developing a form of timely cabaret theater under the banner of his Group Creativity Projects. But in Chicago, in 1957, the Compass was finished, its ensemble members going off to make individual reputations and fortunes.

Meanwhile, Sahlins, in October 1956, leased the 1,250-seat Studebaker Theatre, in the Fine Arts Building at 410 S. Michigan Avenue, which briefly had been used as a television studio, and launched an ambitious new project. Christened the Studebaker Theatre Company, it was founded in the venturesome spirit of Playwrights, and it used some of that troupe's actors, but it was to be produced on a grander, starrier scale. Its noble purpose, Sahlins said in an interview in the old *Chicago* magazine, was "to decentralize, to institute theater of our own, to have our own actors, directors, writers and to be able to make some of our own decisions."

As with Playwrights, the Studebaker held out expectations of a genuine resident theater in Chicago, and with Danny Newman, who had helped boost the city's new Lyric Theatre into the grand opera world two years earlier, pumping out the press releases, all four Chicago daily newspapers gave the new venture their advance best wishes. A *Daily News* editorial hailed the new company as "the restoration of Chicago as a dramatic center for the Middle West," and critic Herman Kogan's salute in the *Sun-Times* said, "Chicago is on the verge of getting a new big-time repertory theater."

Sahlins and three cofounders—Andre Gabor, Theodore Rossman, and the young attorney Lewis Manilow—corralled seventy-five investors to put up a total of "more than fifty thousand dollars" for start-up funds, and Newman, who shared managerial duties with Daniel Goldberg, an old pro theater operator, forged a sixteen-thousand-subscription base for the first series of five plays. In what was to become classic Newman style for his subscription pitches, the Studebaker promised a big bargain ("See five plays for the price of four," beginning with a four-dollar package price) and a lineup of exciting shows. With guest artists such as Geraldine Page, Luther Adler, and Sir Cedric Hardwicke (as director) providing box-office bait, the company had some early, notable critical and audience successes, including Page in Andre Gide's *The Immoralist* and Hardwicke's production of Shaw's *Androcles and the Lion.* Arthur Miller's *A View from the Bridge,* which led off the second series with Adler as its star in a staging by George Keathley, a young director from Florida, did so well that it transferred to the Harris Theatre for a commercial run after its Studebaker engagement ended.

By spring of 1957, however, the theater, which had started with such a big bang, was falling apart from a series of box-office busts. Aristophanes' *Lysistrata,* featuring imported star Vicki Cummings and directed at first by Keathley and then by Sills in its last throes, was a special fiasco. Claudia's May 13 review in the *Tribune* bore the headline (which, as usual, she wrote), "This May Be Worst *Lysistrata* since the Athenian Premiere." She led off the review proper by stating, "Unlikely as it now

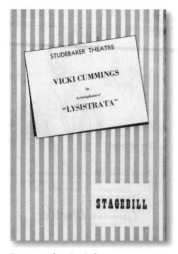

Program for the infamous
Lysistrata at the Studebaker
Theatre, 1957

SPECIAL COLLECTIONS AND PRESERVATION
DIVISION, CHICAGO PUBLIC LIBRARY

seems, there may have been worse performances of *Lysistrata* than the Studebaker Theatre Company's last night. After all, much can happen in 2,368 or so years of an occasional performance." And it got worse. Referring to Cummings's portrayal, she said, "In a sea of ineptitude, she was a Gibraltar of disaster." What could have happened? she wondered. In a production staged by Sills that featured Barbara Harris, Elaine May, Mike Nichols as leader of the men's chorus, and Severn Darden as leader of the women's chorus, Claudia concluded, scornfully, that "the old Playwrights Theatre Club has just moved downtown."

The end came in May 1957 with the company's *Waiting for Godot,* directed by Walter Beakel, with a cast containing Harvey Korman as Vladimir, Louis Zorich as Estragon, and Mike Nichols as the hapless slave Lucky. The Studebaker had come to the end of its "frayed managerial rope" (Claudia's phrase) and was so broke that it closed the box office to save money and played out its brief life strictly to a rapidly dwindling group of subscribers.

In the spring of 1957, deep in debt, without the kind of private and public institutional support that would help sustain not-for-profit theaters in the future, and its investors having lost all their money, the company shuttered amid failed expectations and hard feelings.

Still, that was not the end of the story. Sills, continuing his interest in smart, satirical revues, thought of starting up a new coffee-house-type establishment, popular in those days of the Beat Generation. To prepare himself, he hired out as house manager at the Gate of Horn, a popular folk-comedy club in the Rush Street nightlife area, and he enlisted the aid of Sahlins and Howard Alk, who had been an occasional performer with the Compass, as

Not mentioned on the program cover of the 1957 *Waiting for Godot* is Mike Nichols, who portrayed Lucky in the Samuel Beckett drama.

SPECIAL COLLECTIONS AND PRESERVATION
DIVISION, CHICAGO PUBLIC LIBRARY

his coproducers. For about six thousand dollars, they converted a former Chinese laundry on Wells Street into their cabaret theater and put together their first revue. It was a rush to get the place open. Sahlins remembers that on opening night, in between scenes and applause, he could hear the carpet man still tack-tack-tacking down the rug in the lobby.

But they were, incredibly, a big success. At last, they had found the right theater in the right location. And the time was right, too. Second City did not occur in a vacuum. Comedians such as Mort Sahl and Lenny Bruce, and writers such as the Chicago poet and editor Paul Carroll were stirring up cultural and political discussion, and there was a hip audience for that kind of communication.

Bernard Sahlins outside The Second City on its opening night, December 16, 1959
MICKEY PALLAS, COURTESY OF CENTER FOR CREATIVE PHOTOGRAPHY, UNIVERSITY OF ARIZONA

Then, as in the future, The Second City did no advertising, but the word-of-mouth and the reviews, when they came in, were terrific. Their audiences, which included many urban middle-class eggheads of the day, were delighted with such classic early bits as "Football at the U. of C." and "Businessman," a spoof invented by Roger Bowen about a superman of commerce, opposed by "Collective Man."

It became common, after revue followed revue, for Second City's regular customers to say that the new shows weren't as good as the earlier ones had been. This is not precisely true, and, after all, as Sahlins drolly notes, this complaint first surfaced with the third show. Decades after the founding of The Second City, with a world of changes in cast and audience makeup, streaks of smart hilarity continue in bits dealing with everything from political satire to family relationships. But it is true that some of those early shows were filled with sketches that were stinging bits of social commentary and small masterpieces of improvisation-inspired work. When Barbara Harris and Alan Arkin fleshed out a fifteen-minute scene in which a giddily repressed young woman and a guitar-strumming beatnik meet in the Art Institute, they produced not only laughter but truly touching characterizations. There was a unique, sometimes stupendous air of daft whimsy whenever Severn Darden entered a scene, and when Mina Kolb unleashed her inimitable dottiness as the nice suburban WASP lady trying to stay afloat in this very urban male group, there was something akin to instinctive genius at work.

At least once, Sills transcended the short bits of the revue format with a longer, dazzling act of surreal brilliance. *Peep Show,* the entire second half of the revue *Alarums and Excursions,* concerned two conventioneers looking for "action" and finding it in a bizarre world of fantasy laid out for them by a mysterious stranger. Many years later, certain moments from that scene—a young woman on a swing in a fantasy image taken from a Salem cigarette commercial of the time—are still with me.

However different the content, the form of the presentation remained basically the same. In The Second City's original location at 1842 N. Wells Street and at 1616 N. Wells Street, where the group relocated in 1967, the audience was shoehorned into seating at small tables that were navigated by waitresses serving drinks before and during the show. A slightly raised platform near the rear of the house, with a railing facing the stage, served as a seating site for reviewers and other favored customers. Onstage, the cast of six or seven players (the men always outnumbering the women) worked in a small, plain space, with a pianist on one side providing the music and sound effects. Lighting and scenic effects became slightly more elaborate over the years, but costuming consisted principally and simply of a scarf, coat, or hat to suggest character, and a shifting around of bentwood chairs remained the chief means of changing scenes. Props were minimal and often imaginary. There were no cups or glasses. To take a drink, the actor just cupped his hand, put it to his mouth, and sucked on the thumb knuckle.

Even in those early days, the casts always contained a future star or two. Harris and many later recruits—Darden, Arkin, Paul Sand, David Steinberg, Joan Rivers, Robert Klein, Peter Boyle, and Fred Willard—all went on to greater fame in film, television, and stage careers. Even

The Second City classic "Funeral," from *43rd Parallel or Macabre and Mrs. Miller,* directed by Del Close, 1972: at services for a man who drowned in a can of Van Camp's pork and beans, mourners (left to right) Joe Flaherty, Eugenie Ross-Leming, Harold Ramis, and John Belushi stifle guffaws while the widow (Judy Morgan) and minister (Jim Fisher) try to maintain their dignity.

DICK KLEIN-PHOTOGRAPHY

the busboy ranks had a future star. David Mamet, in between busing tables in the summer beer garden, watched and learned from Second City sketches and improvisations, feeding his hopes of becoming a playwright and laughing helplessly whenever Willard, whom he still calls "the funniest man I have ever seen onstage," took off on one of his wild bits.

A year after it opened, a Second City revue, live from its cabaret, already had been featured in a program presented nationwide on an early form of pay-TV, and in 1961 the troupe landed on Broadway with a special revue, *From the Second City.* But the big breakthrough of fame-through-television came in the seventies with the extraordinary arrival of John Belushi, a student at the west suburban College of DuPage. Spotted by associate producer Joyce Sloane on a visit to the college, Belushi, then twenty-one, was hired without auditioning, and

Audrie Neenan and Tim Kazurinsky chat it up.
JAY KING, COURTESY OF THE SECOND CITY

instantly, he was a clear-cut star, manically energetic and vastly ambitious. "He took over whenever he was onstage," says Harold Ramis,
who appeared with Belushi. "You can imagine how that made the rest
of us feel." At one point, Mamet remembers, Belushi exuberantly used
the f—— word in a skit, and, warned by Sahlins against a repetition, he
made sure that he used it often. "Waiter," he would say, "I'd like a bowl
of f——." And so on.

When *Saturday Night Live* hired Belushi and other Second
City–related players Dan Aykroyd and Gilda Radner as core members
of the Not Ready for Prime Time Players (in 1975), followed by Bill
Murray (1976), Tim Kazurinsky (1981), and Chris Farley (1990), their
immense television success catapulted Second City into its status as a
major comedy factory. More than ever, this haven of comedy was viewed
as a breeding ground of stars. In 1976, the SCTV series, with Second
Citizens Ramis, John Candy, Eugene Levy, Joe Flaherty, Martin Short,
and Dave Thomas, plus Rick Moranis, in hilarious sketches poking fun

at television stars and programs, added to the ongoing impression that, in the words of the critic Clive Barnes, "The entire recent tradition of American theatrical satire can be summed up in three words: The Second City."

With television now a major factor in comedy, The Second City changed. "In the early days," says Sahlins, "we looked to the stage as a goal. Today, they look to television. I'm not saying that's bad. But it's different."

The makeup of the audiences changed too, bringing bused-in tourists and suburbanites to a cabaret that once had been considered the epitome of urban hip.

Sills, always a restless spirit, left after a while, as did Alk, leaving Sahlins to keep the place running as the sole owner, producer, and, for a while, artistic director. Sills, Patinkin, Sahlins, Del Close, and, in briefer stints, Alan Meyerson and Michael Miller directed the shows, the runs of each revue growing longer as the audiences grew larger. In

Forever changing, forever the same: cast and crowd at a performance at The Second City
JENNIFER GIRARD

1985, Sahlins sold The Second City to Andrew Alexander and Len Stuart, partners in the theater's Toronto branch. Today, the place is staffed both on- and offstage mostly by people who had not yet been born in 1959, and the cabaret continues to churn out comic actors who springboard from Wells Street to the vast audiences of television and movies. What began as a small coffeehouse in Chicago is now a monolithic national institution. In addition to the bedrock of the main stage on Wells Street, there are satellite companies in Toronto, Detroit, and Las Vegas; a series of training centers in all of the above, plus New York and Los Angeles, that take in about four thousand students every eight-week term; a junior (and often terrific) revue stage in Chicago called Second City etc.; a string of United States and Canadian touring companies; a Second City Theatricals branch devoted to developing new plays, musicals, and performance pieces; a similar division for television and film projects; workshops for adults and children; a Corporate Services group that customizes Second City–style comedy and workshops for business events; and USO tours for American troops.

There are great ironies in Second City's success. A theater founded on ensemble skills, it is now known mostly for the famous individual stars who came out of the ensemble. And in a form originally aimed at presenting theater for the proletariat, it is now a capitalistic empire of awesome proportions, its skills brought to bear in situation comedies and TV commercials that Shepherd would never have dreamed of as avenues for his theater.

Yet the results remain amazing. Scores of writers, directors, and actors did receive their basic training at The Second City. Ramis says, "It's a comedy school, which is very rare in this country. It's like a flying school; the more you fly, the better you fly. You just work, night after night. Some nights you're good, some nights you're awful, but there's no record of your failure. You just keep on going."

Improvisation, in the theater games of Spolin, handed down through Sills, remained a basic element in creating the shows. In the games, Second Citizens learned to watch one another, trust one another, listen to one another. "Listening is the key," Kazurinsky says. "It's half the battle in building an ensemble. In our casts, we would have some actors who had the best ideas for scenes, others who knew exactly how to perform those scenes. They say improvisation is the bastard child of acting and writing. Well, we had it all. Everybody brought something to the picnic."

Through every change in manners and mores and casts, the laughs kept coming. In the satirized rituals of the movies *Best in Show* and *A Mighty Wind*, in the deft characterizations that people even the most mundane of situation comedies, in the beautifully crafted direction of *Groundhog Day, Analyze This*, and other film comedies by Ramis, and in the supreme dumbo voice of Homer Simpson by Dan Castellaneta on *The Simpsons*, the influence of The Second City and its alumni is essential.

Above all, there is the strong, enduring legacy of improvisation, the empowering force for actors that was inaugurated by Spolin, carried forward by Shepherd and Sills, honed to a fine edge by generations of actors-writers, given individual variations by Close and others in their workshops, spread through a sea of comedy improv clubs in Chicago, and continues apparently without end in every Second City performance.

I once asked Stuart Gordon, who came to Chicago in 1970 as a young director devoted to Sills, what he believed were the essential qualities needed for a Chicago actor. He replied, in an instant, "A sense of humor and a skill in improvisation."

For both, we can thank The Second City.

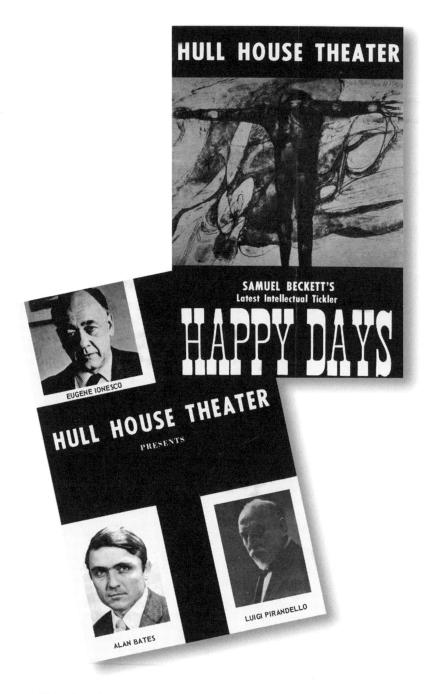

Highlights from the 1960s at Hull House Theater, including Samuel Beckett's *Happy Days* and a triple bill offering works by Eugene Ionesco, Luigi Pirandello, and Chicago playwright Alan Bates

AUTHOR'S COLLECTION AND CHICAGO HISTORICAL SOCIETY (ICHI-37541)

Chapter 11

"It Was an Honor to Work There"

FOR A LITTLE WHILE, BEGINNING IN 1961, The Second City expanded its programming to include a new theater project, Playwrights at Second City. Its purpose was to present the same kind of venturesome material that the original Playwrights Theatre Club had offered. Like its next-door parent, the new 225-seat house at 1846 N. Wells Street was a cabaret theater, serving drinks and snacks. It had a beer garden in the summer, and there were silent movies in the bar in the winter.

Its opening production in May, very much in keeping with Second City's hip image, was *The Explainers,* an original revue adapted from his intellectual cartoons by Jules Feiffer in his first foray into the theater. It was followed by *Big Deal,* a new version of *The Threepenny Opera* set in Chicago, subtitled "An Opera for Politicians," with Paul Sills directing from a scenario (Compass style) by David Shepherd and with music by Second City's composer-in-residence, Allaudin Mathieu. Its cast included Alan Arkin in the lead role of Macheath, plus Del Close, Avery Schreiber, and Dick Schaal, all of whom would eventually shift to Second City casts.

Poster for the "improvised play" *Big Deal*
at Playwrights at Second City, 1961

Later in the year, Playwrights and Second City switched places, the latter taking over the larger space for its expanding audience. In its smaller space, Playwrights produced the Chicago professional premieres of Harold Pinter's *The Caretaker,* Edward Albee's *The Zoo Story,* and Jean Genet's *The Maids,* as well as the world premiere of Bernard Sahlins's *The Puppet.* It was there that I first saw Samuel Beckett's *Krapp's Last Tape,* with a mesmerizing portrayal of a lost life by Severn Darden.

It was not commercially viable, however, and in 1963, in the days before not-for-profit theater was commonplace in Chicago, this important, pioneering place for new and cutting-edge work closed down, its proprietors concentrating on the main business of turning out new shows in what was now their successful revue format at The Second City.

Yet there were signs in the early and mid-1960s that a new kind of resident theater was beginning to take shape throughout the country and, in its own way, in Chicago. As early as 1951, Tennessee Williams had written in a prescient letter to Claudia Cassidy about the need for something better than weak touring productions trundling across the nation from New York. "The only cure," he wrote, "is decentralized theater. So that plays can be done freshly all over again, off Broadway, in place after place, each time created brand new. Why don't you take the stump for it in Chicago? No better place on Earth!"

This had been the goal of Playwrights, which Paul Sills had described as an attempt by Chicago artists "to earn a living as an art form." It had been the aim of Sahlins in the resident troupe of the Studebaker Theatre Company, and it had been the hope of David Shepherd in the popular theater he had wanted to bring into being with the Compass.

Resident theaters, founded and funded by and for their particular communities, had been around for decades, as with the Chicago Little Theatre in 1912. Beginning in 1916, with the first production of the professional Cleveland Play House, there had notably been the Dallas The-

Lou Gilbert and Thomas Erhart in *The Caretaker,* by Harold Pinter, at Playwrights at
Second City, 1961

COURTESY OF THE SECOND CITY

ater Center (1947), Alley Theater in Houston (1947), Arena Stage in
Washington, D.C. (1950), and the Actor's Workshop of San Francisco
(1952). By 1965, when the federal government entered the scene, with
the National Endowment for the Arts committed to supporting work
on a national scale, and with several states, including Illinois, establishing their own state arts councils, the "regional theater" concept took
hold for good. Plans for arts centers multiplied, and their buildings, often
incorporated as part of a mammoth performing arts center, grew larger.
One after another, there were big theaters with big budgets launched in
Minneapolis (Guthrie Theater, 1963), New York (Lincoln Center, 1965),
Los Angeles (Los Angeles Music Center, 1967), Washington, D.C.
(Kennedy Center, 1971), and Denver (Denver Center for the Performing
Arts, 1979).

The drive for larger and more elaborate cultural edifices had a brief
fling in Chicago in 1966, when the Mayor's Committee for Economic
and Cultural Development, a blue-ribbon Establishment group convened

KICKS AND *HAIR*

It's now fairly common for a Chicago-originated show to move on to a New York engagement, but in the early 1960s, it was a novel idea, and it didn't always work out the way it had been planned.

Ad touting the ill-fated premiere of *Kicks & Co.*

AUTHOR'S COLLECTION

In 1960, Oscar Brown Jr., a prolific Chicago composer-writer-director-performer, fashioned a promising neo-Faustian musical that featured a devilish leading character called Mr. Kicks. The show gained national attention and backers' money through a unique on-the-air audition pitch on NBC-TV's *Today* program, and in 1961 *Kicks & Co.* had its much anticipated pre-Broadway premiere in the hangarlike Arie Crown Theatre of McCormick Place, the massive convention and trade-show hall at Twenty-third Street and the lakefront. With Burgess Meredith, as Mr. Kicks, leading an interracial cast, the musical was plunked on the huge Arie Crown stage, its songs and dialogue mushed by a primitive amplification system consisting of dozens of stalactitelike hanging microphones (before the days of body mikes). What had looked and sounded so lively on television died an ugly death in Arie Crown.

In 1964, Brian Bedford, in Chicago at the Harper Theatre to direct the local premiere of the English youth comedy *The Knack,* was "going nuts" in rehearsal, he says, with his male leads, Gerome Ragni and James Rado. According to Bedford, "They were wonderful, but they were not learning their lines. 'Look,' I told them, 'if you don't learn your bloody lines, I'm going to fire you.' They looked at me very sheepishly, and said, well, they were writing a musical. 'I don't care if you're writing the Bible,' I yelled, 'you've got to learn your lines,' and, finally, they did."

A year later, in 1965, Bruce Sagan, owner of the Harper, got a call from Ragni and Rado, who were in New York. They had finished their script for that musical, now called *Hair,* and they wanted Sagan to produce it for a tryout run in Chicago at the Harper. Sagan, who had found these two "nutty guys" a constant hassle to manage during *The Knack's* run, gave an emphatic no to their proposition. "I did everybody, including them, a big favor," says Sagan. "Here, *Hair* would have flopped. In New York, they were able to make the connections that turned it into a hit." One of those connections, however, had a Chicago link. Michael Butler, a wealthy playboy from suburban Oak Brook, became *Hair's* producer on Broadway, a status that earned him the title of "the hippiest millionaire."

Hair, by the way, was not the only new work to be written during the run of *The Knack* at the Harper. The young playwright Sam Shepard was the boyfriend of the play's leading actress, Joyce Aaron, and as he traveled back and forth from New York to Chicago to visit her, he wrote a one-act play called *Chicago,* which had nothing to do with Chicago, but which did very well in 1965 when it was presented off-Broadway in New York.

by Mayor Richard J. Daley, proposed a $31 million, fourteen-year program for growth that focused on a large, centrally located performing arts center.

For a while, after the then-homeless American Conservatory Theater had stirringly presented two short end-of-summer seasons of its repertory in 1966 and 1967 in the Murray (now the Martin) Theatre of the Ravinia Festival in Highland Park, there was a stir about importing this high-quality, ready-made troupe as a resident troupe for Chicago. But that plan, pushed by Hope Abelson, a local lady bountiful in cultural philanthropy, failed to take off, and, in the end, ACT went to San Francisco.

Big, expensive enterprises were not to be the way of Chicago. Instead of having an at-the-top performing arts complex, the city's culture, and in particular the culture of the theater, was to grow organically, from the bottom up, in homes converted from former warehouses, bowling alleys, laundries, and bakeries. These theaters, founded by youthful, ambitious, and poor artists, would spring up away from downtown, without lavish facilities, without big budgets, without stars, and without (at first) much official support.

The key event in realizing this theater of our own was the opening of Hull House Theater in 1963, when into the vacuum of local theater came a whirlwind named Bob Sickinger.

At thirty-five, Sickinger already had attracted attention for his direction of dozens of plays in several Philadelphia area theaters, presenting new works by the young playwright Edward Albee, among others, and working with aspiring actors like Peter Boyle and Robert Prosky and the lighting designer Jules Fisher, who was eighteen and still in high school when he hung lights for the director. Paul Jans, director of the Lighthouse Settlement social agency in Philadelphia and newly appointed executive director of Hull House in Chicago, knew Sickinger's work and asked him to come to Chicago to reinvigorate the theater program that had once been a highlight of Hull House activity.

Sickinger, who had staged his first play, Thornton Wilder's *Our Town*, in a five-hundred-seat theater in the Philadelphia area, was a director of distinct, unusual vision. For *Our Town*, which ends in a scene set among the deceased residents of a cemetery, he did not want to have curtain calls because, he explained, "Dead people can't take curtain calls." (His cast quickly rejected that notion.)

Bob Sickinger in rehearsal for *Who'll Save the Plowboy?*—his first Hull House
production, 1963
COURTESY OF BOB SICKINGER

He had no formal training as a director, and his idea of a director's
job could be extremely whimsical. When Estelle Spector, the choreographer for his Hull House production of the musical *The Boy Friend*,
asked him just what he wanted in one scene, he told her, "If I knew what
I wanted, I wouldn't need myself." He still suspects that Jans hired him
as much for his fund-raising abilities as for his directorial talents. But
actors who worked with him in Chicago swear by his casting instincts,
and Sickinger himself believes that one of his strengths was in knowing
how to pick the right actor for the exact performance he wanted.

Chicago presented Sickinger with a fresh opportunity for innovation, and he eagerly took the job offer. Believing that his theater would
be built in the downtown area, he went to a Philadelphia architect and
proposed a bold plan for a new theater complex. "That was a time when
they were tearing down a lot of theaters and replacing them with parking lots," he explains, so he suggested building an underground theater,
on top of which would be a parking garage, configured so that all the

cars would be slanted down toward an open playing space. It was to be the world's first drive-in legitimate theater.

The plan, whether ingenious or plain goofy, was never realized. Instead, Sickinger moved into Hull House headquarters in a former American Legion post at 3212 N. Broadway and started converting a bowling alley in the building into a 110-seat open-stage theater. First, however, he had to raise money, gather support, and scout talent for his theater project. He began holding weekly breakfast club meetings as a way of networking into the theater community; he held auditions for community theater actors; and, aiming for support from the well connected and the well heeled, he launched a series of fund-raising chamber theater programs. Paul and Suzanne Faberson, who acted in them, explain how they worked: "We performed in the homes of people who were interested in the theater. The hostess would usually have a nice buffet, and then the guests, twenty-five to forty people who each had paid ten dollars or so, would move into the living room, where we had set up our chairs, and we would do what was basically a staged reading of contemporary plays like *After the Fall, Who's Afraid of Virginia Woolf,* and *Gallows Humor.* When we finished, Bea Fredman, who organized the readings, would get up and make the pitch for Hull House Theater."

Handbill for Bob Sickinger's sensational Hull House Theater staging of the drug-addict drama *The Connection,* by Jack Gelber, 1964

When Sickinger came to Chicago, he discovered "the acting pool was not very deep." But he found his actors, and they found him. They were amateurs who performed in community theaters, earning their livings by day and rehearsing and performing at night, without pay. As with most community theaters, at Hull House they performed only on weekends, Friday through Sunday. With three performances a week, that made up a total audience of 330 persons, not counting the squeezed-in extra seats that were sold for overflow houses. That would have been a pathetically meager audience for one night in a large downtown theater, but at Hull House, the impact was immedi-

Pat Terry and Mike Nussbaum in *The Typists,* 1964
COURTESY OF BOB SICKINGER

ate. Moreover, the actors were as good as, and better than, anything that could be seen in a touring show in the Loop.

Robert Kidder, who became a stalwart of the company, was an English teacher in Highland Park. Mike Nussbaum, whose fifty-year-plus career in Chicago theater was nourished at Hull House, owned and operated a pest extermination business. Beatrice Fredman, Stuart Eckhaus, Marla Friedman, Bill Kelly, Diane Rudall, Harvey Rubin, Catita Lord, Bob Curry, Roberta Custer, Jim Jacobs, and David Mamet—they were names that at the time meant nothing to theatergoers. But each one of them, and many more, were prodded and inspired in Sickinger-directed plays and musicals.

Before long, they realized that they were into more than another routine community theater engagement. "We knew something was going on," Nussbaum says, "when we didn't know anybody in the audience."

There were no loyal relatives or friends who attended from a sense of personal obligation; instead, there were people who had paid for tickets just to see the production.

"What energy he had," Nussbaum says of Sickinger. "And what a work ethic. It was nothing for him to go on with rehearsals until three A.M., and he thought everybody should want to stay that long too."

For Michael Miller, a director whose career in stage, movies, and television began at Hull House, "Sickinger had the energy and the hustle of a door-to-door salesman. He was everywhere, urging you on. When the doors to the theater opened, there he was, at the entrance, greeting the customers like a priest at church on Sunday."

Jim Jacobs, who acted in both plays and musicals at Hull House, recalls of Sickinger, "He was in the audience almost every night. You could tell, because you could hear that big, booming laugh out there. After the show, he would come back with notes. One night I told him, 'We're in the last week of the run. Why are you still giving notes?' And he said, 'This is nothing. Once, I gave notes on closing night.'"

Maureen Steindler, who taught acting classes and also performed at Hull House, insists, "I never minded not getting paid for my work. My husband did, but I didn't. It was an honor to work there."

In November 1963, the Chicago premiere of *Who'll Save the Plowboy?*—Frank D. Gilroy's off-Broadway drama about an embittered urban everyman—opened the newly christened Hattie Callner Memorial Theater of Hull House in the Jane Addams Center, and it was a knockout.

This production was a defining moment in Chicago theater life, and a revelatory experience for me. Being young and hungry in the newspaper business and looking for something to write about, I had gone there on opening night expecting little but curious to see what was going on. Decades after I reviewed it in the *Daily News* as "the most exciting, significant and promising Chicago theatrical event in years," I can still hear and see in memory the vivid power of the play's story. In its energy, passion, and commitment, it set the pattern for the bountiful Chicago theater work of the future. Suddenly and powerfully, it proved to me for the first of many times that small mattered, that a piece of theater in a 110-seat converted bowling alley could be wonderful, big time.

Here and in the next few prolific years to come at Sickinger's Hull House, there was no such thing as an "amateur" theatrical. By digging into the core of a play's meaning, by prodding and coaxing a cast of nonprofessionals to work at a high professional level, by fiercely attending to detail in every aspect of production, Sickinger turned out an amazing series of plays and musicals in Hull House outposts scattered through the city.

Taking off from the familiar blue-collar realism of *Plowboy*, he turned to less common clay in *Happy Days* (billed as "Samuel Beckett's latest intellectual tickler"); the Chicago premiere of Albee's *Tiny Alice*; a full-out environmental presentation of *The Threepenny Opera* that turned the stage and aisles of the Callner Theater into a crawling mass of London lowlife; a version of Albert Camus's *Caligula* that opened in a Playboy Club–like setting, with Nancy Sinatra's recording of "These Boots Are Made for Walking" playing at full blast (and which one reviewer damned as "a bad play in a worse production"); a thrilling adaptation of John Hersey's novel *The Child Buyer*; an original shocker of a drama, *Kids' Games*, by Chicago playwright Alan Bates; and even the Greek tragedy *Electra*.

Very little escaped Sickinger's attention. For Harold Pinter's *The Lover*, he sent the prop manager foraging through dozens of second-hand shops in the city to find the right kind of milk bottle that would be used in an English household. For Kenneth H. Brown's harrowing, naturalistic drama of *The Brig*, he persuaded four marines to put the male cast through a hellish kind of boot-camp training. For *Threepenny*, he put tacks at the ends of the hammer keys to give the show's piano the tinny sound he wanted. For a production of Pinter's *The Birthday Party*, presented at the Ravinia Festival in north suburban Highland Park in the tempestuous summer of 1968, he staged the play so that Stanley, the mysterious, reclusive central character, was dressed and played as a hippie, and Goldberg and McCann, the menacing strangers who drag him out of his hiding place, were dressed and played as buttoned-down, black-suited enforcers of the Establishment.

Dissatisfied with the ending of the musical *Flora the Red Menace*, Sickinger got the show's composer-lyricist team of John Kander and Fred Ebb to send him some of their other songs, and he inserted one of them, "I Believe You," to round off the story on a better final note. Ebb came in to see the production and wept with pleasure at its revised form.

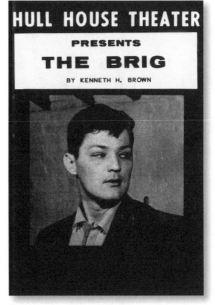

At its peak, in the mid-1960s, Hull House Theater, in addition to its home base at the Jane Addams Center, had four branches in Chicago. On the North Side, the Leo Lerner Theater of the Uptown Center at 4520 N. Beacon Street became a home for musicals, presenting everything from the Chicago premiere of *Take Me Along* to an affectionate revival of the operetta *The Desert Song*. The basement theater in the Parkway Community Center at 500 E. Sixty-seventh Street featured black and racially integrated dramas, such as James Baldwin's *Blues for Mr. Charlie*, many of them staged with tremendous force by Miller, a young director Sickinger had encouraged and tutored. The Hull House

Program for Kenneth H. Brown's brutally naturalistic *The Brig* at Hull House Theater
CHICAGO HISTORICAL SOCIETY (ICHI-37540)

Sheridan Playhouse, 717 W. Sheridan Road, briefly served as a home for the commercial transfer of such successes as *The Connection,* Jack Gelber's sensational drama about a group of drug addicts. A small space in the Henry Booth Settlement House at 2328 S. Dearborn Street aimed to bring theater to residents of the projects.

A playwrights' unit sought to develop new scripts by local authors. A children's theater program came up with delightful, polished shows featuring the adventures of "Captain Marbles." And a few plays went out on a four-state tour.

By 1969, however, the organization had come apart. "I began to wear out," Sickinger says. The plays he directed—and he staged all but a few of the productions at the Jane Addams and Uptown centers—lacked the old fire. The Hull House board, seeing that the theaters—in particular the Parkway and Henry Booth operations—were becoming a financial burden, and wary of some of Sickinger's more violent presentations (Venable Herndon's *Until the Monkey Comes* centered on a wild, chaotic party in which the apartment setting was destroyed at

Bob Curry taunted by Catita Lord in *Dutchman*, by LeRoi Jones
COURTESY OF BOB SICKINGER

every performance) and fearful of the director's free-wheeling, late-night rehearsals, decided that Hull House, a social service agency, should not be in the business of producing avant-garde theater for an audience of basically well-to-do customers. In their view, the tail was wagging the dog.

"They said we weren't reaching any poor people," Sickinger says, "but I told them we were absolutely serving the community of poor actors, directors, and designers who were working at our theaters."

With Jans, his friend and protector, having already resigned under pressure from the board, the end came when Sickinger and his actors were locked out of rehearsals in the Uptown Center. (Bristling at the memory of that incident, Sickinger insists, "One of the board members was angry because he said we had stained the carpet.")

There was a short-lived attempt to keep the theater going under the direction of Chicago actor-director-teacher Robert Benedetti, but when he saw the lack of funding and enthusiasm for the project from the board and subsequently bowed out, Hull House Theater died. The theater space itself, enlarged from 110 to 140 seats by the addition of a small balcony, lived on, however, as a home for itinerant off-Loop groups. Over the years, the rising companies of Steppenwolf, Bailiwick, Famous Door, and About Face all used the theater where Sickinger had worked his miracles. Its end came at last in 2002 when the Jane Addams Center was shut down.

In 1969, Sickinger left Hull House in bitterness, taking with him a film script for *The Child Buyer* that he wanted to direct as his entry into the movie business. Instead, he went to New York, helped found and direct the earliest days of the Manhattan Theatre Club, and eventually set up a telecommunications business specializing in answering services. Out of theater for several years, he came back with all the old enthusiasm in the 1990s, spending much of his time trying to develop musicals based on Willa Cather's novel *O Pioneers* and the films *The Blue Angel* and *The Little Princess*.

In this new life, with a new marriage and a new family, Sickinger one day received a call from David Mamet, who had worked at Hull House Theater when he was a kid. ("Very bright," Sickinger says of Mamet. "He was like a sponge. He absorbed everything. But he wasn't a very good actor.") Mamet, now a Pulitzer Prize playwright, was going to be in New York to give a lecture, and he invited Sickinger to attend. Sickinger went, and he took along with him his fifteen-year-old daughter, Erika. Mamet walked onstage, spotted Sickinger in the crowd, and, pointing him out to the rest of the audience, said, "Ladies and gentlemen, I want you to meet one of the greatest directors I have ever known." Taken by surprise, Sickinger turned to his daughter, who looked at him with wide eyes. "I think," he recalls, "she was impressed."

Candlelight Dinner Playhouse

WILLIAM PULLINSI   ANTHONY D'ANGELO

present

GARY HOLCOMBE   LINDA BALGORD
ANN-MARIE ROGERS   DOUG OKERSON

in

FORTY-SECOND STREET

Music by   *Lyrics by*
HARRY WARREN   AL DUBIN

Book by
MICHAEL STEWART & MARK BRAMBLE

Based on the Novel by BRADFORD ROPES

Original Direction and Dances by GOWER CHAMPION
Originally Produced on Broadway by DAVID MERRICK

with

IRIS LIEBERMAN   MARY BETH DOLAN   LARRY RUSSO
DALE BENSON   JAMES BRAET   MARC ROBIN
TRUDI GREEN   BARBARA EARLY   SETH SWOBODA

Production Choreographed by DANNY HERMAN and TRUDI GREEN

Musical Director NIC

STAGEBILL

RITA MORENO
"The Rose Tattoo"

BECKET

HARPER THEATER

A new breed of Chicago commercial theaters: the Ivanhoe and Harper theaters and
Candlelight Dinner Playhouse, founded in the 1960s

Chapter 12

"We Improvised"

WRITING IN THE 1969 EDITION OF her *Chicago: An Extraordinary Guide,* the where-to-go, what-to-do columnist Jory Graham voiced a familiar complaint about Chicago as a theater town. "Theater here," she wrote, "simply isn't like theater in London or New York. The big shows are elsewhere and Chicago is left out. Left out of the razzle-dazzle of openings, the celebrity game, the taken-for-granted right of the West End and Broadway to make or break plays, authors, new actors, stars. When it comes to professional theater, Chicago is scarcely better off than any other road-show city in America—it takes what New York producers decide will make money outside New York."

She was right, as far as she went. The immediate downtown area was in bad shape, and it would grow worse after 1971, when the 4,400-seat Arie Crown Theatre of McCormick Place, the city's convention center on the South Side lakefront at Twenty-third Street, went after bookings for big touring musicals. Isolated in its setting, airplane hangar–like in its dimensions, and an acoustical nightmare, Arie Crown, under the aggressive programming of manager Betty Kearns, further sucked life away from the already weakened downtown area. Its impact lasted into the 1980s, when long-run bookings of megamusicals moved into the Auditorium, and the folly of putting a show like *Sweeney Todd* into a convention center theater on a remote lakefront site in the dead of a bitter Chicago winter became all too evident.

At the time Graham wrote her assessment, few people regarding this woeful scene believed there could be a "movement" afoot in Chicago theater; but there was indeed movement, in different forms and in different places, indicating that the grass might be getting a little greener in our own backyard. Step by step, in scattered locations and in what seemed to be unrelated progressions, the foundations of a theater community were being laid.

Bruce Sagan
COURTESY OF *CHICAGO TRIBUNE* NEWS ARCHIVE

On the South Side in 1961, Bruce Sagan, publisher of the community newspaper *Hyde Park Herald*, had bought a building on Harper Avenue that contained a former vaudeville/movie house. He moved his offices into the top floors, and in 1964, sensing that the time might be right for a smart, serious theater in the Hyde Park area, he decided to become a producer. "We [Sagan and his then-wife Judy] knew a little bit about the off-Broadway movement in New York," he says. "We had even invested in a show there, and we thought it might be possible to create a kind of off-Broadway theater here, especially after Bob Sickinger had started things at Hull House. The Harper had a proscenium stage, a fire curtain, and exit signs, so I knew we would be all right with the building codes, and we went ahead."

Sagan renovated the building, installed an old drugstore soda fountain as a lobby bar, and reopened the three-hundred-seat Harper with a production of Luigi Pirandello's *Henry IV*, in Eric Bentley's English version, with a brilliant portrayal of the title role by Alvin Epstein, supported by a local cast that included film actress June Travis.

Because this was a new kind of professional theater (not a dinner theater or summer theater or community theater) outside the downtown area, Sagan and the local office of Actors' Equity pieced together a contract based on a heavily edited version of an extant cabaret contract. In so doing, they created one of the very early off-Loop contracts. "Nobody knew how to deal with that kind of theater," he says. "We improvised."

The Harper did not have a long life as a legitimate house. The Sagans produced local premieres of distinction, such as the English youth comedy *The Knack,* but they soon shifted to presenting contemporary dance companies in the theater. In its few years, and with its checkered performance menu, however, the Harper housed two noteworthy, if faltering, attempts at resident theater. One was a brief-lived Second City Repertory effort that featured two plays: Anton Chekhov's *The Cherry Orchard,* directed by Paul Sills, and Norman Mailer's *The Deer*

Alvin Epstein in the title role of Luigi Pirandello's *Henry IV* at the Harper Theater, 1964
COURTESY OF BRUCE SAGAN

Park, with Sills in the cast and Sheldon Patinkin directing. The other was the Eagle's Mere Repertory, staffed by recent Northwestern University graduates and directed by the revered Northwestern University acting coach Alvina Krause. (Frank Galati, an N.U. graduate and a designer and actor in the company, remembers waking up the morning after their opening to the sound of sobs by a fellow cast member who had just finished reading the reviews.)

The same year that Sagan decided to buy the Harper, William Pullinsi, fresh out of college, came home to Chicago, eager to set up his own theater in the bright lights of the city. "Rush Street," he says. "The North Side. That's where the nightlife action was." Instead, on July 7, 1961, he opened the 150-seat Candlelight Dinner Playhouse in a roadside building owned by his grandfather at 5508 S. Archer Avenue, a long way from the action.

Here, Pullinsi resumed an entertainment operation he had invented while he was a student at Catholic University in Washington, D.C. He and his friend Anthony D'Angelo had converted a banquet hall in a downtown D.C. hotel into a space in which customers saw a show while they were still seated at their dining tables. It was the ultimate in one-stop entertainment, the first such dinner-theater operation in the country.

Offering a stock lineup of light comedies, but no guest stars, Pullinsi did well enough on Archer Avenue to open a new Candlelight in 1964 at 5620 S. Harlem Avenue, with a large parking lot attached, in the blue-collar southwest suburb of Summit. On his arena stage, placed on a hydraulic lift so that it could be lowered for quick scenery changes, he soon began a remarkable run of musical productions that, in addition to long-running standards like *Fiddler on the Roof* and *Man of La Mancha,* included high-quality Chicago-area premieres of *Nine* (using designer William Ivey Long's original Tony Award–winning costumes), *Zorba, Phantom* (the Maury Yeston–Arthur Kopit version), *Mack and Mabel, Into the Woods,* a rousing, reworked rendition of the failed Broadway musical *Rags,* and an extraordinary *Follies.*

William Pullinsi

In the late 1960s at Candlelight, satisfying his taste for darker plays, Pullinsi also threw an occasional unconventional surprise into the mix, presenting such edgy fare as *MacBird!*—Barbara Garson's vision of Lyndon B. Johnson as a contemporary Macbeth—and *Everything in the Garden,* Edward Albee's bleak satire of suburbia.

In 1972, Pullinsi opened the adjoining Forum Theatre, a 425-seat regular proscenium house with a lobby bar and a separate dining room. Presented here were the American premiere of Peter Nichols's *The National Health;* the Midwest premiere of the musical *Company* (with Boris Aronson's original setting); the world premiere of *Boss,* a musical with a script by Frank Galati, based on Mike Royko's book on Chicago's mayor Richard J. Daley; the American premiere of the English musical *Robert and Elizabeth;* and the phenomenally popular *Do Black Patent Leather Shoes Really Reflect Up?*—a musical presented by the fledg-

The full cast of *Phantom,* by Arthur Kopit and Maury Yeston, assembled on the
hydraulic lift stage of Candlelight Dinner Playhouse
COURTESY OF WILLIAM PULLINSI

ling local producers Libby Mages and Daniel Golman and adapted by
John Powers from his humorous, sentimental book that looks back on
his life growing up Roman Catholic on the South Side of Chicago.

These were not cut-rate, leftover productions, dumbed down for the
yokels. In Summit, Pullinsi kept his work at a high downtown level.
Along with the Chicken Imperial, Baron of Beef, and Manicotti with
Meatballs on the menu, he served up shows put together with full, often
lavish professionalism. In the process, he developed a widening pool of

THE PRODUCERS

Chicago does not have heavy-hitter producers and theater landlords, such as the Shuberts and the Nederlanders of Broadway, but it does have a few individuals who have made their way with some success in the crap game of commercial theater. Among them:

Michael "Mick" Leavitt, stagestruck since he was in grade school, got his first directing job in 1981 by answering a want ad placed by the non-Equity Pegasus Players. Arlene Crewdson, Pegasus's executive director, says, "He had great energy and a positive attitude. I was very impressed." By 1985, he was taking his first steps toward producing, often expertly directing the shows he presented. At one point in the nineties, he leased four midsize commercial houses in Chicago, but his big leap forward came when he hooked up with the Fox Theatricals organization and became a Broadway player. He was a producer of revivals of the musical *You're a Good Man, Charlie Brown* and the drama *One Flew over the Cuckoo's Nest* (in the 2001 Steppenwolf production), and he shepherded *Thoroughly Modern Millie* from its early development to its Tony Award for best musical in 2002. He was producer for the downtown Cadillac Palace when it reopened in 1998, but sold out his interest to the Nederlander Organization soon after.

Libby Mages

Libby Mages, a shrewd motherly soul with a knack for spotting shows of popular appeal, was a teacher at Northeastern Illinois University in Chicago when she encouraged a young fellow faculty member, John Powers, to turn his nostalgic, semiautobiographical books about growing up Roman Catholic on Chicago's South Side into a stage musical. "It was like Mickey and Judy, and 'Let's put on a show,'" she says. She took Powers to his first musical (*Working,* at Goodman Theatre in 1978) and with her then partner Daniel Golman helped Powers put together *Do Black Patent Leather Shoes Really Reflect Up?*—an instant local hit in 1979 and a continuing annuity since (except for its instant Broadway flop in 1982). She has put money in more hits than failures, and she has the ability to round up loyal fellow investors for the family-friendly shows she likes.

Michael Cullen, soon after graduating from the Goodman School, began producing with his Travel Light Theatre, presenting portable plays in nooks and crannies of Near North Side saloons. In a yo yo career of flops and hits, he had his big success in the 1980s, when he, his partner Sheila

Henaghan, and actor Howard Platt produced the very long running musical *Pump Boys and Dinettes.* An avid theater buff with a topsy-turvy business record, he found a home in 1994 when he and restaurateur Joe Carlucci renovated and took over the 350-seat Mercury Theater, 3745 N. Southport Avenue, using it primarily for off-Loop transfers and small touring shows.

Marshall Migatz, having made and lost a lot of money producing summer theater in the 1950s and 1960s, started a new venture in the 1970s, the Academy Festival Theatre on the campus of Barat College in Lake Forest. In 1973, he assembled a revival of Eugene O'Neill's *A Moon for the Misbegotten,* with Jason Robards Jr. and Colleen Dewhurst, directed by Jose Quintero. The production opened, was acclaimed a classic and transferred to a legendary, Tony Award–winning run on Broadway. But Migatz, passionate in his zest for theater, never saw the production. A few weeks before the opening, always in a hurry, he pulled over to the shoulder of the Edens Expressway when his car ran out of gas. As he ran across the highway in heavy traffic to get aid, he was hit and killed by a car. He was fifty. He had given me my first and only job in the professional theater, when I served as an apprentice at his Chevy Chase summer theater in Wheeling in 1949.

Tony DeSantis knew little about theater when he started his first Drury Lane Theatre in the 1950s as an adjunct to his Martinique restaurant in the southwest suburb of Evergreen Park, and, he says, he has learned little since. But director Gary Griffin, who worked for and admires him, contends, "He knows a lot more than you think he does." A smart investor in real estate, a tough, careful manager of the bottom line, and a restaurateur who gives value for money, he expanded his Drury Lane formula of guest stars in old plays to locations in McCormick Place, Water Tower Place, and north suburban Lincolnshire, but eventually focused on the hugely profitable Drury Lane in west suburban Oakbrook Terrace. Here, the crystal chandeliers and gold trim that decorate his 900-seat theater, which presents musicals and comedies with all-Chicago casts, share space with a restaurant, banquet halls, and mini-convention center. At age ninety, he was busy planning a 2005 return to Water Tower Place with a new 560-seat proscenium-style theater.

Terry James came to Marriott's Theater in Lincolnshire in 1982 as an actor-singer in musicals, moved into administration in 1992, and took over as executive producer in 2000, when Kary Walker, who had built the theater into a thriving operation, retired. Continuing the theater's all-musicals policy, James imaginatively mounted on Marriott's arena stage new productions of recent Broadway hits, such as *Cats* and *Miss Saigon,* mixing them with an occasional new work and a lavish revival. His theater, housed in the Marriott resort in Lincolnshire, runs on an annual budget of $9 million. With a list of close to forty thousand subscribers, it is the commercial giant of Chicago-area resident theater.

musical theater talents, from performers to designers and choreographers such as Lou Conte, who went on to found and develop Hubbard Street Dance Chicago into a world-class troupe.

In 1996, in a pinched economy and a tough season, and with a bank nervous about a large loan it had given him, Pullinsi was forced to close his two theaters. They were leveled, the hydraulic stage was buried under concrete, and a roadside restaurant went up in their place. Pullinsi continued as an independent director, but Candlelight, unfortunately, was over.

George Keathley

On the North Side of Chicago, another kind of venturesome theater, in a conservative, commercial arena, began in 1968 with the arrival of director George Keathley at the Ivanhoe Theatre. The Ivanhoe, named after its adjoining parent restaurant, the Ivanhoe, at 750 W. Wellington Avenue, was opened in 1966 by owner Richard Jansen as a dinner-theater operation, presenting guest stars in tried-and-true, lightweight fare. It had a few hits and a much-ado 1967 revival of *The Philadelphia Story,* which starred Lee Bouvier Radziwill, Jacqueline Kennedy's sister, and which, as an added attraction in the circuslike celebrity proceedings surrounding her debut, featured Truman Capote, flaunting his elfin personality as a member of her entourage. Mostly, however, the Ivanhoe faltered, so Jansen, at the suggestion of one of his stars, Celeste Holm, who knew Keathley's work, brought in the talented director. He proved to be just the right man for putting the Ivanhoe on a serious and successful course of professional theater.

In 1949, Keathley, as a young man in his twenties in Florida, had converted an abandoned Miami garage into his own small theater, Studio M. He soon was spotted as a comer through his direction of an early version of Tennessee Williams's *Sweet Bird of Youth* there in the 1950s.

After moving from Miami to operate out of New York, he landed his first Chicago job in 1957, staging Arthur Miller's *A View from the Bridge* for the old Studebaker Theatre Company.

In Chicago, interviewing for the Ivanhoe job, he looked in on the theater's moldy revival of Noel Coward's *Fallen Angels,* with the badly miscast movie actress Joan Bennett as its guest star. He realized then, he said, "It would not be hard to do better."

He did more than that. He showed his mettle in his third show at the Ivanhoe, using Rita Moreno, a guest star who could act, and a solid Chicago supporting cast in a buoyant production of Williams's *The Rose Tattoo,* a play he loved by a playwright he knew. It was a commercial and critical smash, and in 1969, at the first annual Joseph Jefferson Awards ceremony, initiated to honor professional work in resident theaters, it won three of the six prizes handed out, for production, director, and guest artist.

For the next three years, Keathley had a golden touch at the Ivanhoe, his commercial savvy and artistic taste combining to produce serious work that still had mainstream box-office appeal. He elevated the quality of local professional theater, and he gave a core group of veteran Chicago players—Geraldine Kay, Marrian Walters, Edgar Meyer, Bob Thompson, Donald Marston, and Marji Bank—something more substantial than pap for their acting chops to chew on.

In 1971, in a valiant but eventually futile effort to coax Williams out of personal and professional depression, Keathley staged the premiere of the playwright's latter-day two-character drama *Out Cry,* with Eileen Herlie and Donald Madden. Williams, in a tempestuous residency, became increasingly unstable as rehearsals proceeded. Tom Guerra, the company stage manager, still remembers the shock that came when Williams, given a bottle of red wine he had requested, took one sip and, in front of the cast and crew, emptied the bottle on the stage floor. This erratic behavior took its saddest, strangest turn when, during a wild backstage explosion, Williams lashed out at Keathley and fired his loyal, long-serving literary agent Audrey Wood. Even then, *Out Cry*'s tale of a brother and sister trapped in a ghostly theater had its moments of brilliance. Two years later, when, in a new production with a different director, the play flopped on Broadway, Williams said, rightly, "It was better in Chicago."

Eileen Herlie and Donald Madden in Tennessee Williams's *Out Cry*, 1971
COURTESY OF RICK PAUL

Ironically, the Ivanhoe's biggest success was not Keathley's work. It was *Status Quo Vadis*, a slick, superficial new comedy of social satire, written and directed by Broadway professional Donald Driver. It ran a total of fifty-eight weeks in 1971–72, giving the Ivanhoe an instant box-office fix but interrupting its format and subscription schedule. Brought to Broadway in 1973 by overly optimistic investors, it was a one-performance flop.

Thereafter Keathley's golden touch seemed to tarnish. There were some high-profile shows—Sandy Dennis in *A Streetcar Named Desire*, for one—but the box office had a calamitous falling off. In 1975, Driver's prophetically titled new comedy, *The Last Straw*, was a resounding failure, and that April both theater and restaurant were shut down and put up for auction. Keathley left Chicago ("with some bitterness," Thompson felt) and went on to TV work in New York and a happy fifteen-year term as artistic director of the Missouri Repertory Theatre in Kansas City. The Ivanhoe, eventually acquired by independent producer Douglas Bragan, survived primarily as a rental house until 2001, when Bragan sold the theater and it was dismantled to make way for an addition to the liquor and food business that had taken over the building. (One of its later long-run occupants, before it closed, was the Lookingglass Theatre's production of director Mary Zimmerman's much admired *Metamorphoses* in 1998–99.)

The Ivanhoe in its prime served an important function by boosting the rising sense of pride in local professional theater. It demonstrated that it was possible to hire guest stars who were good actors and that Chicago had a core of resident actors ready and eager to take their talents beyond the usual featherweight material of dinner theater.

Although the Ivanhoe, the Harper, and the Candlelight eventually went under, they nonetheless left behind them a series of productions that helped develop the evolving strength of resident artists and raise the level of performance for audiences in Chicago. And soon, in another, humbler arena of not-for-profit theaters, the genuine "movement" would be under way.

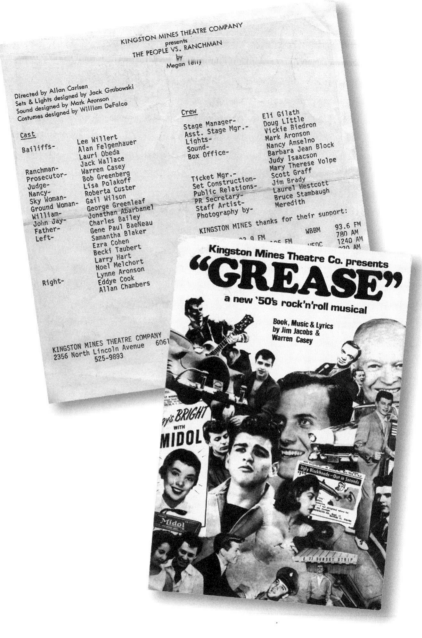

KINGSTON MINES THEATRE COMPANY
presents
THE PEOPLE VS. RANCHMAN
by
Megan Terry

Directed by Allan Carlsen
Sets & Lights designed by Jack Grabowski
Sound designed by Mark Aronson
Costumes designed by William DeFalco

Cast

Bailiffs-	Lee Willert
	Alan Felgenhauer
	Lauri Obeda
	Jack Wallace
Ranchman-	Warren Casey
Prosecutor-	Bob Greenberg
Judge-	Lisa Polakoff
Nancy-	Roberta Custer
Sky Woman-	Gail Wilson
Ground Woman-	George Greenleaf
William-	Jonathan Abarbanel
John Jay-	Charles Bailey
Father-	Gene Paul BaeNeau
Left-	Samantha Blaker
	Ezra Cohen
	Becki Taubert
	Larry Hart
	Noel Melchort
	Lynne Aronson
Right-	Eddye Cook
	Allan Chambers

Crew

Stage Manager-	Eli Gilath
Asst. Stage Mgr.-	Doug LIttle
Lights-	Vickie Biedron
Sound-	Mark Aronson
Box Office-	Nancy Anselno
	Barbara Jean Block
	Judy Isaacson
	Mary Therese Volpe
Ticket Mgr.-	Scott Graff
Set Construction-	Jim Brady
Public Relations-	Laurel Westcott
PR Secretary-	Bruce Stambaugh
Staff Artist-	Meredith
Photography by-	

KINGSTON MINES thanks for their support:

	WBBM	93.6 FM
		780 AM
	WEDC	1240 AM

KINGSTON MINES THEATRE COMPANY
2356 North Lincoln Avenue   6061
525-9893

Kingston Mines Theatre Co. presents

"GREASE"

a new '50's rock'n'roll musical

Book, Music & Lyrics
by Jim Jacobs &
Warren Casey

From a "new '50s rock 'n' roll musical" to a bit of far-out off-Broadway drama at Kingston Mines Theatre in the 1970s

ELAYNE LETRAUNIK AND GUY BARILE COLLECTIONS

Chapter 13

"Let All the Flowers of the Arts Bloom"

Early in his career as a Chicago designer, Rick Paul discovered that there were strange and wonderful ways in which Chicago's community of little theaters could be nourished, unwittingly, by the larger commercial houses of the city. Paul landed a job as an assistant to set designer William Fosser at the then-thriving Ivanhoe, and, whenever an Ivanhoe production ended and its scenery was tossed out, Paul raided the dumpster, gathered up whatever material he thought he could use, and carted it two blocks east to a second-floor church auditorium at 615 W. Wellington Avenue.

Here, in Baird Hall, was Paul's home base: Chicago City Players, a small, poor, but imaginative homegrown avant-garde group established in the 1960s by the Community Renewal Society (CRS), an arts organization sponsored by the United Church of Christ.

Byron Hildreth was the troupe's coartistic director, leaning in his work toward plays of the Theater of the Absurd, such as Fernando Arrabel's *Automobile Junkyard*. Among the directors working with him was June Pyskacek, an alumna of the Goodman School who, before coming to Baird Hall, had been staging "happenings," those 1960s versions of

Jack Wallace leading the cast in Jean-Claude van Itallie's *The Serpent* at Kingston Mines Theatre, 1969
COURTESY OF RICK PAUL

performance art, in North Side art galleries. Pyskacek had a flair for directing what used to be called "far-out" plays, and she had a nose for talent, too. Jack Wallace, a Chicago actor possessed of force-of-nature vitality, was a roofer, "covered in tar," Pyskacek says, when she first met him, and yet she knew on the instant that he had the energy and the exuberance needed for the theater she was producing.

While she was sweeping the theater's floor one night after a performance, a member of the audience came over and asked her if she would like to direct his work. He was Jean-Claude van Itallie, who was emerging as a leading playwright of the sixties counterculture. Pyskacek subsequently staged his 1966 hit *America Hurrah*, a benchmark off-Broadway trilogy of three short nonrealistic works questioning American values, for a long, successful Chicago premiere run. She also brought to Chicago the first productions of several other leading off-Broadway playwrights, including the imaginative works of Maria Irene Fornes.

This was the era of the Vietnam War, a time when many young people were passionate about the arts and wanted to use them as an instrument of protest against, and liberation from, the old political, social, and cultural forms of the Establishment. In Chicago, the violent urban unrest following the assassinations of the Reverend Martin Luther King Jr. and Robert F. Kennedy was compounded by the police-versus-protesters confrontations surrounding the Democratic National Convention in the summer of 1968. Chicago, according to Tom Wicker of the *New York Times,* an astute outside commentator, was "the place where all America was radicalized."

Under these new, radical circumstances, there was a call for a freer, more open, more diversified, and less tradition-bound art form that would be able to speak to the restless, seeking spirits of the sixties generation.

A major response to this demand was the Free Street Theater, founded in 1968 by Patrick Henry, a graduate of the Goodman School who had emerged as a bright young hope in directing at Goodman Theatre, which in the sixties was ending three decades as a house presenting solely student productions.

John Reich

Following the growing resident theater movement taking hold across the country, and encouraged by the new theaters starting up in the city, Goodman in 1969 became a fully professional theater. John Reich, a Viennese producer, director, and teacher who was hired as artistic director of the Goodman in 1957, had been edging the theater toward professionalism for several years, inaugurating a vigorous subscription campaign devised by the indefatigable Danny Newman and importing professional guest artists to add glamour and polish to the student casts. In 1966, he put out feelers toward hooking up with the University of Chicago by presenting a professional production of Molière's *The Misanthrope* at the U. of C., with George Grizzard as its star. The connection was never made, but the reception for the show was encouraging enough to keep Reich working

Free Street Theater in performance, 1973
COURTESY OF *CHICAGO TRIBUNE* NEWS ARCXHIVE

toward his goal of taking the Goodman into the ranks of fully certified
resident theaters. Finally, in 1969, with the approval of the parent Art
Institute, the determined Reich reached his goal. He and the English
actor and director Douglas Seale became codirectors of a resident professional company on the Goodman's main stage, with student productions limited to a smaller, 135-seat studio theater. The opening
production was *Soldiers,* a drama about World War II ethics and politics by the German writer Rolf Hochhuth, with Douglas Campbell, a
veteran of the Stratford (Canada) and Guthrie theaters, taking on the
play's principal role of Winston Churchill.

When Goodman turned professional, it looked like Henry would
become one of its leading lights, a specialist in contemporary and edgy
work. But, although he initially served as producer-director of the studio theater and continued to direct at Goodman and on other professional stages, he chose to focus his energy and creativity in a different
area. With initial funding for a pilot project from the Goodman and the

Illinois Arts Council, as well as from some private donors, Henry gathered an interracial cast of students and very young actors and trucked his shows out in portable "showmobiles" that toured the parks, alleys, and empty lots of city neighborhoods. He fashioned a series of revues that in song, dance, and drama were derived from improvisation and encouraged audience participation. The revues tried to address the gritty issues of urban life, and they expressed the problems and ideals of their youthful casts. In one show, an actor asked for questions from the audience on any of three subjects: sex, human rights, and revolution. In another performance in Grant Park, I remember in particular a tremendously moving monologue by Steve Fletcher, a young actor trying to sort out the emotions of anger and confusion he felt, knowing that he might soon be drafted and sent to Vietnam.

Free Street did not come free, of course. Even with its minimal wages, it required public and private money to keep it going, and this money became increasingly hard to come by. But its touring editions provided an invaluable basic training ground for its actors, and its often joyful revues played to a large audience that would not otherwise have seen (and enjoyed) live theater. Henry, who later expanded his casts and shows to embrace seniors and senior issues, died, too young, in 1989; Free Street continued on a limited basis but with its original spirit of youthful vision intact.

Late in the sixties, the movement toward bold, youth-oriented culture was further strengthened by the founding of the Body Politic, a North Side bastion of offbeat, populist, and experimental work in a two-story building at 2257–61 N. Lincoln Avenue. The director, majordomo, and guiding light here was the Reverend James "Jim" Shiflett, a Presbyterian minister who also was a social activist. A graduate of the McCormick Theological Seminary and former pastor of St. Andrew Church on the Northwest Side, he had taken part in civil rights demonstrations in the South and had come back to Chicago determined to do something more in social work than traditional pastoral responsibilities would allow.

In 1964, he enrolled his children in theater games classes being conducted by Viola Spolin, and through her he met Paul Sills, who had returned to work in Chicago after leaving The Second City for New York in 1960. Shiflett quickly determined that the games, which taught

The Reverend Jim Shiflett, 1972
COURTESY OF *CHICAGO TRIBUNE* NEWS ARCHIVE

their players to trust and rely on one another, could be used as an instrument of social action and cooperation. He attended a few workshops himself ("I couldn't play very well, but I did recognize the value of these games").

As part of his social work, Shiflett became a member of the Broken Jar Center, an ecumenical ministry with a leaning toward the arts. He was asked by the CRS to conduct a survey on the need for a North Side arts center. In response to the survey's findings, the Community Arts Foundation (CAF) was founded in 1966, with Shiflett as director, to act as an audience-building organization that encouraged artists to relate directly to the problems and goals of their community. Chicago City Players was part of his responsibility.

With a grant from the Chicago Community Trust, Shiflett was able to set up theater, writing, film, dance, photography, and art workshops in Chicago schools, and, in 1969, he persuaded a private donor to come up with a down payment of twenty thousand dollars to buy the rundown Lincoln Avenue storefront building for use as a center for CAF. In its new state, the place derived its name from a statement by the nineteenth-century actor-manager Harley Granville-Barker, who had likened theater to "a body politic." Here, Shiflett says, "The mission was to let all the flowers of the arts bloom." And tending this garden was the tall, soft-spoken, bearded, craggy-faced Shiflett, who, in his sandals, jeans, beads, and flowing embroidered shirts, looked exactly right as a guru of grassroots arts.

The Lincoln Avenue building, which included a rent-paying saloon, the Oxford Pub, on its north side, became a home for a swarm of visual and performing arts projects, patronized by a large, enthusiastic, young audience. "Whoosh," Shiflett says. "All of a sudden, the place was filled with people. Socialites started talking about our growing arts community."

For theater work, Shiflett turned to Sills, who in 1968 had set up a temporary base and started experimental work with a fresh group of actors in the old Second City space at 1842 N. Wells Street. That summer, in the tempestuous days of the Democratic National Convention in Chicago, the place became a haven for demonstrators who had been chased by police out of nearby Lincoln Park.

Now, in 1969, Sills was looking for a home for his new form of theater, and Shiflett offered him a spot in the building on Lincoln Avenue. This move effectively sidestepped CAF's original partner, Chicago City Players, and Pyskacek, whom Shiflett describes as "a real go-getter," feeling kicked out of the action, went off on her own. She found a cavernous old three-story former trolley barn up and across the street at

FIRST THINGS FIRST

Money affairs for small, youthful theaters setting up shop in Chicago in the late sixties and early seventies were usually catch as catch can, but as these groups began to settle down in permanent homes, some effort was made to codify their managerial procedures. In 1971, with the Organic Theater installed as a component of the Body Politic space at 2261 N. Lincoln Avenue, the Community Arts Foundation, which owned the building, sent a memo to Stuart Gordon, the Organic's artistic director, setting down their relationship in black-and-white. The document laid out such basic matters as rent and upkeep payments, but at the top of the list came the following paragraph on the mutual rewards and obligations the Organic and the CAF had worked out. Note the final sentence:

> Our last verbal agreement was that you would receive the first $645.00 in receipts each week, the CAF the next $225.00. Any receipts received beyond $870.00 would be split three ways: one third to Organic Theater, one third to Organic Theater Company, and one third to CAF. Also, the Organic Theater was responsible to clean the rest rooms three times per week.

2356 N. Lincoln Avenue, named it Kingston Mines (after a very small Illinois town where Wallace's father had been a miner), and continued producing her inventive work there. Along with more avant-garde work, she produced *Grease,* a new musical by Chicagoans Jim Jacobs and Warren Casey. Premiered in 1971, it became a long-run hit, which, through its hugely successful move to Broadway, called early New York attention to the uniquely energetic work being done in Chicago.

Sills, meanwhile, moved to Lincoln Avenue in 1969, ready to show off his latest theater venture. Always the innovator, he called this groundbreaking creation Story Theater. As he had done many times before, he set up a new theater space. It was small, seating about 150 persons on the first floor of what had been the former home of the U.S. Slicing Machine Company. In a few weeks, the imaginative theatrical narratives of Story Theater, which had the cast telling and acting out stories from Ovid's *Metamorphoses* and Grimm's fairy tales, were enchanting audiences through their simple magic.

Upstairs, in what had been the Monte Carlo Bowling Alley, composer William Russo's Free Theater was drawing crowds to his "rock cantata" of *Civil War.* Other operations of dance, playwriting, mural painting, puppetry, and political activism, briefly including the radical Rising Up Angry group, added to the grassroots fervor. All this arts activity, plus the saloon business, added to the noise and congestion in the neighborhood and to the garbage bags that kept piling up in the alley.

Faced with the possibility of being closed down for building code violations or being bulldozed for an urban renewal project, Shiflett rallied his disparate groups, organized a letter-writing campaign, and, through the advocacy writing of *Sun-Times* theater reviewer Glenna Syse, got significant support for the community art being produced at the Body Politic. "When we had a meeting with Mayor [Richard J.] Daley about amending the building codes for the new, small theaters we were developing," Shiflett says, "he reached into a desk drawer and pulled out a piece of paper that turned out to be the basis for an ordinance that took care of our problems." The ordinance, with new electrical and fire code provisions tailored for the small, nonproscenium spaces that were beginning to open, was voted into law by the City Council. After that, it became a little easier for storefront theaters to exist in Chicago.

The first Story Theater company, in a group portrait of 1968 (and looking very sixties indeed). From left to right, Joseph Bell, Cordis Heard, director Paul Sills, Warren Leming, Eugenie Ross, and Joyce Piven. Kneeling, center, is Thomas Erhart.

TODD CAZAUX, COURTESY OF JOYCE PIVEN

GREASE WAS THE WORD

In the late 1960s, the theater community in Chicago was small enough that everybody in it knew everybody else. "They would come to our shows, and we would go to theirs," says designer Rick Paul. "We all went to the same parties."

One night, in 1969, at one of these parties, director June Pyskacek heard theater buddies Jim Jacobs and Warren Casey singing some numbers they had started to write for a musical about Chicago high school kids in the 1950s. Pyskacek, caught up by the wit and fun of such ditties as "Beauty School Dropout" and "It's Raining on Prom Night," immediately told the two men, "If you guys finish writing this, I'll put it on."

Two years later, on February 8, 1971, *Grease* opened at Pyskacek's Kingston Mines Theatre, 2356 N. Lincoln Avenue, for what was to have been a run of a few weekend

Jim Jacobs and Warren Casey
COURTESY OF DONNA DUNLAP

performances. "Nobody paid any attention to it," says Donna Dunlap, an actress friend of Casey's, "and, to tell you the truth, at first I thought it was a pretty stupid idea." But, Pyskacek insists, "I knew it would be a hit," and she was right. It ran through August in Chicago, with audiences ranging from middle-aged ladies to hippie teenagers filling the theater's collection of chairs, sofas, and seat cushions night after night.

One out-of-town admirer was the New York critic Michael Feingold, who called the show's trip back to the fifties "a loving, funny museum of where we were, perhaps even, when we scream and stomp our feet at it, a gentle attempt to exorcise the parts of ourselves we left back there, a tribute to the many small, stupid things. . . . *Grease* . . . is as honest in its comedy as any great musical of the twenties or thirties. So don't let anybody tell you they don't make shows like that anymore."

Soon, New York producers were coming in to sniff out the little show. It was picked up for an off-Broadway production that opened in New York on Valentine's Day in 1972. It later was transferred to a larger Broadway house, picking up seven Tony Award nominations and winning none. ("But at least," Casey told Dunlap, "I got to hear Ingrid Bergman [a Tony presenter] say my name.") At the time of its closing in 1980, it had piled up 3,338 performances for a Broadway long-run record.

All this had its modest beginnings in 1963 when Jacobs and Casey met and acted together in the community theater group, Chicago Stage Guild. Jacobs, a self-described "Chicago groob" not too long out of William Howard Taft High School, was an office boy on the twenty-fourth floor of Tribune Tower, although he later would become a copywriter for *Advertising Age*. Casey, the older half of their odd couple, was a clerk downtown at Rose Records, although he later would become regional sales manager for a lingerie firm. (Asked what he did for a living, he would answer, "I'm in girdles and bras.") They lived far

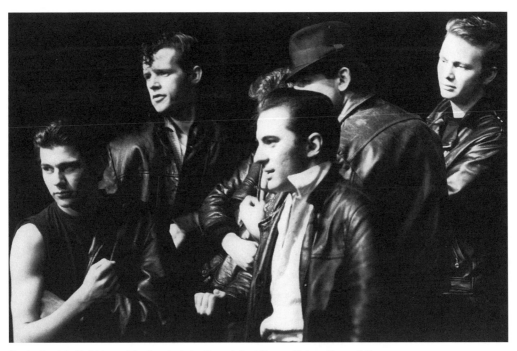

Decked out in T-shirts and leather jackets, the original Burger Palace Boys of *Grease*
DONNA DUNLAP

apart—Jacobs, married, on the far North Side, and Casey, single, in a flat above a Chickenland restaurant on Broadway at Aldine Avenue. (Asked where he lived, he would answer, "Above Chickenland.") But both young men shared a love of wicked nonsense, a zest for the theater, and an affection for old pop music.

The tunes in their "new rock 'n' roll musical of the fifties" started as an offhand amusement, with Casey accompanying their singing on his beat-up guitar. ("He could play four chords," says Ronna Kaye, *Grease*'s original choreographer, "and that was it.") Soon Jacobs told Casey, "We should really put those songs into a situation." The "situation," immediately titled *Grease* by Jacobs, became a story revolving around a gang of greasers and their girlfriends in 1959 at the mythical Rydell (as in teen singer Bobby Rydell) High. Jacobs based many of the characters on the gang he grew up with at Taft. Casey, having bought a second-hand typewriter, started the script rolling by writing the show's pajama party scene as his first typing exercise. After that, they were on their way.

Paul Sills showed some early interest in directing the show, and Jacobs also showed the script to William Pullinsi, director of Candlelight Dinner Playhouse, where Jacobs had worked as an actor. "Every other line had an 'f—— you' in it," Pullinsi says. "When I told Jim that was too much, he said, 'Well, that's the way we talked.'"

continued ➤

(continued)

Hedda Lubin, very blond, and friends in the "Beauty School Dropout" chorale of *Grease*
RON KRAJEWSKI, COURTESY OF GUY BARILE

In the end, it was actor/director Guy Barile who, with Kaye as choreographer, staged the show at Kingston Mines. According to Barile, "I knew there was a show somewhere in that script, but at first I couldn't get anything going. I kept thinking, 'What have I got myself into?' But then it began to take shape, and we got really excited."

Total production costs were a little under $200, Jacobs swears (although Barile believes that's a little conservative), with $70 going toward a 1951 Chrysler that took the role of "Greased Lightning," the gang's car. Too heavy to put on the rickety stage, it was placed to one side. Unfortunately, the actor who drove it couldn't judge distances very well, so at first he was in danger of accidentally zooming forward into the audience, or crashing backward into the scenery.

The original cast included such youngsters as Gary Houston, Jim Canning, Polly Pen, Hedda Lubin, and Jacobs's friend Marilu Henner, then a student at the University of Chicago. The boys portrayed gang members of the Burger Palace Boys, with such names as Sonny LaTierri and Doody, as in Howdy Doody. The girls were called Frenchy, Marty, and (my favorite) Cha-Cha DiGregorio, who explained her nickname this way: "They call me Cha-Cha, because I'm the best dancer at St. Bernadette High." The five-piece band, also perfectly named, was called Johnny Casino and the Gamblers.

Opening night was nearly a disaster. In an overly enthusiastic gang rumble, Canning suffered a nasty forehead cut, which was hastily patched up. Worse, the bulb in the show's sole spotlight burned out, forcing Kaye to cab it a few blocks south to a Rush Street nightspot, where she was able to find a working lightbulb.

The show was long, it was raunchy, and it was an immediate hit, way ahead of the pack in its tapping into fifties nostalgia. When it went to New York, with only Canning of the original cast making the move, it was shortened and smoothed out, and its greaser boys made more "lovable." When it was made into a hugely popular movie, with John Travolta, it suffered the greatest indignity of all: its scene was transferred to Southern California. Nowhere was it ever quite as fresh, funny, and explosive as it had been in its Chicago birthplace.

Casey and Jacobs tried a couple of other musical comedies: an aborted surfer dude spoof for movie director Joel Schumacher, and *Island of Lost Co-Eds,* which had a 1981 student production at Columbia College in Chicago. But they never completed another show. Casey, a victim of AIDS, died at 53 in 1988.

Grease was all they needed.

This first great humungous hit imported from Chicago had a rocky beginning in New York. For Barile and Kaye the move also turned into an unhappy ending. A new director (Tom Moore) and choreographer (Patricia Birch) were hired for the transfer, leaving Barile and Kaye feeling dumped and deserted.

The initial critical reaction to the restaged, recast show was hardly encouraging. The esteemed director/critic Harold Clurman walked out at intermission on opening night. Clive Barnes, reviewing it in the *New York Times,* drolly confessed that all he knew about 1959 was that it was a great year for burgundy, but, he added, "If there is a place in New York for a modern 1950s rock-parody musical from Chicago, then *Grease* might well slide into it." Jacobs was so outraged by the condescending tone of this remark that he threatened, only half jokingly, to track down Barnes and break his legs.

Since then, *Grease* (or *Vaselina,* as it was called in Mexico) has spread worldwide. It became a very long run hit in London, and in 2003, Jacobs signed a contract for a production on the Isle of Man, about as far from Rydell High as it's possible to go.

Dunlap, for whose daughter Casey wrote a separate ditty, "My Barbie Doll's Gone to Barbie Doll Heaven," says she even saw a production of *Grease on Ice* in Knoxville, Tennessee. The show's popularity is so great that, Jacobs says, monthly royalties from Germany alone at one point amounted to $250,000 a month.

In this country, it has been staged, I would guess, by every high school and church group known to man. Albert Williams, who teaches musical theater at Columbia College in Chicago, says that every year, "A couple students audition with songs from *Grease.* Usually I have to sit them down and explain to them that the show started right here in Chicago. All they know is the movie."

A few years back, when Jacobs went to a birthday party for Marilu Henner, she showed him a picture of her two sons, in costume for their grade school production of *Grease.* But the ultimate sign of the triumph of his show came to Jacobs when he was about to turn sixty. His entertainment lawyer told him, "Jim, resign yourself. *Grease* is going to outlive you."

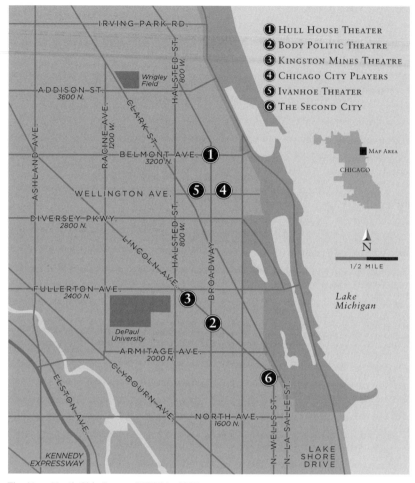

The Near North Side "scene," 1963 to 1969
STEVE RAVENSCRAFT

As Shiflett admits, "We lived on the edge at the Body Politic, in every sense of the word. I never did get a board together. I was no good at it. We were always short on money, the building always needed fixing, and then, in 1974, when we had a bad fire, that put us further in the hole."

For a while, Shiflett maintained his own group, the improvisatory Dream Theater, as a resident and touring troupe. That, added to the burden of administration, was too much for him to handle. Played out and burned out, he retreated from the Body Politic in 1979 and returned to his ministry work. But he left behind an important history of arts activism and a long list of arts organizations that had found a home in his hothouse of the arts on Lincoln Avenue. During his tenure at the Body Politic, the early off-Loop groups of the Dinglefest Theatre Company, Pyskacek's Chicago Theatre Strategy, Chicago City Theatre, Chicago Contemporary Dance Theatre, and Pary Productions, among others, made their homes there. *Lunching,* a yuppie comedy of manners by Chicago playwright Alan Gross, had a three-month run there, after which it moved to the Drury Lane Theatre in Water Tower Place, just east of Michigan Avenue on Chestnut Street, the first off-Loop show to make the transfer to a larger, commercial theater.

But before all that, when Sills and Story Theater left the Body Politic to tour elsewhere in 1970, Shiflett had opened the door for another singular creative force in Chicago theater, a young director who had formed a new company of risk and daring. The troupe was the Organic Theater, its director was Stuart Gordon, and together they ushered in an amazing decade of growth in Chicago's homegrown, homemade theater.

Two of the Organic Theater's triumphs of imaginative, homegrown playmaking in the 1970s

Chapter 14

"We'll Have a Scene"

STUART GORDON'S ORGANIC THEATER Company arrived in Chicago at the start of the 1970s, and for the next few years, in a time of exploding creativity, it was the quintessential Chicago theater group. Venturesome, innovative, energetic, improvisational, and always on the edge of disaster or triumph, it was a small but powerful and influential force in fostering the talent and shaping the personality of the city's theater scene. It produced more than a few duds, but it also presented a handful of Chicago-born masterworks that were both supremely of the moment and way ahead of their time.

Gordon, a Chicago native, developed a hunger for daring theater in his visits to The Second City as a high school kid. While still in his teens, he organized a small improv comedy group, The Human Race, and, by the time he was a student at the University of Wisconsin in Madison in the late 1960s, he had his own theater company.

At Madison, when he was twenty, he wrote and staged his first sensational work, *The Game Show,* a wicked satire that played out as a TV game show in which audience members were forced into increasingly debasing situations—being stripped, beaten, and threatened with rape—

in order to win prizes and money. Those who did not volunteer were dragged onto the stage by brutish ushers, who at one point tore the clothes off a hysterical woman contestant. When a version of *The Game Show* (using Gordon's script but not his actors) later played in a small off-Loop theater in Chicago, Michaela Williams, a smart reporter/writer sent to review the opening night for the *Daily News,* became so outraged at this vicious treatment that she rushed to the aid of a beleaguered contestant and angrily called on her fellow audience members to stop the horror. The contestant, however, was more worried about losing a contact lens than he was about taking a beating. It was then that Williams realized that the man she had pitied was actually an actor who had been a plant and that she and the rest of the real, unsuspecting customers had been suckered into an elaborately conceived hoax.

"The play was supposed to end with the game show host shaming the audience for their apathy," Gordon says, "but it never got that far. The audience always attacked the host and stopped the show." Williams wrote that it had been a most exciting production, and that it should be closed down at once.

Gordon's most infamous show at Wisconsin, however, was his original adaptation of James M. Barrie's *Peter Pan* that, while faithful to the text, inserted a brief nude scene in which the children's trip to Neverland was turned into an acid trip, with dim psychedelic lighting playing on the nude bodies of a few coeds, one of whom was Gordon's future wife, Carolyn Purdy. The show was closed down, Gordon was busted on obscenity charges (later dropped), and the young director decided it was time to move away from the hassles of Madison and head for his hometown. He went down to the Body Politic to see a production of Story Theater directed by his idol, Paul Sills. After the performance he introduced himself to Sills, explained his situation, and asked Sills if he thought it would be okay for him to bring his company to Chicago. Sills's famous reply was: "Sure, come on down. I'm here on Lincoln Avenue at the Body Politic; Kingston Mines is just up the street. When you get here, we'll have a scene. Don't worry. They [the authorities] will leave you alone. Nobody cares."

Gordon made the move, brought a few holdovers from Wisconsin, including Carolyn, and picked up other young actors in Chicago, one of whom, Gordon remembers, went by the stage name of Euclid Hark Life

The Organic Theater Company in its prime, about 1976. Stuart Gordon is fourth from
the left, in the second row from the top, with his wife, Carolyn, at his immediate right.
Also in the picture (can you find them?) are Organic stalwarts Joe Mantegna, Dennis
Franz, Roberta Custer, Brian Hickey, Jack Wallace, William J. Norris, Tom Towles, and
Keith Szarabajka.

COURTESY OF STUART GORDON

but was really named Gerald Kirschbaum. Their first production was an
original, very physical adaptation of George Orwell's *Animal Farm*,
staged in the center of the Holy Covenant Church at 925 W. Diversey
Parkway, a site Sills had helped them secure. "They were wonderful to
us at the church," Carolyn remembers. "They were happy to have us,
just so long as we put the pews back."

The Organics in their beginning were what we used to call hippies or
flower children. In reviewing one of their early Chicago productions,
Tarot Cards, I wrote in the *Daily News* review that the cast consisted of
"six strenuously involved (and some, unhappily, unwashed) performers."

They were very communal ("I was the company cook," Carolyn says), working together on all phases of their productions, splitting up the cash proceeds at the end of the week, and living on cheap food and a little dope. William J. Norris, who was playing an owl in a children's show when Gordon spotted him, was the son of a Chicago policeman and had never taken drugs before he joined the Organic. Then under stress one night when he had to take over a leading role from an injured actor, he walked into the theater and told his fellow players he needed something to calm down. "Where's the dope?" he asked. Right away, he remembers, "Everybody was offering me some kind of drug."

When Sills and Story Theater left Chicago for the road in 1970, Gordon took over his space at the Body Politic, and for the next three years, the Organic staged a remarkable variety of lively, colorful, vibrant shows. Their commedia dell'arte version of *Candide,* presented in clown makeup, had a brief run at producer Joseph Papp's Public Theater in New York; but their breakthrough hit came in 1971–72 with their three-part *Warp!* which they gleefully trumpeted as "the world's first science-fiction epic-adventure play in serial form." Written by Gordon and Bury St. Edmund (aka Lenny Kleinfeld), a bright, sassy writer and friend from their Madison days, the trilogy tells of David Carson, a meek bank teller

CASTING CALL

When the Organic Theater revived its *Warp!* trilogy in 1979, the competition for the leading role of the hero Lord Cumulus came down to two Chicago actors: Bruce A. Young and John Malkovich.

"We kept auditioning them forever," recalls Lenny Kleinfeld, the play's coauthor. "Finally we decided on Bruce, partly because he looked better with his shirt off."

In 1974, when the Organic premiered David Mamet's *Sexual Perversity in Chicago,* the role of Bernie Litko, the hero's hedonistic sidekick, was offered to Joe Mantegna, an Organic regular.

He turned it down.

"I really wanted to do it," Mantegna says, "but I had the chance to understudy downtown in *Lenny,* the play about Lenny Bruce, at $300 a week, and I knew I was never going to make more than $150 a week at the Organic, so I took the *Lenny* job.

"It was absolutely the right choice to make at the time, but I've always been sorry I didn't get the chance to play that role. When I talk to students today, I tell them, 'When in doubt, go with your heart.'"

miraculously transformed into Lord Cumulus, a superhero who ranges through the universe battling the forces of evil—in the confines of a 150-seat theater space.

The production, financed by a $1,500 loan from Gordon's mother, Rosalie, a high school English teacher, was a marvel of do-it-yourself invention. The extreme costumes, featuring space suits made of macramé threads and sci-fi helmets fashioned from metal mixing bowls and rabbit-ears TV antennas, were by Cookie Gluck, a former art major at the University of Wisconsin who was married to Organic actor Cecil O'Neal. She had never worked in the theater before, and, she says, "If the designs seemed imaginative, it was because I didn't know any better. The only reason the men's space costumes exposed their rear ends, which was considered very daring at the time, was that I had no idea how to construct a pair of trousers." The large stage curtain that rose and then spread over the heads of the audience was put together on a sewing machine, in a nonstop forty-eight-hour frenzy, by Andre DeShields, who had played Tiger Lily in *Peter Pan* and who had rejoined Gordon in Chicago to portray Xander the Unconquerable, one of the play's nasty galactic villains.

Gordon, then in his midtwenties, had created a bravura comic strip of a show that, in its roaring adventure, fast-paced storytelling, and ingenious light and sound effects, was fifteen years ahead of *Star Wars*. Its good humor and great energy left Body Politic audiences happily abuzz, leading to a long run in Chicago and, on Valentine's Day in 1973, to a Broadway presentation of the trilogy's first installment, produced by Anthony D'Amato, at the Ambassador Theatre. It received bemused reviews and ran a total of fifteen performances, including previews. Clive Barnes, in his *New York Times* review, suggested, "Go with friends, and go at least a little cheerful, if not actually high."

The show's Broadway failure decimated the company. Most of the actors took off for other ventures. Norris, with one arm badly injured in an opening-night accident, returned to Chicago, as did Stuart and Carolyn. "No theater, no company, no money, no prospects" is how the Gordons describe their situation. For five months, they lived with Stuart's mother.

Then, in September 1973, in a turn of fortune that consistently marked the Organic's history, they were back in business, and they had

Tom Towles (left) and William J. Norris in full cry as intergalactic villains in *Warp!* (1971)

a hit. Gordon landed a home base in the Leo Lerner Theater of the Uptown Center of Hull House at 4520 N. Beacon Street, a former outpost of Bob Sickinger's Hull House Theater. He gathered together a new company of unknowns that included Dennis Franz, Bruce (later Meshach) Taylor, and Joe Mantegna. And thanks to a tip from his brother David, he found a lovely comedy, *The Wonderful Ice Cream Suit*, by Ray Bradbury.

The play, the Organic's one and only production of a script that it had not originated, concerned five urban Latino misfits, alike only in their physical measurements, whose lives are marvelously changed by a magical white suit they take turns wearing. Gordon brought it to the stage with a joyous sense of brotherly unity amid uproarious diversity. It was performed with great zest and great soul, sending out an infectious feeling of goodwill into its audience.

In eight years of work at the Leo Lerner, that joyous, zestful celebration of theater permeated all of the Organic's best work. There were some notable failures: *Campaign*, by advertising writer Richard Harris, a play about an ad agency, opened and closed in one bitterly cold night in January 1979. But there were wonderful nights, too, nights on which the Organic's creativity was at its peak.

Bloody Bess, by Norris and John Ostrander (1974), the story of a woman pirate's revenge on the evil aristocrat who had raped her and murdered her lover, was at once a full-out, stunt-filled evocation of old swashbucklers and an early, bristling feminist statement.

The two-part *Huckleberry Finn* (1975), faithfully adapted by the company from Mark Twain's novel and presented in a simple staging, conjured up both the immense good humor and the inspiring good spirit of Twain's writing. The scene on the raft in which Huck (Brian Hickey) humbly realizes how his spiteful tricks have humiliated his fellow human being, the escaped slave Jim (Taylor), was devastating in its impact, beautifully played by the actors in a superbly balanced duet.

Cops (1976), from a script by Terry Curtis Fox, with Mantegna and Franz as two rough-and-ready plainclothes policemen caught in a shootout in a diner, preceded the gritty TV dramas of *NYPD Blue*, *The Shield*, *The Wire*, and others with its naturalistic look at police manners, mores, and procedures. (When Gordon showed the play to a group of policemen to get their reactions as "technical consultants," they praised his knowl-

Michael Saad, Roberta Custer, and Keith Szarabajka as three of the *Bleacher Bums,* 1977
LISA EBRIGHT, SPECIAL COLLECTIONS AND PRESERVATION DIVISION, CHICAGO PUBLIC LIBRARY

edge of police mentality, but, they told him, "After you shoot the guy, you should kick him." "But he's dead," Gordon said. "Doesn't matter," they answered. "You kick the son of a bitch anyway.")

And, finally, in 1977 came the masterpiece of *Bleacher Bums.* The "comedy in nine innings" was a true company work, taking off from Cubs fanatic Mantegna's belief that there was a play to be formed from the characters who daily fill the right-field bleachers at Wrigley Field. As Mantegna remembers, "Stuart called the company together and told us we had run out of all our grant funding, that we only had a few bucks left, and that there was no money to produce a show. Then he asked, 'Does anybody have any ideas?' So I raised my hand."

After three field trips to the ballpark with Mantegna, the actors came up with their story of a group of die-hard fans who, against all odds, stick to their love of those perpetual losers, the Cubs. (When John Belushi, then performing at The Second City, heard about the show, he told Gordon, "If the Cubs lose, I'll kill you.")

The play was put together for about three hundred dollars. Costumes came from thrift shops, and the setting consisted of the theater's concrete risers, stripped of the audience seats in order to form the bleachers where the action takes place.

Filled with wonderfully bizarre and realistic characters whom audiences love, the play is a proud, metaphorical affirmation of unwavering belief in the infinite possibilities for good, even in the midst of disappointment and disaster. Though firmly anchored in Chicago, it has a universal appeal. When a group of visiting Russian theater people saw the play in Chicago, they knew nothing about baseball. But they knew what the play was about. "It's about hope," they told Gordon.

Ian Patrick Williams trying to handle an ice-cream cup in *Bleacher Bums*

It's a great Chicago show, its city-specific strength made even more evident by the calamity of the 2002 cable-TV movie, a colorless affair that was filmed in Toronto and rendered impotent through its watered-down characters and their devotion to a fictional team.

For all its inventiveness, for all the attention it attracted, for all the acclaim it received during two trips to Europe, the Organic often lived on the brink of extinction. "We were supposed to get $150 a week," Norris says, "but I don't think we ever got that much."

The company had no real administrative staff, and, when it came to producing a show, they all pitched in to build the scenery, hang the coffee-can lights, and sew the costumes. "With Stuart," according to

Richard Fire confers with Susan Gordon-Clark in *E/R: Emergency Room,* 1982.
LISA EBRIGHT; SPECIAL COLLECTIONS AND PRESERVATION DIVISION, CHICAGO PUBLIC LIBRARY

Norris, "a contract was always a handshake. He believed that if a show had an audience, the audience would find it." And, sure enough, the audience found *Bleacher Bums* and ensured the company's survival.

Still, after a while, as the company grew, it needed something more than faith and a handshake to keep it going. There was a need for funding and long-term stability that would ease the fallow periods between the hits. When *Bleacher Bums* moved to New York in 1977, the company lost several members, and Gordon had to reassemble his troupe once again in Chicago. This was a wearing process, and the days of operating on a shoestring were over. In 1978, the cost for *Night Feast,* an adaptation of the ancient epic *Beowulf,* wittily billed as "the Millennium Production," was set at $7,812.

The seesaw fortunes of the company had to be put on an even keel. To this end, Gordon for the first time hired a business manager, assembled a board of directors ("to get grants," he says), started the company's first subscription season, and, with the aid of a substantial start-up donation from arts patron Hope Abelson and a $225,000 Challenge Grant from the National Endowment for the Arts, found a permanent Organic home in the Buckingham Theater, a former movie house at 3319 N. Clark Street. The theater was to be the building's main component, but there also was room for street-level retail shops on busy Clark Street, which meant a small but steady flow of rental income.

It was not an easy transition. The subscription drive fell far short of its goal of eighteen thousand members, and fund-raising for the move to the Buckingham stretched out in suspense over several years. Construction and renovation were accomplished without city permits; the theater's huge air-conditioning unit was lowered by crane onto the roof on a Sunday, when city inspectors did not work. When the theater opened in 1981, inspectors threatened to shut it down, but, Gordon says, he convinced them that this would be a bad public relations move for the city, and they allowed him to go ahead, providing he would eventually bring the building up to code.

The big plans and the large house required more money, of course, and, in the first few months, the productions of *The King Must Die,* an ambitious adaptation of Mary Renault's novel, and *Doctor Rat,* taken from the novel by William Kotzwinkle, did not pull in the audiences.

Things hardly looked better in January 1982, when Gordon and company, working from their improvisations on a scenario of emergency room stories by Dr. Ronald Berman, shaped a new show called *E/R: Emergency Room.* Again, it was something new and risky, a detailed look at hospital personnel and practices that, in its realism, preceded the latter-day hospital series on television.

The company had little ready cash for production values, but scenic designer Rick Paul, with a little leftover drywall from the building renovation, managed a realistic setting for the play, and the actors, who had spent time observing life in hospital emergency rooms, gave the story an urgent sense of authenticity.

Gordon, at his wife's hospital bedside for the birth of Jillian, the second of their three daughters, missed the show's opening, and he opened the papers the next day to find a discouraging mix of reviews. But his theory that a show would find an audience came through. Word-of-

Stuart Gordon with a prop body for his film *Re-Animator,* 1985
AUTHOR'S COLLECTION

mouth from doctors, nurses, and hospital employees who had been invited to see the show in previews kept it going until it clicked with a larger audience. The show became a hit, the longest-running show in the Organic's history. It ran for three and a half years, first at the Buckingham and then in a transfer to the Forum Theatre in suburban Summit.

For Gordon, it was "the catastrophe of success." It interrupted the flow of work at the Organic, and, according to Gordon, it led to his board of directors wanting "the next show to be another *E/R*. They would say things like, 'We think the next show should be a hit.' And I would answer, 'We hope all of our shows will be hits, but sometimes it doesn't work that way.' "

When Gordon proposed an expansion into filmmaking, starting with his adaptation of the horror story "Re-Animator," by H. P. Lovecraft, the board rejected the idea. That, in effect, was the end of Gordon at the Organic. His original, founding free spirit could not fit into the new, controlling demands of institutionalization.

Gordon left for the West Coast and made his *Re-Animator,* released in 1985 and a cult hit ever since. The Organic survived, but dwindled, through several succeeding managements, first under East Coast director Thomas Riccio and then under Richard Fire, a member of the company who took it over briefly and in 1989 brought back *Bleacher Bums,* directed by Mantegna, for a short bit of reflected glory. Later, the company merged with the small Touchstone Theatre of producer-director Ina Marlowe, who (to Gordon's chagrin) sold the Buckingham Building and moved the reduced Organic through a journey to several smaller houses.

After *Re-Animator,* Gordon went his special way in the movies, filming Lovecraft's "From Beyond" and "Dagon" with flamboyantly grisly special effects, shooting *The Pit and the Pendulum* in an abandoned castle in Italy, developing the *Honey, I Shrunk the Kids* movies and TV series for the Disney organization, and directing the inventive science fiction thrillers *Fortress* and the lovably oddball *Space Truckers,* with Dennis Hopper steering a futuristic rig through the galaxy.

Gordon was, and is, as Paul Sills liked to say, "a genius, a comic book genius, but still a genius." In his theater work, he was a maverick and a populist who loathed genteel drama and gloried in shaking up his audience in both their brains and their hearts. For many aspiring theater artists in the 1970s, including a young University of Illinois student named Robert Falls, "Stuart Gordon was it. I tried to see everything he did, because it was so exciting."

Gordon did indeed have a taste for the sensational in his desire to shed the conventional, shallow theater fare that bored him. He wanted to bring theater to an audience that distrusted theater as a stuffy, expensive, boring tribulation. But in addition to having a keen instinct for lively theatricality, he also was a sensitive and tasteful interpreter of classics like *Huckleberry Finn* and a masterful leader of ensemble work in such company-inspired pieces as *Bleacher Bums.* With the Organic, he gave Chicago theater some of its most inspired productions.

And, high among his credits, he took a big chance by acquiring, shaping, and superbly directing a new play by a virtually untried twenty-six-year-old writer who was to become one of the great stars of Chicago theater.

Striking poster for a striking new play: *Sexual Perversity in Chicago* at the Organic Theater, 1974

Chapter 15

"It's Good Writing"

SEXUAL PERVERSITY IN CHICAGO, staged by the Organic in June 1974, was David Mamet's first full-length work to be presented in his hometown of Chicago, but it was not his first excursion into the city's theater scene. That had come two years earlier in the tiny studio theater of the Body Politic with *The Duck Variations*, a short, sweet play, directed by Fritzi Sahlins (Bernard Sahlins's former wife), about a running conversation between two old men on a park bench. It lasted under an hour and was little more than a vignette, but clearly its author was a writer able to structure common language into rhythmic speech for the theater. He had a voice.

Mamet was twenty-four at the time. He had worked at Second City and Hull House Theater when he was a teenager. Going east, he attended Goddard College in Vermont, studied acting with Sanford Meisner in New York, and lectured as a visiting artist at Goddard. He returned to Chicago, he says, "because I was barely hanging on by my fingernails in the East. I didn't have any money, and I always believed that if you can't make it in Chicago, you can't make it anywhere."

He was in the Body Politic lobby for opening night of *Duck Variations,* standing off in a corner, toting a backpack ajumble with notebooks and pens. He had then, as he does now, a look of intensity.

When Mamet brought *Sexual Perversity* to Stuart Gordon, it was a series of Second City–style sketches. Gordon saw the spark there, and he worked with Mamet to shape the sketches into a single play that told of the rise and fall of a love affair amid the careless scene of Chicago singles bars. For the Organic actors, used to improvising, Mamet's complex, precise structure of dialogue caused some problems. At one point, Carolyn Gordon, portraying the show's heroine, questioned a patch of speech she was having trouble getting down right.

"David, what is this?" she asked.

Mamet took the cigar out of his mouth and replied, "It's good writing."

The play began with a bang, an obscenity-filled torrent of loud boasts by the hero's best friend (played by Warren Casey) about outrageous sexual escapades, and it closed on a wordless scene of almost unbearable grief that Gordon staged with infinite tenderness and sadness.

David Mamet

After the two young lovers of the play (Eric Loeb and Carolyn Purdy Gordon) have had a disastrous breakup, they retreat to separate sides of the stage. At center stage is a television set, which they watch from their different vantage points. It is late at night, and "The Star Spangled Banner" is playing, signaling the end of the broadcasting day. The anthem ends, and in its place comes the high whining sound of the station signal. Then just a blank screen and a blur of snow and a humming sound. Slowly, the young woman goes to the television set and turns it off. Suddenly silence, darkness, nothing.

In one startling image, the incredible loneliness and loss of a broken relationship are brilliantly summed up. Thinking about it now, years after first seeing and writing about it, I'm still staggered by its force.

The play also received several negative reviews, which concentrated on its use of foul language, but despite this, *Sexual Perversity* did well,

Carolyn Purdy Gordon and Roberta Custer in *Sexual Perversity in Chicago,* 1974
DONNA DUNLAP

and when the Organic went off to Europe on tour, Mamet took over the Leo Lerner for the rest of the summer and launched his own St. Nicholas Theater Company. He persuaded two of his former students at Goddard, William H. Macy and Steven Schachter, to move to Chicago. Joining them were musician-composer Alaric "Rokko" Jans, a buddy from Mamet's days at Francis Parker School in Chicago; Patricia Cox, an endlessly energetic and engaging manager of all the company's administrative odds and ends; and Linda Kimbrough, an actress newly arrived in Chicago who had heard that a writer named David Mamet (mispronounced, when she heard it, as "Mah-MEH") was looking for a woman to play a small part in a new play he had finished. She tried out for *Squirrels* and got the part of a feisty cleaning lady in an office inhabited by Schachter and Macy.

For about a year after *Squirrels,* the St. Nicholas folks led a scattershot, hectic life. Their headquarters was a small, crowded second-floor apartment on North Clark Street, above the Luv Boutique, and their life, Mamet recalled, consisted of "incredible love-hate crises every day."

In the winter of 1975, Mamet's staging of Eugene O'Neill's 1920 drama *Beyond the Horizon* in a North Side church was such a misfire that, as he accurately reported, "everybody hated it." In the summer of 1975, the whole St. Nicholas crew played a daily triple-header on weekends, starting off at midday by driving up to the Renaissance Faire in Gurnee, Illinois, where they performed both their version of *The Canterbury Tales* and a strolling mind-reading act. Finishing up that gig, they scooted back south to the Lake Street shopping mall of suburban Oak Park, where they inaugurated the village's annual summer festival of outdoor Shakespeare with Schachter's staging of *A Midsummer Night's Dream*, featuring Mamet in the double role of Theseus and Oberon, Kimbrough as Hippolyta and Titania, Macy as Puck, and Cox as one of the fairies. At midnight, they were in the Hull House Theater at 3212 N. Broadway, frolicking through Mamet's ebullient children's play *The Poet and the Rent,* which Macy directed.

"We all hung out together," Kimbrough says, "and part of the hanging out was to have breakfast with David. One morning at the restaurant he pulled out this script that he had not shown to anyone and asked me to read it. 'Now?' I said. 'Yes,' he said. So I read it, and when I finished, he asked me what I thought of it. 'It's an American classic,' I said. And he said, 'God bless you.'"

She had just read *American Buffalo.*

Mamet, gratified by Gordon's shepherding of *Sexual Perversity,* had already volunteered to become the Organic's playwright-in-residence; but after some hesitation Gordon, leery of sticking too much to the work of a single writer in a company known for its improvisational work, had said no to the idea. "Just think," Gordon says, "I turned down David Mamet. We could have produced *American Buffalo.*"

Instead, Mamet took his play to the city's oldest and largest resident theater, the Goodman.

⌒

Much had happened at the Goodman since it turned professional in 1969. John Reich, who had labored long and mightily to bring the theater into the ranks of the country's major resident theaters, was gone, forced into retirement in 1972 after two seasons in which the Goodman piled up a two-hundred-thousand-dollar deficit. After a brief term under Kenneth Myers, a Broadway professional who held the title of produc-

ing director, William Woodman, a man with credentials and connections in several not-for-profit
theaters and a teacher at New York's Juilliard
School of Drama, became artistic director in 1973.
A year later, he brought in a recent Juilliard alumnus, Gregory Mosher, to serve as his assistant.

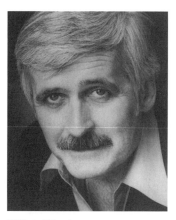

William Woodman

Woodman's tenure was marked by several
important events. His applauded American premiere production of Brian Friel's *The Freedom of
the City* transferred to New York in 1974, making
it the Goodman's first show to play Broadway—for
a disappointing thirteen performances. In 1977, the
theater broke away from the Art Institute, becoming a separate, independent entity with its own
board of directors heading the newly formed not-for-profit parent organization of the Chicago Theatre Group, Inc. In 1978 another link to the
past fell when the Goodman Theatre School, amid some hard feelings,
was dropped. (Fortunately, it was then picked up by DePaul University.)

As part of his agenda, Woodman established Stage 2, a program for
new and experimental works. Mosher took charge of the operation, and
it was to Mosher that Mamet brought *American Buffalo,* promising, in
a bit of vainglory, that he would put five thousand dollars in escrow as
a guarantee that the play would win the Pulitzer Prize. Mosher promptly
scheduled it for Stage 2.

Mosher, a New Yorker, had come as a stranger to Chicago and, at
first, knew little about the city. While working with Mamet in the playwright's $130-a-month room at the Hotel Lincoln, he often heard seals
barking, and wondered how they had migrated to Chicago, not realizing that the hotel was across the street from the seals' home in Lincoln Park Zoo. But Mosher learned quickly. He was bright, eager, and
ambitious, and he formed an alliance with the bright, eager, and ambitious playwright.

They took *American Buffalo* to Stage 2's space in the Ruth Page
Auditorium, 1016 N. Dearborn Street, and on a budget of a few hundred dollars, began rehearsals. Michael Merritt, the scenic designer,
found a stack of chairs in the building's basement and strung them from
the auditorium's ceiling in order to create the play's aura of a Chicago
junk shop.

The cast consisted of three men:

Bernard Erhard portrayed Teach, the tough-talking mastermind of the petty burglary that was the plot's fulcrum. He was a tough guy off-stage as well, and, when Mosher berated his work in one rehearsal, the director, for a moment, was sure that Erhard was going after him with murder in mind.

Macy, who had a youthful "Howdy Doody face" (as described by *Tribune* theater critic Linda Winer), was perfect for Bobby, the simple-minded dopehead gofer of the play's trio. By Mamet's account, the part was "never better acted" than by Macy, who became and remains the supreme interpreter of every pause, contraction, and quirk in Mamet dialogue.

J. J. Johnston was Donny Dubrow, the resale shop's owner and father figure for Bobby. Johnston was an old Mamet pal. (The printed version of the play is dedicated to him.) When he first heard that his friend had written a play called *American Buffalo,* he couldn't make sense of it. "I knew David was a real city boy," Johnston recalled. "I couldn't figure why he had written a cowboy show."

The production opened on October 23, 1975, to very mixed reviews. Claudia Cassidy called it "a foul-mouthed episode" and asked, "Does the Goodman's Stage 2 really believe that filthy language is a substitute for drama?" In the *Tribune,* Roger Dettmer dismissed the play as "almost two hours of bleep-rated dialogue." Glenna Syse in the *Sun-Times* called it "a dreary slice of life that needs tightening, focusing and clarifying," and, she added, "If they took out all the four-letter words, it would last ten minutes." For me, in the *Daily News, American Buffalo* was "a triumph for Chicago theater—and a treasure for Chicago audiences."

Mamet himself believes that *Buffalo,* in its tight, classic structure, is his best work for the theater. Certainly, it's a landmark play of great influence in American theater, one that stamped its author as a significant new writer of American drama. In its taut, poetic handling of common and sometimes vulgar speech, in its depiction of the outsiders and losers of society, in its tragedy of betrayal, particularly of child by parent, and in its mourning for the characters' failure to connect with and care for other human beings, it is Mamet's primary work. As for its famous foul language, its harsh, heightened street speech perfectly captured the futility and desperation of the lives it depicted.

William H. Macy and J. J. Johnston in the premiere production of *American Buffalo*, 1975

The play's origins came in part from the characters and conversations of the poker games Mamet used to play in a Waveland Avenue junk shop. When his fellow players learned that he had a part-time job teaching acting to inmates at Pontiac state prison, they dubbed him "Teacher," a nickname he picked up for one of the characters in the play. More immediately, he based one scene on a burst of temper that had erupted when he dropped in at the apartment Macy and Schachter shared. As he explains it, "I was hungry, so I went to the refrigerator. There was only a piece of cheese, and I started to eat it." Macy said, sarcastically, "Help yourself," and Mamet, enraged by the offhandedly condescending tone of the remark, went crazy. It was a wild scene, both men remember, and it became the basis for the flaming monologue in *American Buffalo* where the volatile Teach rails against a woman who has mocked him for snatching a piece of her breakfast toast.

The play's literary antecedents can be seen in the works of Samuel Beckett and Harold Pinter, whose scripts Mamet discovered as a high school kid on the shelves of the old Oak Street Bookshop and whose plays he saw in production while he worked at The Second City and at Bob Sickinger's Hull House Theater. But the voice is Mamet's alone, a voice from the Chicago streets that soars to beauty. It made his reputation.

It also sent new life into the Goodman. With tickets at $3.50 each, the play grossed $2,878.18 in its three-weekend run at the Page, making it Stage 2's biggest hit. More important, it moved the staid Goodman into the hip, up-and-coming movement of Chicago theater. After its engagement at the Page Center, the play, with Mike Nussbaum replacing Erhard as Teach, opened Mamet's own St. Nicholas Theater in its rented 226-seat permanent home in a former bakery at 2851 N. Halsted Street. Again the show was a hit, but the stress of the play and the frenzy of getting the new theater ready for its December 21 premiere took its toll. At the opening-night party, Macy, exhausted and relieved, broke down. He began to cry and could not stop. "It's okay," Mamet told him. "Don't worry. I know how you feel. It's okay."

For the next few years, Mamet turned out an amazing amount of work for Chicago. At St. Nicholas, there was the one-act *The Reunion* (1976), *The Water Engine* (1977), and *The Woods* (1977). At the Goodman, always with Mosher directing, there was *A Life in the Theatre* (1977), *Edmond* (1982), *The Disappearance of the Jews* (part of a three-play evening in 1983), a double bill of *The Shawl* and *The Spanish Pris-*

Gregory Mosher and David Mamet in rehearsal
COURTESY OF GOODMAN THEATRE

oner (1985), and the American premiere of *Glengarry Glen Ross* (1984), which, nine years after *American Buffalo,* at last earned Mamet his Pulitzer Prize for Drama. The play, about the machinations of a group of salesmen in a sleazy real estate office, was based in part on Mamet's experience as an employee of a similarly sleazy firm. At first uncertain about its quality, he sent it to Harold Pinter in London, asking him if he thought the play needed anything. Pinter read the play and replied, "It needs to be produced." A few months later, in September 1983, it was produced, in its world premiere in the Cottesloe Theatre of the National Theatre in London.

In that string of successes, Mamet produced one big bomb, the disastrous 1979 main stage production of *Lone Canoe, or The Explorer.* Based very loosely on a story by Jack London, it was a semimusical, with a score by Jans, about an alienated white man who discovers truth and beauty among the idealized noble savages of the far north. Its premiere on the Goodman main stage was attended by reviewers from around the country who were gathered in Chicago for the annual convention of the American Theatre Critics Association and were eager to see the latest work of Chicago's hot young playwright. After the first few minutes of droning speech and static staging, there were isolated snickers

A NIGHT TO REMEMBER

At the end of the first act of David Mamet's *Glengarry Glen Ross,* Ricky Roma, a super-slick real estate hustler, unfurls a long, seductive sales pitch aimed at a sucker customer he has just met over drinks in a Chinese restaurant. It's a brilliant piece of writing, knotted with the twists and turns and pauses and rushes of Mametian language, and it offers a splendid opportunity for the actor speaking the speech.

On the February 6, 1984, opening night of the play's American premiere production in the Goodman Theatre Studio, that monologue passed into legend—for the way in which it was not delivered.

Joe Mantegna, as Roma, had been sailing along nicely until he reached that speech, and then, without warning, he fell into every actor's nightmare. He dried up, blanking out on the lines and unable to remember a single sentence.

As Mantegna remembers it, "I could see that Billy Petersen [as the sucker], sitting across from me, was really upset, and I just wanted to hug him and tell him it wasn't his fault. The stage manager was throwing me lines in such a loud voice that everybody in the audience could hear them. But it didn't do any good. I didn't even have a clue."

Finally, Mantegna managed to end the act with a few mumbled words. As he walked off stage, Mamet, director Gregory Mosher, and Mamet's then wife, Lindsay Crouse, were there to hug him and tell him that they loved him. "I think they saved my life," he says.

"It was a wake-up call for me," Mantegna believes. "I learned you can't be vague in learning David's lines. They're poetry, and you have to know every moment."

Mantegna finished the rest of the performance without incident. In retrospect, he says, "It was my worst moment and yet it led to one of my best times. When we went to Broadway, I won the Tony Award for supporting actor."

Gene Siskel, then the movie critic of the *Chicago Tribune,* was in the audience for that memorable performance, and he told Mantegna, "It was the most exciting night I've ever spent in the theater."

Joe Mantegna in his big scene in *Glengarry Glen Ross,* 1984

BRIGITTE LACOMBE, COURTESY OF GOODMAN THEATRE

Mike Nussbaum and Joe Mantegna in *Glengarry Glen Ross*, 1984
COURTESY OF GOODMAN THEATRE

in the audience, and before long, the suppressed laughter had turned into waves of loud guffaws.

It was a night in theater hell, and the next morning's reviews were worse. Mamet went into a blue funk. Appearing on the local television interview program *Kup's Show*, he railed on against the reviewers until Elliot Norton, the venerable Boston theater critic, gently told him to calm down, take his lumps, and get on with his next play. Years later, Mamet said, "I think I was taking myself a little too seriously." The script has never been published.

For a writer who showed much bravado, Mamet could be surprisingly uncertain, Cox says. "David usually wanted me to be in a preview audience, because I have a very loud laugh, and I could sort of prime the pump for the rest of the audience. If the laugh didn't come, he would sit there chewing his knuckles and asking, 'Why isn't anybody laughing here?' And I thought, How can such a talented writer be so insecure about his work?"

Souvenir pin for David Mamet's
Lone Canoe, which premiered
calamitously at Goodman Theatre
in 1979

On the other hand, there was the time when a customer wrote to the Goodman, angrily protesting the rough language in *Glengarry Glen Ross*. Shown the letter, Mamet picked up a red pencil, wrote "Too Bad, You Big Baby" across the page, and returned the letter to its sender.

And Mamet could laugh at his missteps, too. Jennifer Boznos and Cindy Bandle, the Goodman's press representatives, were suitably awed when they first met him in their crowded little office. "He was wearing a hat, smoking a cigar, and he had on this wool shirt," Boznos says. "He looked like a lumberjack. He had this big hunting knife on his belt." Unfortunately, the knife caught on the back of Mamet's chair, and when he got up to leave, the chair swung around with him, knocking over everything in its path. "That's okay," he told the startled Boznos and Bandle. "You can come over any time and f—— up my place too."

Mamet's residency in Chicago, though relatively brief, was of great significance, not only for him but for the many young playwrights who followed him. His success showed that new work by a new writer in a new theater could find an audience—sometimes a very large audience. In the years ahead, works by Alan Gross (*Lunching, The Man in 605*), John Logan (*Never the Sinner, Hauptmann*), Scott McPherson (*Marvin's Room*), Rebecca Gilman (*Spinning into Butter, Boy Gets Girl*), Tracy Letts (*Killer Joe*), Paul Peditto (*Never Come Morning, 1001 Afternoons in Chicago*), and Bruce Norris (*The Infidel*) all premiered on small stages and played to eager, receptive audiences, many shows transferring to larger theaters and other cities.

For Mamet, although Chicago would always permeate his work, the time had come to move on. Other worlds, and the prospect of making movies, were calling him. Mosher realized the inevitability of the move one night when he was watching a performance of *American Buffalo* at St. Nicholas. "It was beautiful," he said, "because it was the last time it was simple, just about the work and not about anybody's career."

Mamet continued to work with Mosher after Mosher, pursuing his own career, left the Goodman in 1985 to become artistic director of Lincoln Center Theater in New York, their last major theater collaboration being the 1988 *Speed-the-Plow*. But increasingly, Mamet directed his

Joe Mantegna and Mike Nussbaum as the two actors, in their dressing room, in *A Life in the Theatre,* 1977

own plays, and, beginning with his script for *The Postman Always Rings Twice* in 1981, he worked much of the time as a writer-director in the movies. (It should be noted, however, that he often used a loose, loyal, unofficial family of production staff members and actors from the Chicago days in his films, including Jans, Merritt, Nussbaum, Macy, Mantegna, Johnston, and Jack Wallace.)

When *American Buffalo,* in a new Broadway production, won the New York Drama Critics Circle Award as best American play of the season in 1977, Mamet was already beginning to shift his work and home away from Chicago. But just before his February 16, 1977, Broadway debut with *Buffalo,* he had one unforgettable moment in Chicago: the February 7 premiere in the Page Auditorium of *A Life in the Theatre,* his loving two-character tribute to the egos and eccentricities of actors.

At the end of the play, while Nussbaum and Mantegna were taking their bows, a cry went up from the audience for "Author!" After a minute or so, Mamet came down from the balcony, where he had been watching his play, and took center stage, joyfully accepting the ovation he was receiving. It was a celebration for the hometown boy who had made good, and it was lovely.

Programs for the Body Politic, reinvented as a producing theater company in the late 1970s, and the Apollo Theater, a new 440-seat house opened in 1978 at 2540 N. Lincoln Avenue with the Chicago premiere production of Albert Innaurato's *Gemini*

PATRICIA MOORE COLLECTION, USED BY PERMISSION OF *PLAYBILL*

Chapter 16

"It Was the Arrogance of Youth"

With David Mamet as its star attraction, the theater scene in Chicago in the 1970s mushroomed from a small cluster on the North Side into a larger community that spread all over the area. People no longer spoke of just Lincoln Avenue theater; now, they called it off-Loop theater.

The growth was helped by several factors. The new building codes for "theatrical community centers" that Jim Shiflett and the Body Politic negotiated with Mayor Richard J. Daley in 1973 made it easier for small troupes to turn their odds-and-ends spaces into theaters. Founding and sustaining a theater was still a risky business for the young artists who planted their flags in the city, but slowly, as they brought in administrative staff, and as boards of directors were formed as an important support group, a sense of some stability and permanence took hold. For some creative spirits, such as Stuart Gordon, the addition of administration and board influence proved more a burden than a blessing. But for others, it meant moving on to a new level of growth.

Adding to this was the advent of the Title VI program of the federal government's CETA (Comprehensive Employment and Training Act), which granted funds for the unemployed. Administered by the city, these

Why are these nine artistic directors smiling? They've learned that their resident
theaters have received ten thousand dollars each from AT&T for the 1987–88 season,
because, as a press release boasts, they "do things they don't do on Broadway."
AUTHOR'S COLLECTION

funds provided up to $10,000 a year, including benefits, to previously
unemployed artists to work on specific projects. In 1977, for example,
CETA funds totaling $2.3 million went to fifty-four Chicago arts orga-
nizations, including twelve theater groups. Kuumba Workshop, an
African American troupe led by Val Gray Ward, received $89,700, and
the Free Street Theater was awarded the highest single amount, $123,790.

Sharon Phillips, business manager for the Body Politic in the 1970s,
believes that the CETA money marked an important psychological transition for theater people. "Before CETA," she says, "everything was cash
on the barrelhead. You made what money you could and split it up at
the end of the week. But the CETA checks changed that. They were real
salaries, $650 a month in two paychecks. They gave us a taste of a real
life. We began to think of ourselves as working at regular-paying jobs."

With permanence, and with the evolution of new theaters into continuing institutions, came organization. The artistic director was still at
the top of a group's personnel chart, but alongside his or her name there

now appeared that of another power person, the managing director, or executive director, the individual who was responsible for guiding the growing administrative staff that planned budgets, sought out subscribers, applied for grants, and drew up marketing strategies.

Gradually, in large and small ways, the public perception of Chicago's resident theaters also began to change. For the first time, foundations and corporations, such as AT&T, that regularly supported the city's giant established cultural institutions gave grants to emerging midsize off-Loop theaters, too. Theater booster groups, such as the Sarah Siddons Society, founded in 1952 to honor female stars of the big downtown touring shows, turned their attention to local students and actors as well.

The theater community at large, which had started with a few small troupes, was growing so fast that it needed a central agency to tend to matters of mutual concern. In 1979, the League of Chicago Theatres, an advocacy and service organization that had grown out of the earlier Chicago Alliance for the Performing Arts (CAPA), was formed. It embraced commercial and not-for-profit houses, Loop and off-Loop theaters. It established HotTix booths to sell discount, day-of-performance tickets. It set up annual "commUnity" meetings designed to address issues common to all its members. It held special events to promote theatergoing. It published a playbill for theaters that signed up and paid for the service. It developed advertising and marketing drives to promote theatergoing. It acted as a liaison between member theaters and the city in dealing with licensing and building code problems.

The move from seat-of-your-pants procedures to a more stabilized agenda was a sign of progress, but the youthful spark that had set the resident theater movement in motion was still there, even stronger now that the number of troupes was multiplying. The wild old days, when an actor who had a handgun in his car gallantly offered Marcelle McVay, Victory Gardens' managing director, a safe ride to the bank, were gone. But there was still a pioneering drive at the most basic level.

For example, when University of Illinois graduates Stuart Oken and Jason Brett were just out of school in 1976, they opened their independent production of Michael Weller's youth drama *Moonchildren*—directed, in his Chicago debut, by their U. of I. chum Robert Falls—at the St. Nicholas Theater. Two years later, with charm, sincerity, and chutzpah, and after making more than a hundred sales pitches to potential investors, the duo, still in their twenties, had put together a financial partnership that enabled them to build the Apollo Theater Center, a new from-the-ground-up commercial house at 2540 N. Lincoln Avenue.

When Falls later settled in Chicago, he auditioned for an acting job in a 1977 open-air staging of Shakespeare's *The Tempest* at Court Theatre at the University of Chicago. He didn't get the job, but after his audition, Nicholas Rudall, Court's artistic director, who had seen Falls's directing work, came up to him and said, "Sorry we can't use you as an actor, but would you like to direct the play?" Falls said yes, staged the production in a kind of Caribbean voodoo atmosphere, and, Rudall says, "He did a very good job on it." For Falls, it was proof that in Chicago "anything could happen—it was very loose in those days."

When Byron Shaffer Jr., artistic director of the Dinglefest Theatre, decided in 1977 that it was time to build a permanent performance space to house his group and others on the North Side, he sent the members

JOHN REEGER AND PAULA SCROFANO, ACTORS: "WE WERE ABLE TO PROVE OURSELVES HERE"

JOHN: We met when we were theater students at Northwestern University, got married, graduated in 1972, and found work almost right away—did some regional work in

John Reeger and Paula Scrofano
FREDRIC STEIN

Wisconsin, went on a USO tour to Asia, and came back to Chicago in 1974. We got our Equity cards then, as understudies in a revue at the old Happy Medium Theater on Rush Street. Ever since, we've only worked in theater, nothing else.

PAULA: We're not big risk takers. I've never even been to Los Angeles or New York. We stayed to work and live in Chicago, because we wanted to settle down and have a family. "I think we should have a home," I told John, and that's what we did. We have two children: Adam, who's a high school math teacher, and Alison, who's a theater major in college. We were careful, never frivolous with our money. And we've been lucky; we've worked everywhere, all over the city.

JOHN: We've never had agents, but as long as we've been here, we've been able to cross over, back and forth between musicals and straight dramas. That helps. Still, even with both of us working most of the time, you hit a financial ceiling here, seven hundred to a thousand dollars a week at the very most. And this is a youth-oriented town; it's hard to be long in the tooth.

PAULA: But we have our home; we've raised our family; we've kept working. We were able to prove ourselves here. And I don't believe we've lost our zest.

of his company out on their bicycles to scout the territory. They found a place, an old warehouse at 3212 W. Belmont Avenue, named it the Theatre Building, and gutted it to hold three small theaters. Shaffer acted as developer and designer for the project, right down to fashioning the kitchen colander lighting shades hanging in the building's central lobby.

Energy, enterprise, and enthusiasm were high. Shaffer and his colleagues had faith in the renaissance. "It was the arrogance of youth," says Roche Schulfer who, shortly after graduating from Northwestern University, joined the Goodman Theatre staff as a box-office assistant in 1973. "We were going to change the world on a budget of a buck and a quarter." As the Goodman's Gregory Mosher said, "Everything seemed possible. The forces were all there. We believed the only limitations were the bounds we would set for ourselves."

At least part of this determination, Mosher believed, came from the antiwar movement that so many of these new theater artists had been a part of in their immediate past. "After the Vietnam War ended," Mosher said, "many people still had this crusading spirit. It needed an outlet, and what better place than the theater for that idealism and adventure?"

Whatever the causes, the 1970s saw a boom in the development of off-Loop theaters. The middle and last half of the decade saw the founding of several key resident groups: Victory Gardens, Wisdom Bridge, and Northlight in 1974, Steppenwolf and St. Nicholas (in its permanent home at 2851 N. Halsted Street) in 1975, and Remains in 1979.

Some twenty years later, the off-Loop landscape these youthful theaters shaped had radically changed. By the end of the twentieth century, hard times, artistic and financial, had closed down some of them, while others had managed, through a combination of luck and wisdom, to squeak by, survive, and even prosper.

The life span of a resident theater is usually short. The Group Theatre in New York, for example, the most celebrated ensemble of the 1930s, home to directors Harold Clurman, Lee Strasberg, and Elia Kazan and actors John Garfield and Luther Adler, lasted barely a decade. And in Chicago in the last quarter of the twentieth century, variations in the economic climate, tensions caused by ensemble needs versus personal careers, and shifts in leadership helped turn the renaissance of the 1970s into the long, hard haul thereafter. As Lou Contey, a director who started in Chicago theater in the 1980s, has wisely said, "Off-Loop is not for the faint of heart."

Some of the enterprising midsize theaters that emerged in Chicago in the 1970s did not survive, but others endured and even pospered, leaving behind them an archive of programs (and memories) recalling their work.

Chapter 17

"The Field Is Littered with Bodies"

AMONG THE SMALL, BUSTLING not-for-profit troupes that blossomed in the seventies, none had more glamour, more prestige, or more support than St. Nicholas. Like most small theaters, it started poor. But after the theater was up and running, its founders were able to organize and survive. David Mamet's association with the company initially lent it a certain cachet, of course, but even after he withdrew from his leadership role in 1976, protesting the selection of Julian Barry's florid satire *Sitcom* as a production choice, the St. Nick crew for a while set the pace and raised the bar for ambitious, aspiring off-Loop companies.

From its start, St. Nicholas appeared to be a model of organization. It set up a subscription season, launched a late-night series of short and experimental works, established an outreach program, began an acting school (with John Mahoney as one of its students), developed a touring children's theater (in which Bob Falls portrayed a roller-skating panda in Mamet's *The Revenge of the Space Pandas, or Binky Rudich and the Two Speed Clock*), and, with the hiring of the young, hard-driving managing director Peter Schneider, kept up a vigorous fund-raising effort in the private and public sectors.

Program for Lanford Wilson's
The 5th of July, 1978

PATRICIA MOORE COLLECTION

The subscription schedules held a varied lineup: an American classic (*A View from the Bridge, You Can't Take It with You*), a recent off-Broadway success (*Uncommon Women and Others, The Collected Works of Billy the Kid*), a new Mamet play (*The Water Engine, The Woods*), and an occasional premiere by a Chicago author (Kathleen Lombardo's *Joplin*). Steven Schachter, as artistic director, also matched *The 5th of July,* Lanford Wilson's searing drama of post–Vietnam War angst among a group of disoriented youths, with a cast drawn from the still-young Steppenwolf Theatre. It was a perfect fit, giving St. Nicholas one of its finest hours.

WHAT THEY DID FOR PAY

Rehearsing and performing at night for little or no pay, most young theater people rely on day jobs to provide enough money to keep them going. Waiting tables, with its flexible hours, is a reliable source of income, but there are many other ways of earning subsistence wages. Herewith a list of some eminent theater professionals and the day jobs they took in their early years in Chicago:

Robert Falls, director: Earth Shoes salesman in a store on Clark Street, and, he insists, "I was pretty good at it."

John Malkovich, actor-director: Clerk in the old Chandler's bookshop in downtown Evanston, where, according to former customers, he was "very helpful and courteous."

Laurie Metcalf, actress: Typist doing temporary secretarial jobs (being an excellent typist, she never lacked work).

Dennis Franz, actor: Security guard at the Pick-Congress Hotel on South Michigan Avenue.

Mike Nichols, director: Staff announcer, at seventy-five dollars a week, at WFMT, a classical radio station, where the script he wrote for announcer auditions is still in use.

Frank Galati, director: Rejected for a sales job at Kroch's and Brentano's downtown bookstore (because, with a Ph.D. from Northwestern University, he was "overqualified"), he existed on unemployment checks and a job in the stock room of Swallow Press, a local book publisher.

Philip R. Smith, Doug Hara, David Kersnar, and Raymond Fox, ensemble members of Lookingglass Theatre Company: Picture framers, which explains why, no matter where their troupe played during its early peregrinations, the lobby always had a display of beautifully framed production photos.

But there were problems with the theater's ambitious expansion plans. Already carrying a deficit, St. Nicholas in 1979 opened an expensive original musical, *The Enchanted Cottage*, in the nine-hundred-seat Athenaeum Theatre, 2936 N. Southport Avenue, for what was hoped would be a profitable Christmas holiday run. It didn't work. The show, received with mixed reviews and indifferent audiences, closed with a heavy loss. The theater's board, so optimistic a few months before, canceled plans to buy and renovate the Ivanhoe Theatre as its new home. St. Nicholas was unraveling.

Schachter and Macy, heading out for their careers, had left the theater, and Schneider resigned in 1980. New leadership took over. Cynthia Sherman, the theater's former literary manager, as artistic director and newcomer William Conner as managing director tried to turn the

---

David Mamet, playwright: Cabdriver, poker player, and, for a brief time, waiter in a gay bar.

Jeff Perry, actor: Waiter and cook at Egg Rolls, Etc., a fast-food restaurant in suburban Northbrook.

John Mahoney, actor: Associate editor of the *Quality Review Bulletin of the Joint Commission on Accreditation of Hospitals.*

Amy Morton, actress-director: In "either the most degrading or most hilarious point of my career," she and actress-roommate Glenne Headly posed as mermaids in a large pond set up in the lobby of the Hyatt Regency Hotel for the lavish food-and-drink premiere party of the 1980 movie musical bomb *Can't Stop the Music.* "Some of the guests," she remembers, "threw cocktail shrimps at us."

Joe Mantegna, actor-director: Shoe salesman at the Brass Boot on Oak Street, and also a freelance photographer.

William L. Petersen: Bartender in north suburban Wilmette; he also trimmed trees and delivered rugs for a North Side carpet store.

John C. Reilly, actor: Waiter who waited on so many tables at weddings and bar mitzvahs that "I learned the complete lyrics to 'Hava Nagila.'" According to a fellow catering service employee, "We never assigned John to the head table, because he was not very good at it."

Gary Sinise, actor-director: Groundskeeper at the Ravinia music festival in suburban Highland Park and loading-dock worker at Neiman Marcus department store in the Northbrook Court shopping center.

theater around. But in 1981, in a final blow, the Internal Revenue Service demanded tax money that the theater had failed to pay. In debt and unable to make the payment, the board of directors in late 1981 voted to close St. Nicholas.

Macy, as a much applauded, always working actor, and Schachter, as a director in theater and on film, went on to do good work elsewhere, reuniting in their Emmy Award–winning cable TV movie of 2002, *Door to Door*. Schneider, who had left Chicago under a cloud because of his handling of the theater's tax problems, emerged for a few years in the nineties as a top-line Hollywood executive, supervising theater projects within the Disney organization.

But St. Nicholas was over. In answer to a query about the theater's status, Dean Corrin, then the company's literary manager, had to reply, "Financial problems have forced the theater to suspend operations."

Survival, as the once-golden St. Nicholas proved, was not easy. There was more to it than talent and imaginative programming. It required a

St. Nicholas founders (from left) David Mamet, Steven Schachter, Patricia Cox, and William H. Macy, 1975

COURTESY OF *CHICAGO TRIBUNE* NEWS ARCHIVE

Frank Galati and James O'Reilly in Ronald Harwood's *The Dresser* at the Body Politic, 1983
JENNIFER GIRARD

delicate balance of many other factors—economic planning, personal chemistry, advantageous location, and a streak of luck—in order to continue its work, and in the process it could go through several crises and configurations.

This was certainly the case with the Body Politic, which under Jim Shiflett had started out as a community arts center, housing the Story and Organic theaters as part of its mission. Such self-produced shows as director Joseph Slowik's sensitive staging of Oliver Hailey's *Who's Happy Now?* and the charming one-man *Banjo Dancing* of Stephen Wade, directed by Sharon Phillips, had sustained hit runs, but it wasn't until 1981, when James O'Reilly officially took charge of the theater, that it became a resident theater for a distinctive ensemble-driven troupe.

O'Reilly, a hard-drinking, chain-smoking, curmudgeonly rapscallion, had been involved with Chicago theater since the 1960s, giving a powerful performance in the title role of *King Lear* at Court Theatre in the days when it was a summer outdoor theater operation at the University of Chicago. He was an erratic performer, and as he grew older, he would sometimes nod off during a quiet stretch of a play. Phillips remembers that in Brian Friel's *Translations,* when O'Reilly was draped over with

Dennis Zacek, artistic director of Victory Gardens (in a traditional pointing pose), and Marcelle McVay, Victory Garden's managing director (to his right), are bracketed by artistic director James O'Reilly (far left) and managing director Sharon Phillips (seated at far right) of the Body Politic as they go over plans with their board presidents to share the building at 2257 N. Lincoln Avenue in 1981.

a sheet after his death scene in the final act, the audience could see the rise and fall of the sheet over his face as he went into a deep sleep. But, Phillips says, "At his best, Jim was so smart, so sharp, such a good actor. There was nobody like him."

With his artistic partner Pauline Brailsford, O'Reilly for a few years turned a mixed group of veterans such as Edgar Meyer and Joan Spatafora and youngsters such as Tom Amandes, James McCance, and Lucy Childs into a cohesive troupe of skilled players. Specializing in contemporary Irish and English plays, they were able to transform the Englishness of Ronald Harwood's *The Dresser* and Alan Ayckbourn's comedy *Taking Steps* into the stuff of Chicago hits, no mean feat. And when O'Reilly and company hit home in the modern Irish works of Brian Friel, they were transcendent.

Watching Friel's masterpiece *Translations* at the Body Politic in 1982, I was thrilled by the realization that, in the unlikely event a touring production of the play would be sent out to Chicago, it could not possibly have topped the performance I was seeing in the 225-seat upstairs theater at 2257 N. Lincoln Avenue.

Artistically solid but perpetually dogged by debt, the Body Politic went from one financial crunch to another. Some relief came when it sold 53 percent of its building to Victory Gardens Theater after the Gardens moved there from its Clark Street address in 1981. But there were times when Phillips and other staff members gave back their salaries in order to keep the place open. ("Chicago theater," Phillips believes, "has been built on a lot of sacrifice.")

O'Reilly, in declining health, retired from his post in 1986, returning to play a final *King Lear* in 1989. A year later, at home after taking part in a theater panel in which he had extolled the glory of great language in the theater, he was dead, the victim of a heart attack. Phillips left the Body Politic in 1988; Brailsford, who took over as artistic director, resigned in 1990. For a while, director Terry McCabe, whose defunct Stormfield Theatre once had been an effective entry post for young Chicago playwrights, tried to resuscitate the Body Politic, but, struggling with what he believed was an ineffective board, he eventually withdrew, and the theater limped its way to dissolution in 1996. All that's left is a memorial wall of photos and posters in its old second-floor quarters that recalls the theater's best days.

Victory Gardens Theater, which took over the entire building on Lincoln Avenue when the Body Politic folded, had a similarly rocky history, but with a happier ending. It had started out as a collective effort by eight Chicago theater artists: Warren Casey, Cordis Fejer, Stuart Gordon, Roberta Maguire, Mac McGinniss, Cecil O'Neal, June Pyskacek, and David Rasche. Its original home was the Northside Auditorium at 3730 N. Clark Street, and for the first few years, its founders acted as a kind of group artistic director. This was not a manageable management method, however, and in 1977, Dennis Zacek, a native of Chicago's Southwest Side, who had taught theater at Loyola University and worked well as both actor and director at the Gardens, was appointed artistic director. His wife, Marcelle McVay, served as managing director. The hand-in-glove, mom-and-pop teamwork of the low-key Zacek

The cast of playwright James Sherman's *The God of Isaac*: Bernie Landis, Sherman, Roslyn Alexander at bottom; Petrea Burchard, Dennis Cockrum, and Barbara Gaines at top
COURTESY OF VICTORY GARDENS THEATER

and the ebullient McVay kept the theater on course through its many ups and downs.

In its early years, Victory Gardens presented its share of classic plays. Zacek, for starters, had staged an excellent 1976 production of Harold Pinter's *The Caretaker,* with William J. Norris as the cantankerous title character, Michael Saad as a sadistic leather boy, and Frank Galati, whey-faced and lead-footed, in a stunning portrayal of his brain-damaged brother.

But the theater's mission always leaned toward new work. Its first show was an original melodrama, *The Velvet Rose,* by Stacy Myatt. Among its early hits were more originals—*The Magnolia Club* (1975), a country-western musical; *Three Women* (1975), a trio of interweaving monologues derived from improvisatory sessions that was coproduced with Goodman Theatre; and *All I Want* (1976), the story of the trials of a Chicago blue-collar family by the young playwright Bruce Hickey.

Zacek, a common-sense visionary, brought several innovations to the mostly white mainstream of off-Loop theater on the North Side. He staged the African American plays of Steve Carter, using local actors and directors. With director Ramiro Carillo, he mounted a Latino Chicago production, also with all Chicago talent. And, at an early stage, he made a commitment to new plays, with an emphasis on works by Chicago playwrights.

Local writers William J. Norris, David Blomquist, Jackie Taylor, Nicholas Patricca, Alan Gross, Alan Bates, Stuart Flack, Denise DeClue, Tom Sharkey, Jeff Berkson, and John Karraker all had premieres at Victory Gardens. And in 1996, Zacek made his commitment official by establishing the Playwrights Ensemble, a group of twelve members who could call the theater their home.

Jeffrey Sweet, one of the ensemble members, had his one-act play *Porch* produced at the Gardens in 1980 through a typical bit of Chicago community networking. Joyce Sloane, a producer at Second City and a VG board member, referred Sweet to Zacek, who read the play and scheduled it for the theater's small second-stage space in a production directed by Tom Mula. Nobody expected too much of it. Sonja Lanzener, the actress portraying the unhappy heroine who comes back to her small-town home to visit her ailing father, told Zacek, "It might make a good radio play." But it also made a good theater play, launching Sweet on a long, prolific, fruitful relationship with the Gardens. "The Ensemble," Sweet says, "sends a signal that we writers aren't transients."

The continuing effort to bring new work to the audience produced some failures, some long runs, some notable guest-artist appearances (Esther Rolle, Julie Harris, Fritz Weaver, William L. Petersen, and the duet of Shelley Berman and Byrne Piven in Sweet's *The Value of Names*), and one runaway success, the 1989 comedy *Beau Jest,* by Second City alumnus and future Playwrights Ensemble member James Sherman. The story of an out-of-work actor hired by a young woman to pose as her Jewish fiancé for the benefit of her parents was the biggest of Sherman's many hits at the Gardens, and it repeated its success in other

Byrne Piven, a Chicago actor since the 1950s, in his 1978–79 portrayal of *The Man in 605,* by Alan Gross
AUTHOR'S COLLECTION

Shelley Berman as the embittered blacklisted actor and Jill Holden as his daughter in the Victory Gardens production of Jeffrey Sweet's *The Value of Names*, 1985
COURTESY OF VICTORY GARDENS THEATER

Roslyn Alexander, Bernie Landis, Linnea Todd, and Peter Curren in a romantic crisis in James Sherman's comedy hit *Beau Jest,* 1989
COURTESY OF VICTORY GARDENS THEATER

Tony time for Victory Gardens in 2001: executive director Marcelle McVay, artistic
director Dennis Zacek, associate artistic director Sandy Shinner
COURTESY OF VICTORY GARDENS THEATER

stagings in New York and elsewhere. It wasn't avant-garde, but it was
solid entertainment in its home truths and folksy wisdom, and it worked
like a charm on its audiences.

This mission of producing new work was good for the soul, and in
2001 it paid off in a more material manner when Zacek, McVay, and
associate artistic director Sandy Shinner accepted the annual regional
theater prize given by the Tony Awards. Eleven of the twelve ensemble
members were there in New York to celebrate with them.

It was sometimes said of Zacek that he was more dogged than
dynamic, that he was too conservative. It was one of the reasons members of his board, chafing at his tough-minded "bigger is not necessarily
better" reservations about their overly ambitious expansion plans, tried
to demote him to a lesser role in a fortunately aborted coup in 2002. But
if he was plodding, Zacek patiently plodded on all through the seventies,
eighties, and nineties and rode into the twenty-first century with a fresh
burst of speed, augmenting Victory Gardens' operations with a $15 mil-
lion campaign to buy and renovate the old Biograph movie theater,
2433 N. Lincoln Avenue, as a home for a new 299-seat main stage and a
128-seat studio theater.

The perils of too much expansionism, and of a changing leadership, are strikingly illustrated in the history of Wisdom Bridge Theatre, which was very much on the fast track in the seventies and eighties, but moved to a dead end in the nineties.

Wisdom Bridge was founded by David Beaird, a lanky kid from Louisiana who was nineteen when director George Keathley picked him to play the leading role in the Pulitzer Prize–winning *Look Homeward, Angel* at the Ravinia Festival's Murray Theatre in 1971. An actor who wanted to be a writer and director, Beaird in 1974 found a spot for his theater at 1559 W. Howard Street. It was a former karate school, on the second floor "up a precipitous flight of steps" (as Claudia Cassidy neatly put it), in a scruffy area of Chicago's Rogers Park neighborhood at the city's northern border with Evanston. (The theater's slightly mystic name came from a painting the impressionable Beaird had seen in the Art Institute of Chicago.)

Beaird, by then a graduate of the Goodman School, ran the theater as a kind of one-man operation for two years but had to leave because of ill health. That looked like the end for Wisdom Bridge, but in April 1977, Robert Falls, another youngster in his twenties who had made his

Robert Falls

mark with his direction of *Moonchildren* at St. Nicholas in 1976, scrounged up fifty dollars and put on a powerful production of John Steinbeck's *Of Mice and Men* that became a solid off-Loop hit. In the autumn, Falls took over as artistic director, leading the theater for nine productive years until he left to become artistic director of Goodman Theatre.

From the beginning, when the Bridge was a non-Equity (nonunion) house with a decrepit backstage area, Falls showed a daring, dashing flair for theater. He zestfully staged *The Idiots Karamazov,* a wildly erratic, zany farce/satire by Christopher Durang and Albert Innaurato, which the theater trumpeted as a story of "the rise and Falls of Western literature." It had a cast of sixteen actors (plus "the entire Russian Army") that included Larry McCauley, a farceur

Sonja Lanzener in Bertolt Brecht's *Mother Courage* at Wisdom Bridge Theatre, 1981
JENNIFER GIRARD

supreme, as the translator Constance Garnett, zipping on and off the stage in a wheelchair. Among its songs was "Moscow," a verse of which went "We gotta go to Moscow, San Francisco or L.A. We'll sell the cherry orchard, and throw the pits away."

As the theater went Equity, Falls directed *Bagtime,* a new musical based on the adventures of a Chicago supermarket bag boy—played by B. J. Jones—from a series of newspaper stories originally written by columnists Bob Greene and Paul Galloway in the *Sun-Times*. He staged Marsha Norman's harrowing Pulitzer Prize–winning drama *Getting Out,* with brilliant portrayals by Steppenwolf ensemble members Laurie Metcalf and Gary Sinise. He formed an alliance with another young director, Michael Maggio, who delivered sparkling versions of Tom Stoppard's contemporary *Travesties* and Molière's classic *Tartuffe*. He brought in director Shozo Sato from the University of Illinois to stage a series of strikingly designed Kabuki-stylized renditions of *Medea* and *Macbeth*. He vibrantly put Bertolt Brecht's epic *Mother Courage* on the theater's

A STAR AND AN ACTOR

William L. Petersen, born and raised in Evanston, came to acting only because, as a college jock, he wanted to raise his grade point average with a few easy courses in theater. His first public performance was in Neil Simon's comedy *The Star-Spangled Girl.* "I went onstage, said my lines, got my laughs, and that was it," Petersen says. "I was hooked."

After school and a brief fling in politics in Idaho, he chose not to join the family furniture business in Chicago, spent a year in Spain, married (later divorced), became a father, returned to the States, and took on odd jobs in the West. Unhappy there, and hearing of theater work in Chicago, he packed up and came back home in 1976. He took acting courses with Dennis Zacek at Victory Gardens, played Francis of Assisi in *Canticle of the Sun* and the title role in *Dillinger,* both by William J. Norris, and appeared as Sebastian in *Twelfth Night* under Zacek's direction, at the summer Illinois Shakespeare Festival of Illinois State University in Bloomington.

In Chicago, he became friends with other young actors his age, Gary Cole and Tom Irwin among them, and lived in the odd basement, in a girlfriend's apartment, and in a house near Wrigley Field. For a brief period, he lived in a corner of the MoMing dance center on the North Side. "I decided to give it a shot at being an actor in Chicago," he says, "even if that meant living on a park bench."

He also listened well to a bit of friendly counsel given to him by the sage actor-director Mike Nussbaum. "If you want to be an actor and you want to have a career," Nussbaum said, "I advise you to stay in Chicago and build your foundation. Chicago is a place for an actor to grow. You can fail here. You can make mistakes and not be sent away."

Petersen stuck to it and hit his stride as a leading man and Chicago actor in the 1980s with Remains Theatre, a troupe he cofounded in 1979. He played Hoss, the aging rock star, to Cole's Crow, the upstart rocker, in Sam Shepard's *The Tooth of Crime* (1982), and Ahab in the audacious adaptation of *Moby Dick* (1982). But his big breakthrough came in 1983 with his portrayal of the condemned killer Jack Abbott in director Robert Falls's production of *In the Belly of the Beast* at Wisdom Bridge Theatre. "It was a transforming experience for me," Petersen says. On the opening preview night of a production that was to run off and on in various venues in Chicago and abroad for the next couple years, he told himself, "Well, if you want to be an actor, tonight's the night, pal. Go ahead and do it."

It was an astounding performance, so fierce that Petersen suffered four minor concussions in the course of the engagement as he banged his head in fury against the wall of Abbott's cell. It's a portrayal that hit me especially hard. Driving back to the office to file my review after the play's opening night, I had to pull my car over to the side of the road and rest there for a few minutes in order to collect myself.

Beast led to a run at the Stratford Festival of Canada in Tennessee Williams's *A Streetcar Named Desire,* and from there Petersen went into the movies, starring in director William Friedkin's *To Live and Die in L.A.* (1985), Michael Mann's *Manhunter* (1986), and Joel Schumacher's *Cousins* (1989).

William L. Petersen in *In the Belly of the Beast* at Wisdom Bridge Theatre, 1983
JENNIFER GIRARD

Up and down in his film work in the nineties, Petersen returned to Chicago several times to work on the stage: in the Chicago premiere of Mamet's *Speed-the-Plow* at Wisdom Bridge (1989), in the premiere of Jeffrey Sweet's *Flyovers* at Victory Gardens (1998), and in Falls's galvanizing revival of Williams's *The Night of the Iguana* at Goodman Theatre (1994). In 2000, he starred in and coproduced *CSI: Crime Scene Investigation,* a hit CBS series that made him a genuine, bankable TV star.

Wherever his career led him, Petersen remained a Chicago actor at heart. A natural star, he was also a skilled actor who had paid his dues and learned his craft. On location for *To Live and Die in L.A.* in 1984, he met a young man who said that he, too, was a Chicago actor. Petersen asked him where he had worked in the city, and the answer was that, though the man had never really acted in Chicago, he had been there and he wanted to be an actor. Outraged, Petersen yelled, "You can't just say you're a Chicago actor. It's not that easy. You have to earn the right to call yourself a Chicago actor. It's something to be proud of."

Aidan Quinn as *Hamlet,* 1985
JENNIFER GIRARD

small stage, and he imaginatively set *Hamlet,* with Aidan Quinn in the title role, in a technocratic, media-saturated kingdom of lies and deceit.

In 1985, Falls began a long, happily volcanic association with actor Brian Dennehy by presenting the well-known film and television actor in a production of Ron Hutchinson's modern Irish drama *Rat in the Skull.* And in 1983, he directed a memorable staging of *In the Belly of the Beast,* adapted from the prison memoir of Jack Abbott, with William L. Petersen unforgettably portraying the dark, tormented convicted killer.

From 1979 on, Falls worked in close partnership with Jeffrey Ortmann, a fellow U. of I. alumnus who became Wisdom Bridge's executive director. Undaunted by the theater's unfavorable location, Ortmann determinedly pitched for grants, resolutely renovated the theater auditorium, expanding it from 150 to 225 seats, and conscientiously put together an outreach program for nearby schools and community groups. He was a strong believer in the possibilities of off-Loop theater moving into the Loop, and with ten thousand subscribers and a $1.5 million annual budget, his optimism was unbounded. At a meeting in the downtown Civic Theatre in early 1986 to herald the upcoming staging there of a short season of two Wisdom Bridge shows, Falls's *Hamlet* and Sato's *Kabuki Faust,* he got a bit of wise advice from Ardis Krainik, then general director of Lyric Opera of Chicago, which occupied the larger, next-door, thoroughly unionized Civic Opera House. "This is all very well," Krainik said, "but bear in mind that when you come downtown, you're playing with the big boys."

It turned out to be a fateful warning. The two-play season lost a lot of money, and that, combined with Falls's departure to become Goodman's new artistic director, left Wisdom Bridge in suspension. The selection of Richard E. T. White, a liberal director from Seattle, as Falls's successor, did not help. The theater, in need of a hit, had none, and White and Ortmann soon were on a collision course over management and direction. After two years, White was out, and Ortmann stayed on as producing director, also taking on many of the responsibilities of artistic direction.

"Jeffrey was a very good executive director," says Sharon Phillips, who was then in charge of the Bridge's outreach program, "but he did not have the necessary talents for an artistic director." Still, Ortmann moved ahead. He directed plays; he acted and sang in them; he arranged for coproductions with other troupes. With Remains Theatre, Wisdom Bridge in 1989 produced the Chicago premiere of David Mamet's *Speed-the-Plow,* with Petersen and Gary Cole starring in a staging by Hollywood director Joel Schumacher. When the Howard Street neighborhood further deteriorated, Ortmann left the building, wandered from rented space to rented space, and, hoping to find a permanent home, sought (unsuccessfully) to move the theater into the new North Shore Center for the Performing Arts in suburban Skokie. Meanwhile, he rented the Ivanhoe Theatre for the 1994–95 season. Nothing worked. Finally, in late 1995, the theater sank into nonexistence with an adaptation of *Little Women* in the auditorium of the downtown Harold Washington Library Center that was put together with students from Roosevelt University and was barely up to acting school standards. Wisdom Bridge, having lost its winning leadership team and its continuity, was out of business.

On the other hand, there was Northlight Theatre, which went through several perilous times and changes in leadership and venues and yet managed to endure.

City on the Make, original musical by Jeff Berkson, Denise DeClue, and John Karraker, based
on the writings of Nelson Algren, directed by Michael Maggio, at Northlight Theatre, 1984
LISA EBRIGHT, SPECIAL COLLECTIONS AND PRESERVATION DIVISION, CHICAGO PUBLIC LIBRARY

Originally called the Evanston Theatre Company, then North Light
Repertory in 1978, and finally Northlight Theatre in 1984, it opened in

1974 in the auditorium of the decommissioned
Kingsley Elementary School at 2300 Green Bay
Road in Evanston. Gregory Kandel, just out of
Northwestern University and its founder, served as
producing director. Mike Nussbaum, the artistic
director, was the star of the premiere offering, Tom
Stoppard's *Jumpers,* directed by Frank Galati. The
wood bottoms of the theater's 289 seats were
barely softened by slim, pale green corduroy cushions, and the house had "almost nothing" in the
way of technical equipment, according to Nussbaum. But after a nervous, ill-prepared start, the
theater settled down into a respectable organiza-

Michael Maggio
AUTHOR'S COLLECTION

tion, and two of its best shows, Sam
Shepard's *Buried Child*, staged by
Kandel, and the musical *The Club*,
directed by Maggio, moved to Chi-
cago for encore engagements at the
Body Politic in 1980.

Kandel, who left in 1981, was suc-
ceeded for two seasons by the Canadian director Eric Steiner, and in 1983
Maggio became artistic director,
wryly noting, in a bow to the theater's grade school location, that he
was leading an organization of "high
standards and low urinals." Frail in
health but vigorous in imagination,
Maggio had made a name for himself
in 1977 by mounting a shoestring-
sumptuous non-Equity version of the
musical *Candide*, presented by SCT
Productions in the Athenaeum Theatre. Since then, he had gained
increasing respect as a freelance
director at Wisdom Bridge and

B. J. Jones, a Chicago actor since the 1970s and
artistic director of Northlight Theatre since 1998, as
an aspiring young clergyman in *God's Man in Texas*,
by David Rambo, at Northlight in 2000
MICHAEL BROSILOW

Goodman theaters. He did well at Northlight, too, directing *City on the
Make*, a new musical adapted from the writings of Nelson Algren, and
his big hit, *The Real Thing*, by Tom Stoppard, a playwright for whom
he had an affinity.

The wear and tear of running a theater became too much for Maggio, however, and in 1987, Russell Vandenbroucke, a scholarly director
and playwright, took over leadership. Soon, he found himself without
a home, as the Kingsley building was to be reactivated as a school. Moving operations south in 1990 to the old Coronet movie theater in downtown Evanston, an unhappy home until 1994, Northlight management
spent thousands of dollars renovating the inhospitable space, fought
with the landlord, absorbed the subscription membership of the failed
National Jewish Theater in Skokie, and tried unsuccessfully, in fumbled
negotiations, to move into new quarters at National-Louis University in

Evanston. For two seasons, the theater shuffled through seven different sites in Chicago and Evanston. Its subscription rolls diminished, and it went deeper and deeper in debt. At one point, Vandenbroucke was ready to suggest to his board that perhaps Northlight was like an old dog that should be taken to the back of the house and put out of its misery. Richard Friedman, the managing director, said, "There wasn't a day when you came to work and knew what was going to happen."

Yet after many a false start, and before he left to go back into the academic world, Vandenbroucke in 1997 was able to see Northlight established as the resident theater company of the North Shore Center for the Performing Arts. When actor-director B. J. Jones, *Bagtime*'s star, who had been active in Chicago theater since the early 1970s, zestfully embraced the job of artistic director in 1998, he gave the theater an invigorating surge of fresh life with a programming blend of new musicals, new plays, rediscovered classics, and recent hits from the off-Broadway and regional theater circuit.

Remains Theatre came to the 1970s party fairly late, and it had a relatively short history, 1979 to 1995; but it was an important troupe in off-Loop activity, both for its plays and its players. These included Gary Cole, D. (for Donald) W. Moffett, Amy Morton, and William L. Petersen, all of whom established substantial careers for themselves after working together at Remains.

They chose the name Remains because they were all that was left of an earlier group that had split apart. They set their sights on staging new and avant-garde work because, as Petersen explains, "We didn't have the chops to do the classics, so, hey, why don't we do Beckett?"

They found themselves a small wedge-shaped space at 3744 N. Clark Street, adjoining the Ginger Man saloon, which became their hangout away from home. "I remember we were always around each other," Morton says. "We were very tight." And, sure enough, one of their early productions was Samuel Beckett's *Waiting for Godot,* with Morton in the leading role of Estragon. "Tragically awful," she recalls, shuddering.

In those early days, Petersen remembers, "We took our clothes off a lot, especially in the late shows. Guys who wandered in from the street or the bar thought we were running some kind of strip joint." The

The cast of *Moby Dick* gathers around William L. Petersen's Captain Ahab in Remains Theatre's production of 1982.

troupe's offstage life was fairly carefree too. Petersen's chief extracurricular activities were playing (barefoot) on the Remains softball team and hanging out at the Ginger Man, where he ran up "a huge tab" and looked out for "a date and a drink." Even then, however, the Remains folk were serious about their work. "We wanted to add our voice to the choir," Petersen says.

They did some marvelous work, too: *Seduced,* Sam Shepard's surreal spin on the bizarre life of Howard Hughes, starring Cole and directed by cofounder James Roach, and Richard Foreman's *Book of Splendors: Part II.* After they lost their lease in 1981, they continued to produce terrific shows as they moved from place to place: Franz Xavier Kroetz's dark *Farmyard* at MoMing Dance and Arts Center; Shepard's *The Tooth of Crime* and Caryl Churchill's *Traps* in the Theatre Building; an original adaptation of *Moby Dick,* staged in contentious conjunction with the English director Stephen Rumbelow, in the Goodman Theatre Studio; William Saroyan's *The Time of Your Life,* directed by Moffett, on the Goodman main stage; the two-person *The Mystery of Irma Vep;* Bertolt Brecht's *Puntilla and His Hired Man;* and two witty, biting contemporary comedies, *Highest Standard of Living* and *Big Time,* by the smart, young American satirist Keith Reddin, both presented in their Chicago-area premiere.

The Remains group maintained a high average of quality work throughout, but as the ensemble moved through the eighties, the founding members started their individual movie and television careers. In 1986, the appointment of twenty-five-year-old Larry Sloan, a former associate director at Goodman, as its first artistic director, gave the group some stability, and the theater moved into what it hoped would be permanent quarters in a new retail and restaurant complex at 1800 N. Clybourn Avenue. But Sloan, a very good producer and only a fair director, left in 1989 to work with Gregory Mosher at Lincoln Center in New York. (Sloan returned to Chicago in 1991 to lead Season of Concern, the Actors' Equity Association program providing care to persons in the theater community living with AIDS. He died from complications of AIDS in 1995.)

After Remains lost its home in the failed Clybourn building, new artistic director Neel Keller in 1995 threw all his efforts into presenting the premiere of the dark farce *Moon under Miami,* by the brilliant, erratic, prizewinning New York playwright John Guare. The production was staged in the Organic space and cost $180,000, part of which went for scenery by the pop artist Red Grooms. The play opened on April 30, 1995, and it was a train wreck (described in my *Tribune* review as "a rash, undisciplined, ill-conceived lollapalooza"). The high-risk gamble of creating a high-profile new work that would rejuvenate the company did not pay off.

Nothing remained of Remains.

Surveying the deaths and catastrophes that had come upon the off-Loop community, John Walker, managing director of Victory Gardens, said, succinctly, "The field is littered with bodies." And Remains was not the only theater to go under. Once-productive off-Loop groups such as Stormfield, Huron, Econo-Art, Blind Parrot, Interplay, Immediate, Commons, Blue Rider, Practical, Center and Absolute theaters, igLoo the theatrical group, and Pary Productions all faded away, mostly because of financial problems and/or ensemble breakups.

The disappearance of St. Nicholas, Wisdom Bridge, Body Politic, and Remains, all midsize (up to 250 seats) houses that had played key roles in spurring the remarkable growth of activity in the seventies, created a void in the theater community, unfortunately widening the gap between new, small, low-income troupes and older, larger, more prosperous institutions.

All was not doom, however. Victory Gardens and Northlight survived, and the departed St. Nicholas, Body Politic, Wisdom Bridge, and Remains had enjoyed moments of glory that raised the standards, developed the talents, and made the reputation of Chicago theater.

And then, of course, there was the amazing story of a group of ragtag actors who in 1975 set up their theater in the basement of a Roman Catholic grade school, up the hill on Deerfield Road in north suburban Highland Park.

Steppenwolf on the ascent. In 1987–88, the company presented the Broadway-bound *Burn This,* by Lanford Wilson, with John Malkovich and Joan Allen, whose work would win her a 1988 Tony Award for best actress in a play; the deliciously pulpy *Killers,* by John Olive, with a full-out gonzo ensemble performance; and Frank Galati's adaptation and staging of John Steinbeck's *The Grapes of Wrath,* future Tony winner for best director and production of a play, 1990.

"We Needed to Tribe Up"

THEY CALLED THEMSELVES STEPPENWOLF, a name they inherited from a novel few of them had read. Their location, in that legendary basement in Highland Park, "was not the best spot to call attention to ourselves," cofounder Jeff Perry admits. But it became a good base for them, and, Perry adds, "We needed to tribe up, to be together. This was the place where we could start."

Highland Park, moreover, was home territory for Perry and Gary Sinise. Both had grown up there and had developed their interest in theater while attending Highland Park School. (Perry actually had made his professional stage debut as a child actor in 1966, when he briefly appeared in a production of Luigi Pirandello's *Six Characters in Search of an Author*, presented by the touring American Conservatory Theater at the Ravinia Festival.) After his high school graduation, Perry went on to Illinois State University in downstate Bloomington, while his buddy Sinise, never the great scholar, stayed on to graduate in January 1974.

Soon after, Sinise got together a group of fellow actors to present an in-the-round staging of Paul Zindel's *And Miss Reardon Drinks a Little* in the North Shore Unitarian Church at 2100 Half Day Road, just

Gary Sinise, flushed with the pride of ownership, and Steppenwolf's first sign, 1976
LISA EBRIGHT, COURTESY OF STEPPENWOLF THEATRE

outside Deerfield. "After rehearsal one night," Sinise remembers, "I suggested we pick a name that would give us identity as a company. One of the other leaders of the group, Rick Argosh, held up the book he was reading, *Steppenwolf,* by Hermann Hesse. I said great, everyone agreed, and we moved on to other business."

Perry, meanwhile, met and became friends with fellow actor Terry Kinney in the theater program at I.S.U. As Perry recalls it, "I told Terry that he had to meet this friend of mine, this really great actor. So we went up to Highland Park to see Gary act." The show was *Grease,* staged in the gymnasium of the Indian Trail Elementary School, and Sinise was playing, or overplaying, the lead role of Danny Zuko. "He was totally wild," Perry recalls. "I thought to myself, Wait a minute. Here I'm bragging about this guy who's such a great actor, and there was Gary up onstage, in a musical, acting like a madman." Says Kinney, "It was not what I had expected."

Nevertheless, they took to one another, and in that summer of 1974, the three of them got together for a production of Tom Stoppard's

Rosencrantz and Guildenstern Are Dead. They liked the experience so much that they decided to go on. In 1975, with the idea of adding more friends from I.S.U. to make an ensemble, they picked the old name of Steppenwolf for their own new company because, Sinise says, "This name was already incorporated and had an identity in Highland Park, be it a small one." Their only plan, Sinise recalls, "was to get out of school and put on some plays. In our meetings, if somebody talked about drawing up a five-year plan, we would say, 'What five-year plan? We're not going to be here in five years.'"

Among the new recruits in 1976 were Laurie Metcalf (whom Kinney was dating at the time), Moira Harris, Alan Wilder, John Malkovich, Nancy Evans, and H. E. Baccus, who became their first artistic director. Joan Allen joined in 1977, but Rondi Reed, also at I.S.U., took a pass, she says, because, "I thought they were all nuts." Instead, she took a job as a bank teller in Minneapolis and didn't join the company until 1979, when the company had lasted far longer than she—and everybody else—had anticipated.

In 1976, after a meeting at Perry's house, Sinise took the group over to the Immaculate Conception School and showed them their new home. They also had their first group picture taken. There were nine of them.

They moved into the school basement and, with the aid of designer Kevin Rigdon, built their own light booth, took out a twelve-thousand-dollar loan to put in a sprinkler system and risers, lugged in eighty-eight seats from the old Arie Crown Theatre of McCormick Place, and were still painting the walls just before the audience came in on their opening night. "Everything was new, uncharted soul-searching for us," Sinise says.

I got my first sampling of the Steppenwolf impact in their production of Israel Horovitz's one-act *The Indian Wants the Bronx,* which tells of two punks (Sinise and Kinney) who terrorize an innocent man, an Indian (Baccus), lost in the Bronx. To prepare for their roles, Sinise and Kinney dressed up as urban goons and prowled the manicured streets of Highland Park, looking tough—"If you can imagine that," says Kinney, with a smile. On the night of each performance, they ran around the outside of the theater screaming and carrying on in order to fire up their energy. Then, on a signal from the stage manager, they raced down from the top of the hill, roared into the backstage area, and rocketed onto the stage, where, laughing maniacally, they confronted the

BEING JOHN MALKOVICH

From the beginning, "intensity" was the word for John Malkovich's work as an actor. It was a description well deserved, as he demonstrated several times, onstage and offstage.

One night during the 1976 Steppenwolf run of Hugh Wheeler's youth drama, *Look, We've Come Through,* Jeff Perry came offstage after getting a sigh of audience approval in one of his scenes and immediately got a sharp rap on the back of his head from Malkovich, who hissed, "That kind of reaction should be reserved solely for puppy dogs and fireworks."

"Naturally," Perry says, "I tried to get that same audience reaction every night—and to dodge John when I came backstage."

In 1979, in Sam Shepard's *Curse of the Starving Class,* directed by Robert Falls and presented by Goodman Theatre in a Stage 2 production in the auditorium of the Latin School of Chicago, Malkovich had a scene in which his character, with his back to the audience, urinated. "Most actors," says Roche Schulfer, Goodman's general manager at that time, "would have used the small syringe of water attached to the costume for that scene, but John, being John, actually urinated. Oh, yes, I spent many an afternoon in the headmaster's office on that one."

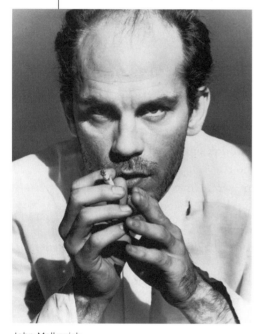

John Malkovich
COURTESY OF STEPPENWOLF THEATRE

In 1981, in a Steppenwolf performance for students of John Steinbeck's *Of Mice and Men,* Malkovich extended his intensity to one unfortunate customer in the audience: a high school kid in the front row who had sprawled out in his seat and plopped his feet on the stage where Malkovich was playing a scene. As the lights went down for a scene change, Malkovich grabbed the kid by his ears and snarled, "If you put your f——ing feet on this stage again, I will tear your f——ing head off." When the lights went up, Malkovich had vanished, and the stupefied young man was sitting straight up, his eyes big as saucers and his feet firmly planted beneath his seat.

Occasionally, however, Malkovich could be upstaged. When one of the actors in the 1979 comedy *Say Goodnight, Gracie* became ill, Austin Pendleton, the director, filled in. Before going onstage, Malkovich whispered to Pendleton, a professional actor since the fifties, "You know, we're very competitive out there. You'll have to hold your own." Pendleton nodded, awaited his cue, made his entrance, and, according to Malkovich, "In two minutes, he had blown us all away."

hapless Baccus. It was so convincingly terrifying I was sure that, when they had finished messing with him, they were going to come after me and the rest of the audience.

This was what came to be known as the gonzo style of Steppenwolf performance, a huge, raw outpouring of energy, slammed across with take-no-prisoners force. It gained the group instant identification, much as David Mamet's use of rough, coarse language had stamped his writing style. But, as with Mamet, there was more to Steppenwolf than that.

Sinise takes some credit, and blame, for the style. "I was performing onstage in a rock band until I was twenty-two," he says, "and I was drawn to plays that gave me that heightened energy, the same kind of energy a rock concert has. But we did many plays that were much more sensitive. It wasn't all 'rock 'n' roll' theater."

Gary Sinise and Terry Kinney trying to look very tough for *The Indian Wants the Bronx,* 1976

LISA EBRIGHT, SPECIAL COLLECTIONS AND PRESERVATION DIVISION, CHICAGO PUBLIC LIBRARY

Indeed it wasn't, and the results were definitely mixed. In 1977, in response to their board's request that they put on something a little lighter than the dark, gloomy works that were their early specialty, they produced *Mack, Anything Goes over the Rainbow,* a musical revue of songs by Kurt Weill, Cole Porter, and Harold Arlen that failed to take into account that none of them, except Perry, could sing. But in 1982, Allen, an actress who deserves the adjective "radiant," turned in a lovely, impeccably modulated performance under Kinney's sensitive direction in *And a Nightingale Sang,* a nostalgic drama of homefront England in World War II.

Still, in those early years, they kept close to the gritty, edgy, contemporary works that made their reputation. When Austin Pendleton, the New York–based actor-director who joined the Steppenwolf ensemble

The Steppenwolf kids, smiling and in plaid, in 1978. Front row: Joan Allen, Terry Kinney. Middle row: Moira Harris, John Malkovich, Jeff Perry, Laurie Metcalf. Rear row: Bob Biggs, the company's administrative director and grant writer; Alan Wilder; H. E. Baccus. Absent: Gary Sinise.

COURTESY OF STEPPENWOLF THEATRE

in 1987, urged the company to tackle *The Crucible*, Arthur Miller's drama set in a Puritan community of seventeenth-century New England, Sinise dutifully read the play but reported back, "I just can't see us doing a play where people are called 'Goodie' and wear buckles on their shoes."

They lived and worked in what Perry aptly describes as "incestuous isolation" in a "Peyton Place" (Metcalf's phrase) lifestyle of personal attachments. Staunchly supportive and fiercely competitive, extremely individualistic but absolutely dependent on each other, they argued about everything from artistic policy to cleaning chores. It was a risky business, as Metcalf discovered in 1977 when she was suddenly called to fill in for Moira Harris, who had become ill, in Edward J. Moore's two-character drama *The Sea Horse*. Metcalf learned her lines on a nonstop auto trip from downstate to Highland Park. When she showed up at the

John Malkovich as the son, Laurie Metcalf as the daughter, and Anne Edwards as the mother in Tennessee Williams's *The Glass Menagerie*, directed by H. E. Baccus, 1979

theater, Sinise sketched out the action for her, explaining that he and Harris had been playing it pretty rough in Moore's tough love romance. Thus prepared, Metcalf stepped onstage, and, for the next two hours, she says, "Gary threw me all over the place."

With them, the energy and the arrogance of youth were in full bloom, and, in truth, they had something to be arrogant about. Their production of Tennessee Williams's *The Glass Menagerie*, for example, was a daring revelation of a familiar text. Baccus, who directed, was determined not to sentimentalize Williams's semiautobiographical family story, and he pulled extraordinary portrayals from Malkovich, as the memory play's narrator, Tom, and Metcalf, as his handicapped sister

Laura. Malkovich's Tom was clearly a homosexual trapped in a bleak home life; Metcalf's Laura was a thumping cripple, pathologically shy and obviously destined for a mental institution.

Before long, their ensemble performances were getting them jobs outside their own theater—in 1978 at St. Nicholas in *The 5th of July,* in the Theatre Building in 1979 with the comedy *Say Goodnight, Gracie* (directed by Pendleton), and, for Sinise and Metcalf, Jeff Award–winning portrayals in Robert Falls's 1980 staging of Marsha Norman's *Getting Out,* at Wisdom Bridge. A few ensemble members—Francis Guinan, Kinney, and Wilder—even hired out for *The Littlest Elf,* a one-hour children's Christmas holiday show presented in 1980 in the underground auditorium of the First National Plaza in the Loop. Patricia Cox, who produced the show, recalls, "It was my job to tell them that, as part of the arrangement with the bank, they had to appear on a float in the downtown Christmas parade. When they heard that—well, oh my, I had never had anybody talk to me like that. Those boys didn't hold anything back."

They were making no money, hanging on when they did well, and just barely existing when a show failed to draw customers. In one bad patch in 1979, their then business manager advised them to shut down permanently. Their solution was to fire the business manager and look for a larger theater.

They had already made those brief excursions into Chicago as guest actors in other theaters, and they had presented one show on their own, Wallace Shawn's *Our Late Night,* directed by Gary Houston, in 1977 at the Jane Addams Center of Hull House. In 1980, with their acclaim growing, they moved down to the city for good, making the Jane Addams Center their new home, with Sinise as artistic director. Here, they did some of their best work, the talents of Glenne Headly, John Mahoney, Tom Irwin, Guinan, and Reed now added to the ensemble.

Not all their shows in the next eleven years were winners. There was a strange 1986 musical, by singer–song writer Tom Waits, called *Frank's Wild Years* (at Briar Street Theatre), and a bizarre 1981 staging, by Malkovich, of Christopher Hampton's *Savages,* in which the roles of the play's South American natives were portrayed by several seminude Northwestern University students. Martha Lavey, one of these students and Steppenwolf's future artistic director, also joined an acting class, taught by Malkovich, that included among her dozen or so

John Malkovich and Jeff Perry as the battling siblings of Sam Shepard's *True West*, 1982
LISA EBRIGHT, SPECIAL COLLECTIONS AND PRESERVATION DIVISION, CHICAGO PUBLIC LIBRARY

classmates Mr. T. ("He came to every class wearing all his jewelry," she says.)

Disregarding those oddities, the Hull House years were rich in splendid shows, filled with some of the company's best individual and ensemble work: *A Prayer for My Daughter,* marking the professional acting debut of Chicago Police detective Dennis Farina (1982); Allen, Harris, and Molly Regan as Anton Chekhov's *Three Sisters* (1984); Mahoney's breakthrough portrayal of the sinister father figure of Lyle Kessler's *Orphans* (1985); a luminous revival of George S. Kaufman and Moss Hart's *You Can't Take It with You* (1985), directed by Frank Galati, who would join the ensemble in 1986; Lynn Siefert's uproarious *Coyote Ugly* (1985); Wallace Shawn's *Aunt Dan and Lemon* (1987), with brilliant performances by Regan and newcomer Lavey; the delirious pulp thriller *Killers* (1988), by John Olive, in which almost everyone in the

A STEPPENWOLF MASTERPIECE

If Steppenwolf symbolized the power of theater in Chicago, then the power of Steppenwolf itself was epitomized by its production in 1980 of *Balm in Gilead*.

Lanford Wilson's 1964 off-Broadway drama was a favorite text of Steppenwolf cofounder Terry Kinney. "He was always talking about it," Gary Sinise says. But when the company finally decided to present it in their home at the Jane Addams Center of Hull House, it was John Malkovich who was given the job of staging it. "Nobody wanted to direct it," Malkovich says, "They all wanted to act in it."

With a cast of twenty-nine actors, including three children, the play dealt with the lives of a sprawling mass of lower-class humanity who swirled in and out of the grungy interior of an all-night New York greasy-spoon diner. Its realistic tone, its ensemble unity, and its electric flow of energy were perfect for the Steppenwolf actors, and Malkovich gave it a brilliant presentation.

Sinise, scruffily dressed in soiled army fatigues, with a peace medallion hanging from his neck, portrayed Dopey, the zonked-out narrator and ringmaster for the story. Other ensemble members—Jeff Perry as a haughty transvestite, John Mahoney as the diner's boss, Joan Allen as a rough lesbian, Laurie Metcalf as an awkward, innocent waif lost in the city, and Glenne Headly as a sympathetic whore—memorably wove themselves into the narrative threads, and Malkovich underscored their turbulent action with background music of recordings by Bruce Springsteen and Tom Waits.

Gary Sinise as Dopey, the spaced-out narrator of Lanford Wilson's *Balm in Gilead*, 1980

There wasn't a weak link in the show. The Steppenwolf style of acting, realistic and in the moment, was at its zenith, and, in that small theater space, with the customers sitting on three sides of the square thrust stage, the action in the diner seemed to be taking place right in front of, or in the midst of, the audience.

There is one indelible moment I shall never forget. In an extraordinary, extended monologue, Darlene, the young woman portrayed by Metcalf, told the story of her bizarre, doomed affair with an albino lover. The pain of her experience was almost palpable in her telling of it, and it was made all the more compelling by Headly, who listened to the story with such rapt attention that it drew everyone in the theater into the sad tale. I have never seen anything like it, anywhere.

The play was remounted in the summer of 1981 at the Apollo Theater Center, and in 1984, in a collaboration with Circle Repertory Theatre, it scored a great success off-Broadway at the Minetta Lane Theatre, cementing Steppenwolf's New York reputation as a troupe of immense talents.

cast got naked; and Lanford Wilson's *Balm in Gilead* (1980), the pinnacle of Steppenwolf ensemble performance.

Among these shows, none was more crucial to Steppenwolf than the 1982 production of Sam Shepard's *True West*. It nearly tore the company apart, and it launched the troupe into the stratosphere.

The play, directed by Sinise in his high rock 'n' roll mode, and with Perry and Malkovich as two battling brothers, was such a huge, long-run hit in Chicago that it attracted off-Broadway producers who wanted to bring it to New York. At the time, however, Steppenwolf was preparing to make a big move into the old St. Nicholas space at 2851 N. Halsted Street, and the ensemble, fearing that the transfer of *True West* to New York would drain energy from their Chicago plans, was dead set against it—except for Sinise.

"It was," Sinise says, "a real time of challenge." He had felt all along that Steppenwolf had to be more than a local phenomenon, that it had to have a New York presence if it was to be nationally recognized. But the other members of the ensemble, leery of New York and seeing that two of its principal actors, Perry and Malkovich, would be out of action in Chicago, fought the plan. Perry decided not to make the trip to the Cherry Lane Theatre, and when the New York producers vetoed Tom Irwin as a replacement and Sinise decided to take on the role himself, many ensemble members looked on the New York journey as Sinise ego-tripping. They did not want Steppenwolf's name to be associated with the production.

"I really felt all alone; I thought everyone was against me," Sinise says. One afternoon, in a crazy burst of energy, and bitterly determined to show his fellow ensemble members that he did too take an interest in looking after things in Chicago, he took a chainsaw over to the St. Nicholas space, where the old risers that held the audience seats had to be dismantled, and single-handedly began to rip them apart with the chainsaw. Soon, Stephen Eich, the company's managing director, walked into the theater and asked, in amazement, "What the hell are you doing?" Sinise, exhausted, turned off the saw and left the room.

True West, with Malkovich and Sinise, opened in New York on October 17, 1982, and scored the kind of sweet success that only a New York hit can have. It catapulted Malkovich into a movie career, it made Steppenwolf a hot item in theater circles, and, as Sinise says, "The door was open."

Terry Kinney and Kevin Anderson look after their captive, John Mahoney, in *Orphans,*
by Lyle Kessler, 1985.

In the next few years, Steppenwolf sent Manhattan a series of transfers from the home base in Chicago: *And a Nightingale Sang* in 1983,
Balm in Gilead in 1984, *Orphans* in 1985, and the Tony Award–winning
play of 1990, director Frank Galati's adaptation of John Steinbeck's *The
Grapes of Wrath*. Steppenwolf was now a recognized Broadway force,
receiving the 1985 Tony for regional theater excellence, and Chicago, in
turn, was now a magic town for theater.

The ways of New York were far different from what the ensemble
had experienced in Chicago. *Balm in Gilead* was a coproduction with
Circle Repertory Theatre in New York, and Kinney remembers being
mystified by the fact that the New York actors in the cast started the
day by lining up at the theater's pay phone. "We wanted to start
rehearsals, and they were calling their agents," he says. "We couldn't
understand it." As they too received television and movie offers, Kinney

and the rest of the Steppenwolf crew soon learned to understand that game, and as they did, the old pull of personal careers versus company values began to click in. When talk arose that the troupe might dissolve or move to New York, they held a press conference asserting that they were in Chicago to stay. But, Perry says, "It was a little like 'the lady doth protest too much,' because we all knew then that our tight little commune was going bye-bye."

For Bruce Sagan, Steppenwolf's board president and a former chairman of the Illinois Arts Council (and the same man who had opened the Harper Theater on the South Side in 1964), there was one clear way to keep the company together: build a theater, and they will stay—at least for part of the time.

It was Sagan's belief that a new state-of-the-art theater would effectively turn the troupe into an institution and would act as enough of a

Gary Sinise and Terry Kinney in *The Grapes of Wrath,* 1988
MICHAEL BROSILOW, COURTESY OF STEPPENWOLF THEATRE

Jeff Perry in the center of the swirl of *The Time of Your Life*, 2002

MICHAEL BROSILOW, COURTESY OF STEPPENWOLF THEATRE

lure to keep ensemble members coming back periodically to act or direct in Chicago. Whatever the demands of their separate movie, television, and Broadway careers, and however far afield those careers took them, they could reserve a few weeks to return home and exercise their theater chops in a proud mother ship of size and substance.

As early as 1985, the company had talked about moving to a larger home. "If we hadn't grown and evolved," Sinise says, "it would have been only a matter of time before people went off entirely on their own." In 1991, therefore, at a cost of $8.28 million, with Sagan raising state and private funding, hustling things along, and keeping a tight rein on expenses, Steppenwolf moved into its new building at 1650 N. Halsted Street. It was comfortable, utilitarian, and user-friendly (thirteen stalls in the ladies' room), containing an acoustically sound five-hundred-seat auditorium with a Broadway-size stage plus an upstairs studio theater. (Unfinished retail footage in a garage just south of the building also was converted into a flexible theater room, giving Steppenwolf three performance spaces.)

It wasn't a foolproof solution. The days of the seventies and eighties, when you could see many Steppenwolf actors in the same show, were gone, and some of the finest ensemble talents, such as Allen and Headly, never performed in the new building. Moreover, the new building harbored duds of all kinds (*Inspecting Carol, Everyman, The Road to Nirvana, Supple in Combat*) and journeyman work (*Closer, Skylight, A Slip of the Tongue*), as well as inspired hits (revivals of *Buried Child* and *Glengarry Glen Ross* and the 1992 premiere of *The Song of Jacob Zulu*, with the South African choral group Ladysmith Black Mambazo).

As Sagan had hoped, several ensemble members, including Mahoney, Malkovich, Sinise, Perry, Metcalf, and Kinney, have made it a point to touch home base on a fairly regular basis. And added ensemble talents—directors Eric Simonson and Tina Landau, playwright-actor Tracy Letts, and actress-director Amy Morton—brought welcome new shadings to the Steppenwolf style. If the intimacy of the early productions was gone, director Landau, in such galvanizing new works as Charles L. Mee's *The Berlin Circle* and in her brilliantly revitalizing 2002 revival of William Saroyan's *The Time of Your Life,* showed that the large size and technical facilities of the new theater could be imaginatively used.

Sinise once called Steppenwolf "a unit, a cooperative, a team, a family." Eich, who left his post as executive director of the company after a messy 1995 family feud in which Randall Arney was deposed as artistic director, modified that description to call the ensemble "a dysfunctional family."

Yet for a dysfunctional family, Steppenwolf has survived with amazing lack of fatal injury. Lavey, who became artistic director in 1995, kept in close touch with the "executive artistic board" of founders Perry, Sinise, and Kinney, while at the same time collaborating in productions with smaller, younger companies and bringing in new writers such as Letts and Bruce Norris and directors such as Anna D. Shapiro. Productions such as the 2000 *One Flew over the Cuckoo's Nest,* starring Sinise in Kinney's staging, continued to make their way to New York and multi–Tony nominations.

Steppenwolf had become a major force in American theater, riding the tide of its particular success and serving as a prime example of Chicago theater in general.

Years before, Sinise had asked a New York agent to "come here to Chicago to see our work." The agent replied, "Young man, we are here in New York, you are out there." Now, as Steppenwolf had shown, "out there" was "where it's at."

eclipse theatre company
one playwright-one season

Anish Jethmalani*
Artistic Director

Thomas Jones+
Board Director

presents
The Midwest Premiere of

FRAME 312
BY KEITH REDDIN

*Directed by Steven Fedoruk**

Featuring
John Byrnes, Donna McGough, Nora Newbrough, Krishna Saltman,
Gary Simmers*, Frances Wilkerson

Nathaniel Swift*
Joel Ebarb
Costume Design

Mike Winkelman
Set Design
Kevin Scott*
Scenic Consultant
Jason Breitzman
Projection Design
Maren Robinson
Dramaturg

FRAME 312 had
and its

Eclipse Theatre Company
City Arts Program!, from
a state agency,
The Ri

Apple Tree Theatre

evers
ic Director

Ross Lehman
Artistic Director

presents

...of No Importance

...ook by Terrence McNally
...lyrics by Lynn Ahrens
...usic by Stephen Fl...

---

n Kiely, Artistic Director

Anthony Roberts, Managing Director

american theater company

proudly presents

Part four of the American Century Project: the 1920s
STRICTLY DISHONORABLE
BY PRESTON STURGES

Directed by Damon Kiely

Scenic Design

Lighting Design

...tax-deductible,
...organization of
...ember of the

...heatre.

TimeLine
Theatre Company

2002-2003 Season

Hannah and Martin

World Premiere
By Kate Fodor

Directed by Jeremy B. Cohen*

Produced b...
Associate Directe...
Assistant Directed by...
Scenic & Lighting Design...
Costume Design by...
Sound Design b...
Properties Design...
Dramaturgy by...
Stage Managed by...
Assistant Stage Manag...

May 3 –

TimeLine T
615 W. Wellin
(312)
www.Time...

HANNAH AND MARTIN is spo...

TimeLine Theatre (
Council, a state ag...
Affairs, the Richard...
the Alphawood Fo...
Foundation, the G...
ous individual do...

ssdc

WRITERS' THEATRE

MICHAEL HALBERSTAM
Artistic Director

JENNIFER BIELSTEIN
Managing Director

presents

MY OWN STRANGER

Adapted from the writings of ANNE SEXTON

by MARILYN CAMPBELL and
LINDA LAUNDRA

Directed by
KATE D...

YMBERLY MELLEN*
Lighting Designer
TA PIETRASZEK, USAA

Properties Master
STEVE HINGER

ociation.

T&T and

ommunity Trust and

JULY/AUGUST 2004

Chicagoplays
THEATER GUIDE

See page G1 inside for complete show listings.

The theater community expands through the city and suburbs, with troupes of varied sizes and missions presenting a year-round schedule of classics and contemporary dramas.

AUTHOR'S COLLECTION AND *CHICAGOPLAYS*, PUBLISHED BY AND COURTESY OF THE LEAGUE OF CHICAGO THEATRES

Chapter 19

"The Vast Chicago Theater Market"

STEPPENWOLF'S SPECTACULAR ASCENT to stardom forever changed the playing field of resident theater in Chicago. There had been earlier breakout success stories, from *Grease* to David Mamet, but it was the tale of this bunch of scraggly youths who had emerged as rich and famous stars that dramatically stamped Chicago as a booming theater town. Within the city, there was, for a time, a futile guessing game as to which new group would turn into "the next Steppenwolf," as if the unique chemistry of the real Steppenwolf could be duplicated. And there was some whining that the big new Steppenwolf on Halsted Street was not the same as the little old Steppenwolf in Highland Park. But those days were gone forever.

Still, even if there were no new Steppenwolfs, there were certainly plenty of new theaters. Throughout the eighties and nineties, scores of companies were born and developed, replacing theaters that had closed, replenishing the supply of fresh talent, and staking out new paths to glory. Their goal, as noted in the mission statement of the Eclipse Theatre Company, founded in 1992, was "to stay competitive in the vast Chicago theater market." (Eclipse's strategy for finding its audience,

Barbara Gaines urging on her cast in Shakespeare Repertory of Chicago's production of *Troilus and Cressida*, 1987
BILL HOGAN, COURTESY OF *CHICAGO TRIBUNE* NEWS ARCHIVE

adapted from a similar program of the Signature Theatre in New York, was to devote each season to a particular playwright. It gave the company focus, set it apart from the rest of the pack, and helped it to develop an ensemble unity.)

The big, brand-name theaters rolled on, with new, talented groups bearing such varied names (and goals) as Raven, Lifeline, Corn Productions, New World Repertory, Porchlight, Trap Door, the Hypocrites, Rogue, Remy Bumppo, the House, Circle, Curious, Profiles, and 500 Clown running in to stake a claim, carve out a niche.

Not only was the scene bigger, it was more diverse. The blue-collar image that had become a cliché in describing Chicago acting was no longer viable. The energy, the work ethic, the sense of community, were still

Steven Rishard, Linda Kimbrough, and Scott Parkinson in jolly seventeenth-century form for *The Gamester* at Northlight Theatre, 2001
MICHAEL BROSILOW

Larry Yando as Richard M. Nixon and William Brown as Henry Kissinger in *Nixon's Nixon,* by Russell Lees, 2000

COURTESY OF WRITERS' THEATRE

there, but the style was broadening into areas far removed from the early naturalism.

In 1986, Barbara Gaines, a Chicago actress who had returned home after a spell in New York, put together a Shakespeare workshop that she developed into a small company. Their first production, *Henry V,* was staged on the roof of the Red Lion Pub, 2446 N. Wells Street. From there, the newly minted Shakespeare Repertory of Chicago moved to the Ruth Page Center, put a thrust stage in its gymnasiumlike auditorium, and presented to a growing audience a series of productions of gathering strength that articulated the canon in clear, crisp, muscular performance.

In 2001, Northlight Theatre uncovered and presented the American premiere of *The Gamester,* an all-but-forgotten comedy of manners written in 1696 by Jean-François Regnard. The adaptation by Freyda Thomas was staged by director Michael Halberstam with energy, wit, clarity, and elegant period style. Again, Chicago energy and invention were there, perfectly put to the service of the genre. Linda Kimbrough, an actress who had been working in Chicago since the midseventies, portrayed an aging, still-lusty seventeenth-century noblewoman as if to the manor born.

The previous season, in 2000, Halberstam had unearthed *Spite for Spite,* a sixteenth-century Spanish romantic comedy in verse by Augustin Moreto, translated by Dakin Matthews, and rousingly presented it with Chicago verve and suave panache on the wedge-shaped stage of his fifty-seat Writers' Theatre in the back of the Books on Vernon store in downtown suburban Glencoe. (Born and raised in Nottingham,

Dale Benson menaced by Michael Halberstam in Joe Orton's *Loot,* 2000

COURTESY OF WRITERS' THEATRE

Jeff Still and Howard Witt in Arthur Miller's *The Price,* 2002

England, Halberstam came to the United States as a teenager in 1980 and, after settling in the city, smoothly wed his inherent theater talent to Chicago hustle. In 2003, still keeping his bookstore quarters, he added an elegant new 110-seat, million-dollar theater nestled inside a Glencoe women's club.)

Court Theatre, a place for classic drama on the University of Chicago campus since its beginnings as a summer theater operation in 1955, had become a professional theater under artistic director Nicholas Rudall in 1975 and in 1983 had opened a new from-the-ground-up theater at 5535 S. Ellis Avenue. When Charles Newell became artistic director in 1994, he further defined the 251-seat theater's mission by introducing a post-modern edge to the staging of the classics. His directing collaborators included guest artists such as JoAnne Akalaitis, the Budapest-based Laszlo Marton, and the Chicago-based Gary Griffin. The core cast of actors, who were comfortable in both the classics and musical theater, gave familiar texts new and novel twists, sometimes in a forced, strained manner, but at other times, as in 2002, with Griffin's sparkling two-piano, stripped-down version of *My Fair Lady* and Newell's virtuoso Christmas holiday staging of the musical drama based on James Joyce's "The Dead," to dazzling effect.

Theaters—commercial and not-for-profit, large and small, professional and community, on the North Side or the South Side or in the sub-

Barbara Robertson and Jenny Bacon as the dueling royalty of Friedrich Schiller's *Mary Stuart,* directed by JoAnne Akalaitis at Court Theatre, 2001

Christmas cheer from the cast in *James Joyce's "The Dead,"* directed by Charles Newell at Court Theatre, 2002
MICHAEL BROSILOW

urbs—had learned to find their target audience and to program accordingly, whatever and wherever that audience might be.

Abena Joan Brown, head of the eta Creative Arts Foundation, had gone through most of the career changes in her South Side African American community that many members of the predominantly white off-Loop theaters had experienced. A dancer and an actress, she entered the theater scene in the 1950s, enrolling in Drama, Inc., a group aspiring to give "the professional touch to little theater" that had been organized by Lillian Thompkins, a former wardrobe mistress at the Shubert Theatre. Unreported by the white press, several little theaters at that time dotted the South Side, including the Skyloft Company, Penthouse Players, Center Aisle, and the Tempo Players of Washington Park. And the area had such pioneer leaders as the teacher-playwrights Theodore Ward and Eugene Perkins.

Brown became involved in the black arts and civil rights movements of the sixties, working in several seminal theaters in her community. She and her fellow players moved from site to site, turning makeshift spaces

Stacie Doublin, J. J. McCormick, and Carolyn Nelson in *When the Ancestors Call*
COURTESY OF ETA CREATIVE ARTS FOUNDATION

into performance areas. "If we needed a stage," she says, "we built one." She and her Drama, Inc., colleague Okoro Harold Johnson founded eta in 1971. All along, she knew, "If we wanted to last, to become truly visible, we would have to secure a permanent location, a place where people knew they could find us." In 1979, she found the place, a former storm-door and storm-window factory at 7558 S. South Chicago Avenue, and she turned it into an arts center containing classrooms, a library, an art gallery, a community room, office space, and in 1983 a two-hundred-seat theater. "Now," she says, "we had credibility, legitimacy, and accountability. We didn't have a landlord who could throw us out in some capricious fashion."

From the start, her motto was "Always Different, Always Good." Oscar Brown Jr. wrote the first show, *Journey through Forever,* a musical presented in the new theater, and the fare thereafter, in addition to classic works from African American literature, consisted of original dramas, musicals, and children's plays. The theater has a small subscription base, Brown says, with about 70 percent of the customers coming from church and social groups. It is a system that works for them.

Jackie Taylor, a child of the city's housing projects, was an established young actress when she founded her Black Ensemble Theater in 1976 in the Uptown Center of Hull House, 4520 N. Beacon Street, the old home of the Organic Theater. In the first year of her Ensemble, Taylor created a popular family show, *The Other Cinderella,* an African American version of the fairy story. But she found her theater's niche, and a continuing source of box-office returns, when she began writing, directing, and producing a series of original musicals based on the careers of African American pop artists, capped in 2002 by *The Jackie Wilson Story,* with a star-making performance in the title role by the young actor Chester Gregory II.

The goal here was to present theater that spoke directly to its particular audience, that reflected the life of the people who came to see the shows, or, as Brown says, "to do plays telling our stories."

Such also was the goal of Northwestern graduates Eric Rosen and Kyle Hall in 1995 when they founded the About Face Theatre as a group doing plays that told stories dealing with gay and lesbian matters. "We felt we had come along at a changing historic moment," Rosen says, "when *Angels in America* had transferred gay and lesbian issues from the margin to the center of cultural and political discussion, and we wanted to explore that field with new works and new ways of working." Original works (*Xena Live!*), adaptations (*Dream Boy*), classics (*The Boys in the Band*), and visiting productions (*Another American: Asking and Telling* and a pre–New York version of *I Am My Own Wife*) were all presented, as well as a yearly, groundbreaking Youth Theatre production of true life stories of gay, lesbian, bisexual, and transgender young people that evolved over weeks of improvisatory sessions.

Jackie Taylor in *Indigo Blues*
COURTESY OF BLACK ENSEMBLE THEATER

Bailiwick Repertory Theatre had started out in 1982 as a non-Equity troupe that staged inventive productions of musicals (*The Threepenny Opera*) and classics (*Animal Farm*), but when it settled into its own Bailiwick Arts Center at 1229 W. Belmont Avenue, it developed several specialized areas of interest. The goal of director David Zak's theater, put forth in its mission statement, was "to embrace the wide diversity of our community." An early presenter of gay and lesbian theater, it also offered in its diverse programming children's theater, productions that combined hearing and hearing-impaired actors, original musicals, festivals that showcased new directors and new writers, and, in the midst of all this edgy mix, a sweet and enduring annual family holiday show, *The Christmas Schooner*.

There was room enough in the large Chicago community for all sorts of wild cards, odd phenomena, venturesome seasons, and idiosyncratic enterprises. There was always a next theater—a fact that in 1981 prompted Harriet Spizziri, a North Shore housewife who wanted to be a director, to name her newly founded troupe the Next Theatre.

Along with the actor and cofounder Brian Finn, producing director Spizziri went to work in the Noyes Cultural Arts Center of Evanston. "Our niche," she said, "is 'state of the art' theater. We want to introduce tomorrow's voices, tomorrow's stars." Toward that goal, Next made a smashing debut with her staging of Nigel Williams's English drama of angry youth, *Class Enemy*, and in 1986 it mounted a long-run, first-rate Chicago premiere of Larry Kramer's AIDS drama, *The Normal Heart*.

Harriet Spizziri
AUTHOR'S COLLECTION

Always working with a small budget, sometimes coming up with a clinker, and often in precarious financial straits, Next nonetheless held on to its high-risk programming. When Spizziri retired from the action in the 1990s, the little theater attracted daring leadership from the successive tenures of artistic directors Steve Pickering, Kate Buckley, and Jason Loewith. It presented the early work of rising directors Dexter Bullard (*Bouncers*) and Eric Simon-

Harry Lennix in Pegasus Players' Chicago premiere production of *Ma Rainey's Black Bottom,* 1984
JENNIFER GIRARD

son (*Bang the Drum Slowly*). It staged the 1993 premiere of Tracy Letts's sensational first play, the melodrama *Killer Joe.* And with Buckley as director, it mounted exciting ensemble performances of *Among the Thugs* and *The Laramie Project.*

Amid this profusion of theaters, Pegasus Players occupied a special niche of stick-to-it enterprise. Founded in 1978 and sustained ever since by Arlene Crewdson, a Chicago City Colleges teacher and staunch theater advocate, the non-Equity organization first played in a ninety-seat second-floor auditorium in the Edgewater Presbyterian Church at 1020 W. Bryn Mawr Avenue, where every once in a while the overloaded light board would blow a fuse and the cast would finish by candlelight.

Here, and since 1984 in the 250-seat auditorium of Truman College at 1145 W. Wilson Avenue, Crewdson, using what she calls her "fools rush in" approach as executive producer, presented an amazing number of Chicago theater firsts, including *Ma Rainey's Black Bottom* (1984), the first production in the city of a play by August Wilson, with Harry J. Lennix, then a substitute teacher in the Chicago public school system, in a smashing debut performance. (Thirteen years later, Lennix, by then an elegant, accomplished film and stage actor, returned to reprise his starring role in the play in a main-stage revival at Goodman Theatre.)

Pegasus also took the lead in staging the Chicago premieres of Stephen Sondheim musicals: *The Frogs* (1987), performed in the college's swimming pool; *Saturday Night* (2000), a resurrection of Sondheim's first, previously unproduced show of 1955; *Merrily We Roll Along* (1984), in its first production since its 1981 Broadway flop; *Pacific Overtures* (1986); *Anyone Can Whistle* (1989); *Assassins* (1993); and *Passion* (1996).

Also premiered by Pegasus were *Snow* (1987), an original script by Chicago playwright (and later scenarist of *Gladiator* and *The Last Samurai*) John Logan about the Russian Revolution; a reconstructed version of the Duke Ellington musical *Jump for Joy;* the first Chicago

Into the swimming pool: actors singing and floating in Stephen Sondheim's *The Frogs,* 1987

COURTESY OF PEGASUS PLAYERS

staging of Neil Simon's *Broadway Bound* (1987); and *Muscle* (2001), a new musical by James Lapine and William Finn.

All this, in addition to several tours to Egypt and the Middle East, and an annual Young Playwrights Festival of original works from Chicago high school students, adds up to a remarkable achievement in perseverance and enterprise.

The zigzag career of Famous Door Theatre is proof enough of the diversity, resiliency, and audaciousness that are a part of the perils and glories of off-Loop theater. Named after a jazz club on Fifty-second Street in New York that cofounder Marc Grapey thought was cool, the theater began operations in 1987 in a ramshackle site at 1052 W. Buena Avenue, within easy earshot of the clattering trains of the El. In the decade of roving existence that followed, Famous Door hung on to its core ensemble members, staging several venturesome main-stage productions, such as the German playwright Manfred Karge's *Conquest of the South Pole*. In a gem of late-

Cabbie Danny McCarthy copes with Steve Schine, Scott Anderson, and Maura Pheney as his crackhead fares in Famous Door's long-running *Hellcab*.
JEFF PINES

night invention that ran for more than a decade in Chicago and even traveled to Singapore for an out-of-town engagement, Will Kern's lusty, echt Chicago *Hellcab* told of a cabby's adventures with various urban characters on the wild side of the city.

In 1998, director Griffin's production of *Beautiful Thing*, Jonathan Harvey's tale of two working-class English boys discovering their love for each other, scored a big hit in Chicago and moved on to an off-Broadway run in New York.

In 1999, however, Anthony Minghella's *Two Planks and a Passion*, a saga of medieval players, was a box-office flop that threatened the company's existence. Late in the year, in a miraculous turn of affairs, the company went ahead with another large-cast production, Joshua Sobol's *Ghetto*, about a theater troupe struggling for survival in the Warsaw Ghetto. In a thrilling staging by director Calvin MacLean, the show

Frank Nall, as a brutal Nazi officer, confronts Roderick Peeples, as a Jewish leader, in *Ghetto*, 1999.
JEFF PINES

A flabbergasted Dan Rivkin, in the forefront, with a wounded Marc Grapey in the background, in Famous Door's comedy *Early and Often,* 2001
JEFF PINES

gave Famous Door its biggest success and placed it on track for a new series of daring, ambitious works.

Early and Often, an exuberant, rough-and-tumble political comedy by ex–Second Citizen Barbara Wallace and Thomas R. Wolfe, set during the 1960 presidential election, was, in Karen Kessler's high-speed staging of 2001, a vastly entertaining only-in-Chicago delight. And the 2003 two-part *The Cider House Rules,* based on the novel by John Irving and codirected by Grapey and David Cromer, brought off-Loop production to a new peak of excellence in its ensemble performance and its invention-within-economy production design.

THE FOOD CHAIN

About the time he and his fellow actors were getting ready to open their newly christened Famous Door Theatre in 1987, Marc Grapey was working in the box office and doing general cleaning at the genuinely famous Steppenwolf Theatre. One night, noting the many extra towels, tissues, and rolls of toilet paper in the Steppenwolf men's room, Grapey began stuffing them into a bag, planning to take them away for use by his brave-but-poor troupe. Just as Grapey was about to leave, into the bathroom walked Steppenwolf cofounder Gary Sinise, who naturally wondered what Grapey was up to. The red-faced young actor explained that his small, struggling group had no money for anything, including washroom supplies, and that he thought maybe Steppenwolf could spare a few rolls of toilet paper.

To Grapey's surprise, Sinise laughed and told him, "When we started Steppenwolf in Highland Park, I had a job as a groundskeeper at the Ravinia Festival, and I used to throw all that stuff over the park fence, pick it up when I left work and take it back to the theater. Now you're doing the same thing. You're a part of the food chain."

A few years later, when Famous Door was established as an important off-Loop theater, Grapey walked into its washroom and found a member of the small, talented, struggling Shattered Globe Theatre stuffing towels, tissues, and toilet paper into a bag. And Grapey, reveling in a great new tradition of Chicago theater, told the embarrassed fellow, "That's okay. You're a part of the food chain. In a few more years, somebody will be stealing *your* toilet paper."

Dan Kuhlman and Larry Neumann in Famous Door's epic *The Cider House Rules,* 2003
MICHAEL BROSILOW

⌒

The Neo-Futurists, situated in the Neofuturarium on the second floor of 5153 N. Ashland Avenue, above a funeral parlor, specialized in audience interactive spectaculars, the most famous of which is *Too Much Light Makes the Baby Go Blind,* billed as "an ongoing attempt to perform thirty plays in sixty minutes." Opened originally in 1988 as a late-night show, it consistently sold out in its home base and has been repeated successfully in venues throughout the United States and abroad. Whenever the show sells out, which is all the time, the audience gets treated to pizza, a feat hailed in the show's motto, "If We Sell Out, We Send Out."

ImprovOlympic, started in 1981 by Charna Halpern, drew a large and largely youthful crowd of weekend audiences to its home at 3541 N. Clark Street for its ongoing programming of full-length "long-form" shows developed through that great Chicago tradition of improvisation as interpreted by director Del Close.

Defiant Theatre, originating in 1993 and thereafter hailing itself as the bête noire of Chicago theater, developed a chest-thumping, raw-meat style of performance that roared forth in everything from Shakespeare to original works such as *Action Movie: The Play—the Director's Cut.* British director Michael Bogdanov, seeing *Titus Andronicus* in the company's rented space at the Viaduct Theater, 3111 N. Western Avenue, in 2003, saluted it for "the best use of stage blood I've seen in years."

Redmoon Theater, founded in 1990, made highly imaginative use of masks and puppets of all types and sizes in striking adaptations of literary classics (*The Hunchback of Notre Dame* and *The Old Man and the Sea*) and in its annual Winter Pageant, a lively and endearing community affair that allowed members of the troupe to mix with the men, women, and children of their North Side neighborhood.

A Red Orchid Theatre, down a hallway and next to a Chinese restaurant at 1531 N. Wells Street, was practically a one-man band, operated by the dauntless actor (and Chicago fireman) Guy Van Swearingen, whose risk-taking tastes resulted in the premieres of potent new Chicago works (Brett Neveu's *Eric LaRue* in 2002) and inventive versions of the European avant-garde and new American works (Tracy Letts's *Bug*).

Live Bait Theater, in its seventy-seat home at 3914 N. Clark Street, with playwright-artist-performer Sharon Evans as artistic director, mounted dozens of original works, many of them solo pieces, and orig-inated the unique and highly successful annual fund-raiser of *Doodles from the Stars,* auctioning off doodles donated by celebrities.

Late-Nite Catechism, one of the unstoppable late-night phenomena of Chicago theater, originated at Live Bait in 1988. The audience inter-active show, by Maripat Donovan and Vicki Quade, which milks every bit possible about a comical Roman Catholic nun, has been playing more or less forever in various Chicago locations and has been repeated, with unfailing success, in different productions in dozens of cities and states.

Even in small shows, such as *Late-Nite Catechism* and *Hellcab,* Chi-cago works by Chicago theaters were getting around. And at the city's largest theater, the Goodman, the productions were really starting to move, fast forward.

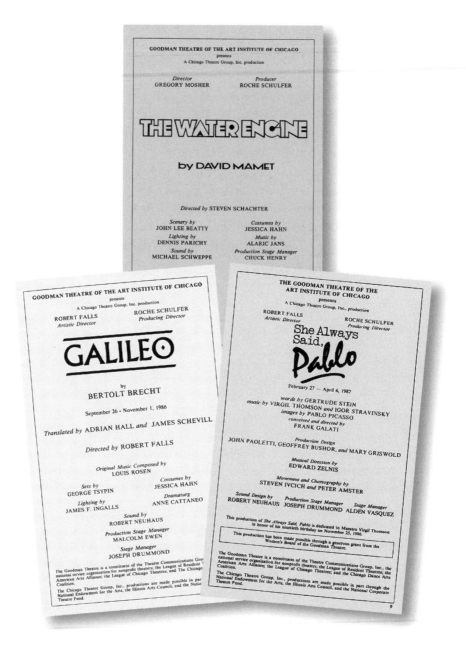

GOODMAN THEATRE OF THE ART INSTITUTE OF CHICAGO
presents
A Chicago Theatre Group, Inc. production

Director
GREGORY MOSHER

Producer
ROCHE SCHULFER

THE WATER ENGINE

by DAVID MAMET

Directed by STEVEN SCHACHTER

Scenery by
JOHN LEE BEATTY

Costumes by
JESSICA HAHN

Lighting by
DENNIS PARICHY

Music by
ALARIC JANS

Sound by
MICHAEL SCHWEPPE

Production Stage Manager
CHUCK HENRY

GOODMAN THEATRE OF THE ART INSTITUTE OF CHICAGO
presents
A Chicago Theatre Group, Inc. production

ROBERT FALLS
Artistic Director

ROCHE SCHULFER
Producing Director

GALILEO

by
BERTOLT BRECHT

September 26 - November 1, 1986

Translated by ADRIAN HALL and JAMES SCHEVILL

Directed by ROBERT FALLS

Original Music Composed by
LOUIS ROSEN

Sets by
GEORGE TSYPIN

Costumes by
JESSICA HAHN

Lighting by
JAMES F. INGALLS

Dramaturg
ANNE CATTANEO

Sound by
ROBERT NEUHAUS

Production Stage Manager
MALCOLM EWEN

Stage Manager
JOSEPH DRUMMOND

The Goodman Theatre is a constituent of the Theatre Communications Group,
national service organization for nonprofit theaters; the League of Resident T
American Arts Alliance; the League of Chicago Theatres; and The Chicago
Coalition.

The Chicago Theatre Group, Inc., productions are made possible in par
National Endowment for the Arts, the Illinois Arts Council, and the Natio
Theatre Fund.

THE GOODMAN THEATRE OF THE
ART INSTITUTE OF CHICAGO
presents
A Chicago Theatre Group, Inc. production

ROBERT FALLS
Artistic Director

ROCHE SCHULFER
Producing Director

She Always Said, Pablo

February 27 — April 4, 1987

words by GERTRUDE STEIN
music by VIRGIL THOMSON and IGOR STRAVINSKY
images by PABLO PICASSO
conceived and directed by
FRANK GALATI

Production Design
JOHN PAOLETTI, GEOFFREY BUSHOR, and MARY GRISWOLD

Musical Direction by
EDWARD ZELNIS

Movement and Choreography by
STEVEN IVICH and PETER AMSTER

Sound Design by
ROBERT NEUHAUS

Production Stage Manager
JOSEPH DRUMMOND

Stage Manager
ALDEN VASQUEZ

This production of *She Always Said, Pablo* is dedicated to Maestro Virgil Thomson
in honor of his ninetieth birthday on November 25, 1986.

This production has been made possible through a generous grant from the
Women's Board of the Goodman Theatre.

The Goodman Theatre is a constituent of the Theatre Communications Group, Inc., the
national service organization for nonprofit theaters; the League of Resident Theatres; the
American Arts Alliance; the League of Chicago Theatres; and the Chicago Dance Arts
Coalition.

The Chicago Theatre Group, Inc., productions are made possible in part through the
National Endowment for the Arts, the Illinois Arts Council, and the National Corporate
Theatre Fund.

9

Changing times, changing directors, changing programs at the Goodman Theatre

Chapter 20

"It All Came Together with *Salesman*"

GOODMAN THEATRE, WHICH OPENED in 1925, had operated first as a professional repertory theater, then as an arena devoted strictly to student work, and finally, beginning in 1969, under the crucial leadership of John Reich, once again as a fully professional theater. William Woodman, who came on board as artistic director in 1973, had further broadened the theater's scope with prestige productions on the main stage and with a Stage 2 program for developing new works that meshed with the talents of the city's emerging youthful theater scene.

When Gregory Mosher, who was brought to the Goodman by Woodman in 1974, took over leadership of the theater in 1978, he was still in his twenties, and he was on fire to accelerate both the prestige and the daring of the theater's growth. His first season's first main-stage offering set the tone for his ambitions. It was a full-scale, large-cast production of *Native Son,* Paul Green's 1941 dramatization (with further adaptation by David Mamet) of Richard Wright's novel about a young Chicago black man (portrayed by Meshach Taylor) who murders a white woman and is sent to death for it. It was a flawed, unwieldy production, but in its attempt to present a big, bold theater statement with a diverse,

Mike Nussbaum tells the story in Gregory Mosher's epic staging of *Native Son*, 1978.
COURTESY OF GOODMAN THEATRE

all-Chicago cast, it was a strong, courageous beginning for the young artistic director.

In the seasons to come, Mosher made several adventurous choices. He brought to the Goodman plays of new international scope: *Death and the King's Horseman,* written and directed by Wole Soyinka (produced in 1979, seven years before its Nigerian playwright won the Nobel Prize for Literature); Mustapha Matura's *Play Mas,* directed by Derek Walcott (1981); *Panto,* a 1978 drama by Walcott (staged in 1982, ten years before this West Indian writer won his Nobel Prize); and *Red River,* a history play by the French author Pierre Laville, in a translation by Mamet. From American writers came the pre-Broadway premiere of John Guare's *Bosoms and Neglect* (1979); *Two-Part Inventions,* by the Pulitzer Prize poet Richard Howard, directed by Michael Feingold (1979); the premiere of Edward Albee's *The Man Who Had Three Arms* (1982); and, also in 1982, after two earlier studio productions, the premiere of Tennessee Williams's last major full-length drama, *A House*

Not Meant to Stand, cruelly dubbed by some customers as "a show not meant to open."

These risky choices produced some misfires. Michael Weller's comic-strip fantasy *Dwarfman: Master of a Million Shapes* (1981) was an elaborately staged clinker, and Mamet's *Lone Canoe* was a famous flop. "You're always going to roll the dice with a new play," says Mosher, in retrospect, "but I thought it was essential for David [Mamet] to have a show on the main stage, and we fooled ourselves into believing it was a good play."

On the other hand, the dice sometimes came up right. Under pressure to produce a Shakespeare play, Mosher in 1983 took up a suggestion from Roche Schulfer, who had become managing director in 1980, and cast *The Comedy of Errors* with the Flying Karamazov Brothers, a counterculture vaudeville act that gave the production a burst of zany energy. (For the occasion, the busts of classic playwrights perched within niches of the Goodman auditorium's walls were outfitted with false noses, horn-rimmed glasses, and Groucho Marx eyebrows.) Returning again to a reliable classic, Mosher put on *Cyrano de Bergerac,* hiring Michael Maggio, an up-and-coming off-Loop director with no main-stage experience, to direct it. The show was a 1980 box-office hit and a breakthrough production for Maggio.

In the Studio, Mamet's *Glengarry Glen Ross* and *Edmond* maintained the winning Mamet-Mosher collaboration; a triple bill in 1983 offered comedies by Mamet, Shel Silverstein, and Elaine May; and the 1984 pre–New York production of David Rabe's *Hurlyburly,* directed by Mike Nichols, with a star-filled cast of Sigourney Weaver, William Hurt, Harvey Keitel, Cynthia Nixon, Jerry Stiller, Christopher Walken, and Judith Ivey, gave the Goodman a glamorous smash. "Just think," Mosher says. "We brought Nichols and May back to Chicago."

Virgil Johnson, who worked on many of these shows as costume designer, contends that Mosher was "a great impresario," a man able to mix the new and the famous in his lineup of plays. But Mosher, whose success at Stage 2 had gotten him the job of artistic director, was less assured as a main stage director, and his risk-taking policies, despite the occasional hot show, more often than not did not pay off at the box office. He was soon engaged in what he calls "an ongoing warfare with the board."

Jerry Stiller and William Hurt as two denizens of lowlife Hollywood in David Rabe's *Hurlyburly,* directed by Mike Nichols and premiered in the Goodman Studio in 1984
COURTESY OF GOODMAN THEATRE

"Every day I was sure I would get fired," he says. "I thought the board was lazy and didn't want the Goodman to be better, and they thought I was an arrogant son of a bitch. It was impossible. It made me cranky. I was a kid, and I was fighting everybody all the time. Oh, man, I should have taken a deep breath and calmed down."

Things came to a head when Mosher, wanting to increase earned income, decided to move the perennial cash cow of *A Christmas Carol* from the Goodman to the much larger Auditorium Theatre in 1984. "It seemed to me," he says, "that if the Milwaukee Repertory Theater could move their *Christmas Carol* to a bigger house every season, we in Chicago should be able to do that easily."

But the ambition was too great for reality. "We didn't have the resources," Schulfer says. "We didn't have the financial resources, we didn't have the management skill resources."

Trying valiantly for rainbow casting that would reflect the diversity of the city in the traditional holiday show, Mosher put an African American youngster in the role of Tiny Tim, a move that generated a shameful amount of hate mail. (Years later, the theater was still getting the occasional vicious note on the casting of African American and Latino actors in the annual production.)

Practically speaking, as Mosher admits, "We were technically unprepared"—among other things, the turntable designed for the show's scene changes broke down, causing huge overtime labor costs—"and we hadn't done the marketing well enough." Moreover, Schulfer points out, the Goodman had suddenly lost its scene shop, because the Art Institute, which owned the building, sold the property, forcing the theater to job out the work at a much higher cost. That took the Goodman deeper into debt, "an agony" for Schulfer, according to Mosher, and a further cause for conflict between the artistic director and his board.

Some of the stress, Schulfer believes, came "because we were all very young. Greg and I were young, and the board was young, only a few years old in its independence from the Art Institute. We were still learning."

Trying to ease some of the problems, Mosher in 1985 set up the New Theatre Company to do more experimental work independent of the main-stage programming. It produced a Mamet translation of *The Cherry Orchard* and a double bill of two short Mamet plays, *The Spanish Prisoner* and *The Shawl,* which was staged away from the Goodman in the Briar Street Theatre at 3133 N. Halsted Street.

That did not resolve the conflict, but later that year, Mosher removed himself from the field by accepting an offer to become artistic director of Lincoln Center Theater in New York, where he worked until 1991. After several years as an independent director and producer, in 2004 he took on the post of director of the University Arts Initiative of Columbia University, a program designed to heighten arts awareness on the campus. He left Chicago, he says, with mixed feelings, proud of the fact that he had tried to give Goodman "at least a chapter in the history of American theater," and regretting that, "in all my seven years there, nobody on the board ever told me I was doing a good job."

Faced with a seven-hundred-thousand-dollar deficit at Mosher's departure and the need for a new leader, the board narrowed its choice for artistic director to two Chicago directors, Robert Falls and Frank Galati, both of whom had experience with Goodman and were highly regarded veterans of the off-Loop community. In the end, after much

Colin Stinton (below) contemplates his grim future and his menacing cell mate (Paul Butler) in David Mamet's *Edmond* at the Goodman Theatre, 1982.
COURTESY OF GOODMAN THEATRE

agonizing by the board, Falls got the job, with Galati signed on as associate artistic director.

Falls's first season in 1986–87 produced a year that rousingly backed up his promises to investigate musical theater, to present new works, and to "see what Chicago actors can do in big, classic dramas." The first show was Bertolt Brecht's epic *Galileo,* staged with assuring confidence by Falls, with Brian Dennehy in the title role, joining the director for the first of their several rewarding main-stage collaborations. Galati, who had played Pope Urban VIII in *Galileo,* directed a stunning, shimmering presentation of his original work *She Always Said, Pablo,* based on the life and writings of Gertrude Stein. And Maggio triumphantly closed the subscription schedule with the Stephen Sondheim–James Lapine musical *Sunday in the Park with George.* By the end of that season, thanks in part to a five-hundred-thousand-dollar grant from the John D. and Catherine T. MacArthur Foundation and the box-office success of the shows, the theater was showing a surplus.

Not all of Falls's projects worked out that neatly. New prestige works by well-known American playwrights Steve Tesich (*The Speed of Darkness* in 1989 and *On the Open Road* in 1992) and Eric Bogosian (*Griller* in 1998) failed to catch fire, as did Falls's forays into new musicals (*Book of the Night* in 1991 and the expensive, clumsy *Riverview: A Melodrama with Music* in 1992).

In Shakespeare productions, Peter Sellars, the bright, innovative, and constantly controversial director, came up with a 1994 version of *The Merchant of Venice* that featured a racially mixed cast, a battery of television monitors, and a homosexual kiss. It caused a stir at home and in a subsequent European tour. But *Twelfth Night,* staged with a mostly female ensemble by the English writer-director Neil Bartlett in 1992, was an out-and-out disaster. (Lynn Baber, a member of the cast, remembers, "In rehearsals we spent hours barking like dogs and singing 'The Twelve Days of Christmas.' Don't ask me why. The one thing we did not do was read the script.")

The theater suffered a significant loss of artistic spirit with the death of Maggio. A victim of a wasting lung disease, he had made a miraculous recovery after undergoing a double lung transplant in 1991 and was working at full speed in his post of resident director until the summer of 2000, when his body finally failed him. His management skills, his ability to stage large-scale musicals, his deft hand in directing the intricate plays of Tom Stoppard (*Arcadia* in 1996), and his rewarding relationship with playwright Keith Reddin (*Black Snow* in 1993 and *All the Rage* in 1997) were gone with his passing. As the years went by, the contributions to the Goodman by Galati, who increasingly directed and acted mostly with Steppenwolf Theatre, were unfortunately reduced, although he did return to stage the premiere of the musical version of Friedrich Durrenmatt's drama *The Visit* in 2001.

Under Falls's leadership, however, the Goodman increased its scope and its national recognition, winning the 1992 Tony Award for a regional theater. Pushing ahead, Falls dramatically added to what he now called the theater's staff of "resident directors." The diversity that Woodman and Mosher had sought to encourage under the wide umbrella of the Goodman organization was further broadened with the arrival of Chuck Smith and Henry Godinez, Smith through his direction of African American plays and Godinez most prominently through his expert handling of the Latino Theater Festival he inaugurated in 2003.

CHUCK SMITH, DIRECTOR:
"I STICK MY CHEST OUT WITH PRIDE"

I'm black. I grew up in a black community. I was born, raised, and have lived all my life on the South Side. Directing black plays is my choice. But I've always remembered what Theodore Ward, the teacher and playwright and my mentor, told me: "Expand your knowledge. Don't get locked up in one place. There's so much more that you don't know. Go out and find it."

Chuck Smith
FREDRIC STEIN

I started in the midsixties with a group that put on shows for patients at Michael Reese Hospital. That went so well that we expanded into a Black Actors Guild, put on plays at the Parkway Community House. In those days, in the early seventies, I knew every black actor in the city, because there weren't very many of them. These days, I find it hard just to see all the black shows produced in Chicago. If I want to do a black play today, I rarely have to hire outside the city. All the good actors I need are right here, and they're all part of a larger theater community in Chicago. It's fantastic.

I think I always wanted to be in the theater. It seemed the right path for me. But after I got out of school, I still had to earn a living, so for twenty years I worked for the Illinois Department of Public Aid. I earned enough money to set up my daughter as a beautician, and on the day she told me she thought she could support her own business, I quit my job and devoted myself entirely to theater. Now, besides directing, I teach acting at Columbia College.

I first worked at Goodman Theatre as an understudy in 1971. I fell in love with it then, and I had my eye on working there. The time was right for me, because the theater wanted to diversify, and in 1992 I became an artistic associate there. I've worked everywhere, beginning with some of the very early off-Loop theaters, from Chicago Theater Company on the South Side to Victory Gardens on the North Side. I was there at the beginning. I've seen the whole thing happen. I stick my chest out with pride.

Enter the new Goodman team: Michael Maggio, resident director; Robert Falls, artistic director; Frank Galati, associate artistic director

COURTESY OF GOODMAN THEATRE

The young, hot directors David Petrarca and Mary Zimmerman were other welcome new elements in the Goodman "artistic collective" mix. Petrarca's masterful staging in 1996 of *The House of Martin Guerre,* with music and lyrics by the Canadian composer Leslie Arden, gave the theater a substantial, beautifully staged new musical, and Zimmerman brought her splendiferous visual elegance to main-stage productions of *Journey to the West* and *All's Well That Ends Well* in 1995 and *The Odyssey* in 1999. In the studio in 1998, she ingeniously devised a strikingly designed and staged theater piece from *The Notebooks of Leonardo da Vinci.*

And though the main stage did not produce many hits from new works, the little Studio Theatre, a seedbed of creativity from the days of director Patrick Henry in the seventies to the series of Mamet plays in the eighties, yielded two original works of outstanding merit by two relatively unheralded young playwrights.

One of director Mary Zimmerman's stunning stage pictures for *The Notebooks of Leonardo da Vinci*, 1998
COURTESY OF GOODMAN THEATRE

Scott McPherson, a writer whom Falls rightly proclaimed as "a genuine original voice," in 1990 delivered *Marvin's Room*, a family drama of great hilarity, infinite tenderness, and heartbreaking pathos, which was magnificently staged by Petrarca. (McPherson died of AIDS in 1993, the disease robbing us of the wonderful plays he surely had ahead of him.)

Rebecca Gilman took the Studio by storm in 1999 with her *Spinning into Butter*, a play about a white liberal dean of students in an eastern college who runs smack into her own prejudices while investigating a nasty racist incident in her school. Her long second-act monologue confronting her deep-seated dislike of black people, powerfully delivered by the actress Mary Beth Fisher, was, and is, a sensation.

These two shows, which quickly were reproduced all over the country, spread the fame of half of the menu of "classics and new plays" that Falls came to see as the Goodman's agenda. Falls himself directed the 1997 pre-Broadway production of Horton Foote's Pulitzer Prize–winning *The Young Man from Atlanta*, but more and more he turned to the classics (Anton Chekhov's *Three Sisters* in 1995 and Williams's *The Night of the Iguana*, with William L. Petersen and Cherry Jones in revelatory portrayals, in 1994). As with Galati, who had moved into big-bucks Broadway theater with his staging of the epic 1997 musical *Ragtime*, Falls made a commercial killing with his directing and coauthor credits for the Disney production of the 1999 Elton John–Tim Rice musical *Aida*.

James Leaming and Mary Beth Fisher in Rebecca Gilman's *Spinning into Butter,* 2001
COURTESY OF GOODMAN THEATRE

But some of his most important work came when he directed Brian Dennehy in a series of American classics: Eugene O'Neill's *The Iceman Cometh* (1990) and *A Touch of the Poet* (1996) and Arthur Miller's *Death of a Salesman* in 1998. (O'Neill's *Long Day's Journey into Night*, presented with mixed results at the Goodman in 2002, evolved into a major Tony-

Family gathering at Disney World in Scott McPherson's 1990 *Marvin's Room:* Jane MacIver, Lee Guthrie, Laura Esterman, Karl Maschek, Mark Rosenthal
LISA EBRIGHT, AUTHOR'S COLLECTION

winning Broadway production in 2003, with Dennehy and a new cast that included Vanessa Redgrave.)

"It was *Salesman* that really increased our visibility," Falls says. "It all came together with *Salesman*." And it happened in the happiest of ways.

There had been no plans to take the show any farther than the stage of the Goodman. Falls told the cast up front that this was to be strictly a Chicago show; and, at Miller's command, the theater was forbidden from promoting the production as one that would mark the play's upcoming fiftieth anniversary. "All I know," Falls says, "is that I hadn't had such a good time in rehearsal since *Griller* [a flop] the season before."

When the show opened on September 28, 1998, instead of being just another revival of a proven and perhaps tired American drama, it turned out to be a spectacular reassessment and reaffirmation of the play's greatness, with Dennehy, Elizabeth Franz, Kevin Anderson, Ted Koch, and Howard Witt all giving fresh, passionate performances. The production moved to Broadway in 1999, and fifty years after *Salesman* had won the 1949 Tony for best new play and best director (Elia

Elizabeth Franz, Brian Dennehy, and Allen Hamilton in *Death of a Salesman*, 1998
COURTESY OF GOODMAN THEATRE

Playwright and star: Arthur Miller and Brian Dennehy
COURTESY OF GOODMAN THEATRE

Kazan) of the season, this revival won Tonys for Dennehy, Franz, Falls, and the production.

"Who knew?" a bemused Dennehy had asked at a pre-Broadway opening party. "Who knew?" No one had known the show would be such a success, of course, which made its glory all the more surprising and rewarding.

Salesman, which went on to Los Angeles and London engagements, brought Goodman the greatest acclaim in its history. It was also one of the last celebrated productions to be staged in the theater's home in the rear of the Art Institute. Goodman was on the move, and the move was on to downtown.

New and old-made-new-again playhouses brought bright lights and a high-profile mix of classics and commercial productions to the central theater district that began to take shape in the 1990s.

Chapter 21

"The New Theater Capital of the United States"

WHEN PAUL SILLS ENCOURAGED Stuart Gordon to bring his Organic Theater to Chicago in 1970, because, Sills said, "They will leave you alone," he was not entirely correct. The city of Chicago did little to directly subsidize the arts, and Mayor Richard J. Daley never had the reputation of being an arts advocate, but he was not unaware of the value that a flourishing arts scene could bring to the city. He paved the way for building code revisions that made it easier for small theater companies to exist. He had failed to stop the destruction of the Garrick Theatre in 1961, but in the struggle to raise funds for the restoration of the Auditorium Theatre later in the 1960s, he encouraged local big business to donate money for the project. And when the Chicago Symphony Orchestra and its music director Georg Solti returned home from their first overseas tour in October 1971, he threw a huge conquering heroes parade and presented them with a trophy worthy of a Super Bowl champion.

In the following years, Mayors Michael A. Bilandic, Jane Byrne, and Harold Washington each raised public consciousness of the arts in Chicago. In 1984, during Washington's term in office, the Department of Cultural Affairs, with a mandate "to serve the people of Chicago by

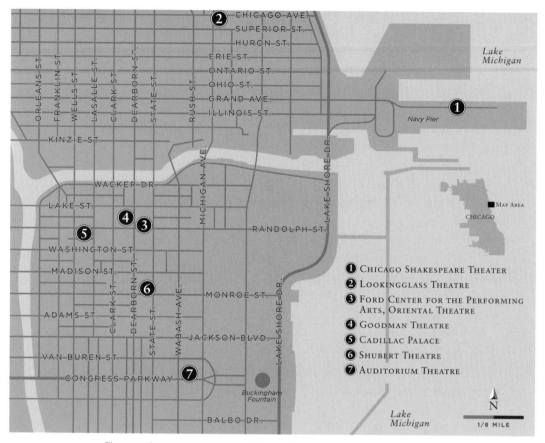

The new downtown territory of Chicago theater
STEVE RAVENSCRAFT

nurturing, enhancing, complementing, and marketing Chicago's cultural resources," was set up as an integral part of city government, with Fred Fine, a sage arts advocate, as its first commissioner.

Daley's son, Mayor Richard M. Daley, first elected to the office in 1989, was acutely aware that good arts help make a good city—and that they generate income. The League of Chicago Theatres, promoting this financial benefit, in 2004 trotted out a commissioned study of the advocacy group Illinois Arts Alliance showing that between 1996 and 2002 the city's live theater industry generated about $823 million in direct spending and that in 2002 alone the theaters had a total economic impact (direct, indirect, and induced spending) of $347 million.

These are statistics that city officials love to see; and in frequent public utterances and campaign remarks, Daley made a point of noting that municipal governments had "come to understand, to appreciate" that the arts are an important part of the city's social and economic fabric. He repeatedly called Chicago's artists "our best ambassadors."

Accompanied by Maggie, his arts-aware wife, Daley took to attending major performing arts events, and in the 1990s he turned his attention to restoring at least some of the old money-generating bustle and the prestige-garnering glamour of the theater scene in the long-neglected Loop.

The Shubert Theatre, erected in 1906 at 22 W. Monroe Street, and the only house of that era still standing in the Loop, had continued in business through the decades, except for the period of 1932 to 1945, when the Depression forced its closing. From 1945 on, first under the Shubert Organization and then, beginning in 1991, under the Nederlanders Organization of New York, it was still booking shows on a fairly regular basis. But in the rest of the downtown area, the theatrical pickings were mighty slim.

An early move toward revival of Loop theater had been made in the 1980s with the reopening of the city's most famous surviving movie palace, the Chicago Theatre at 175 N. State Street. Originally opened in 1921 as the flagship of the Balaban & Katz movie house chain, the 3,500-seat theater had fallen on sad days with the general decline of the downtown business and entertainment district in the 1960s and was threatened with demolition in the 1980s. With financial aid from the city, Chicago Theatre Restoration Associates spent nine months and $25 million to bring back the French Renaissance splendor that the architects George and Cornelius W. Rapp had lavished on the house.

Lewis Manilow, a cultural philanthropist with an interest in drama that dated back to his investment in the Studebaker Theatre Company of the 1950s, saw the Chicago as the possible anchor of a new "Theater Row" area he envisioned for the North Loop. And in 1980 and 1985, city-sponsored studies favorably considered restoration of the Selwyn, Harris, and Woods theaters on Dearborn Street, joining the Chicago as a new hub of activity. But after a flashy September 10, 1986, opening-night program that featured Frank Sinatra, the Chicago, which has a shallow stage, proved hard to book for the large, technically heavy musicals that formed the core of money-making shows on tour. Erratic, infrequent booking led to insolvency, and the downtown area still was without a large theater that could handle the demand for big new pro-

Showtime crowd at the restored Ford Center for the Performing Arts, Oriental Theatre
FREDRIC STEIN

ductions. The Disney organization, after a brief fling at managing the theater, turned over operation to the presenting organization, Chicago Alliance for the Performing Arts, and in 2004, a new group of investors and producers, TheatreDreams, bought the building from the city for $3 million, with a promise to keep the big house lit with a variety of diverse programming.

To give the Loop that aura of nighttime activity that the flashing lights of theater marquees can generate, the scene in the 1990s finally shifted to Randolph Street. Chicago theater had gained its first permanent home in the city with the opening of Rice's Theatre on Randolph Street in 1847, and it was Randolph Street that became the anchor of the newly dubbed "Downtown Theatre District" supported by the Daley administration.

First to reopen there was the 1926 Oriental Theatre, 24 W. Randolph Street, on the site of the old Iroquois Theatre and across the street from where Rice's Theatre had been. Extravagantly designed by the Rapp brothers in what restoration architect Daniel Coffey called "Thai-Baroque," the neglected Oriental had fallen into evil days as a movie house and was in great disrepair, its upper balcony devastated by fire and water damage.

The Oriental project was a joint effort of the city of Chicago and Livent, Inc., a Canadian company headed by producer Garth Drabinsky. The city put up roughly half the $32 million needed to acquire the Oriental Building and the adjoining Butler Building and to transform the old house into a new performing arts center.

Drabinsky had enjoyed success with similar renovation projects in his home base of Toronto, and he had found Chicago a welcoming market for his productions when he brought a lively new version of the Tim Rice–Andrew Lloyd Webber musical *Joseph and the Amazing Technicolor Dreamcoat,* with Donny Osmond, to the Chicago Theatre in the 1990s. He set to work revitalizing the Oriental with his customary passion, proudly showing it off in various states of its renovation. The Ford Motor Company kicked in a few million dollars, and, in return, Drabinsky renamed the building the Ford Center for the Performing Arts, Oriental Theatre.

Drabinsky never got to see the theater reopen, however. He was ousted from his position as head of Livent because of alleged "financial irregularities," and by the time his bountiful production of the musical *Ragtime* officially opened the theater on November 8, 1998, he was completely out of the picture, retreating to Canada and removed from his legal problems in the United States.

The next big movie palace to be converted to a center for live performance was the Palace at 171 W. Randolph Street, a few blocks west of the Oriental. Another house designed by the Rapp brothers (in much less flamboyant French Renaissance style), the Palace, which opened in 1926, had been dormant for several years, used intermittently for banquets, meetings, pop concerts, and boxing matches.

In 1996, the Palace and the adjoining Bismarck Hotel and Metropolitan Office Building were acquired by the Chicago-based PalMet Venture, which renamed the Bismarck the Allegro Hotel and restructured, renovated, and restored the Palace as a 2,250-seat legitimate theater. Total cost for the work on the Palace—renamed the Cadillac Palace,

The shining lights of theater signs brighten up Randolph Street in the revived downtown entertainment district, 2004.

thanks to a large contribution from another automobile manufacturer—was about $24 million, including city funding. The theater, with its newly deepened stage house, officially opened December 9, 1999, with the premiere of *Aida,* a megamusical presented by the Disney organization, with music by Elton John, lyrics by Tim Rice, and staging by Robert Falls.

Even the old Shubert Theatre, part of the "Broadway in Chicago" commercial operation in the Loop, got into the act with a scheduled 2005 rehaul and rechristening as the LaSalle Bank Theatre, named after the refurbishment's corporate sponsor.

~

The first major theater to consider a home in the Loop but the last to fall into place in the revived district was the Goodman, which moved downtown in late 2000 after more than a decade of planning and fund-raising.

Since 1925, the Goodman had been attached to the rear of the Art Institute, its gray, neoclassic, mausoleumlike entrance on Columbus Drive looking like an afterthought to the museum. Its main stage and small studio had housed many ambitious and applauded productions, but in the 1980s, with its staff offices crammed into inhospitable space, its auditorium plagued with tricky acoustics, and its stage lacking facilities to fly scenery, the place was judged inadequate for the Goodman's growing production demands.

The theater management in 1986 announced its intention to move, and in 1990, the Selwyn-Harris-Woods site was officially selected as the Goodman's new home. But it was not until 1998 that construction finally began on the new house. The site picked for the theater was on the west side of Dearborn Street, between Lake and Randolph streets. Part of this strip was occupied by the old (1922), unoccupied Selwyn and Harris, which possessed landmarked terra-cotta façades. In the construction process, these were preserved, but the interiors and the rest of the buildings on the street were demolished to make way for a modern complex containing an 856-seat proscenium house and a smaller, flexible auditorium of about 400 seats. Total cost was about $50 million, $18.8 million of which (a little less than 40 percent) came from city funds.

Predictably, the move downtown meant some wage renegotiations with the stagehands union (International Alliance of Theatrical Stage

Roche Schulfer
COURTESY OF GOODMAN THEATRE

Employees), but after a brief strike in March 2001, the new contract clicked in, and the Goodman's house was in order. The premiere production in the new complex was *King Hedley II,* by August Wilson, the eighth in the playwright's series of dramas dealing with African American life in each decade of the twentieth century. Standing in the spanking-new lobby, taking tickets from the customers for those first performances in December 2000, was Roche Schulfer, Goodman's executive director. Twenty-seven years earlier, he had reported for work at the Goodman box office, and now, here he was, proudly collecting tickets for old times' sake in the new state-of-the-art theater he had guided to completion.

The city's aid in helping to rebuild the downtown theater district was not confined to big houses. The Noble Fool Theater Company, a troupe founded in 1988, received $1 million in city funds for its $2.5 million conversion of the former Old Heidelberg restaurant at 16 W. Randolph Street, just east of the Oriental, into a space that tucked in a 150-seat main stage, a 100-seat studio, and a basement cabaret. The large clock on the façade of the neo-Bavarian building was put back in working order so that it reassuringly chimed on the hour, and the theater, specializing in comedies, opened for business in April 2002, with its late-night, audience-interactive staple, *Flanagan's Wake,* as part of its programming. Two years later, however, in a setback to Loop plans, this modest spot on the new white way went dark. Noble Fool had to shut down the company's Chicago operation, its small theater and uneven programming unable to bring in enough revenue to keep up with big-time downtown expenses, which included $15,000 a month in rent.

In all, the city government put in nearly $60 million for the new/old Randolph Street theaters, plus about $7.7 million more for street decoration and signage heralding the new district. This was small potatoes when compared with the hundreds of millions of dollars poured into other Richard M. Daley–era projects such as the huge, shiny band shell designed by architect Frank Gehry for the downtown Millennium Park and the gargantuan, restructured Soldier Field, south of downtown on

Chicago Shakespeare Theater's main stage on Navy Pier, set up for the production of *Love's Labour's Lost,* 2002
LIZ LAUREN

the lakefront. But the payoff in consumer spending that came with this newly revived entertainment area was big. The Loop would never regain the abundant supply of prime restaurants, nightclubs, and theaters it had housed up to the 1940s, when it stood unrivaled as a center of nightlife activity for the Chicago area; but the restored and new theaters brought back a substantial measure of exciting entertainment activity into the district. And with that excitement came a welcome ripple of after-dark spending.

The Loop, however, was not the only choice location singled out for a theater scene. And now, the city not only provided funding; it provided the space.

Since its founding by director Barbara Gaines in 1986, Shakespeare Repertory of Chicago had maintained a steady artistic and administra-

Scene from director Gary Griffin's galvanizing revival of *Pacific Overtures* in Chicago
Shakespeare Theater's studio theater, 2002
MICHAEL BROSILOW

tive growth. Changing its name to Chicago Shakespeare Theater (CST),
it had mounted a series of crisp, confident productions on a thrust stage
it had heroically fashioned in the initially ill-equipped, barnlike auditorium of the Ruth Page Center at 1016 N. Dearborn Street. Audience size
and acclaim increased rapidly, and in the midnineties, Gaines and executive director Criss Henderson went looking for a new home that would
house their needs for top-flight production facilities.

At first, they looked at the underused Royal George Theatre at 1641
N. Halsted Street, a commercial house just across the street from Steppenwolf, which real estate developer Royal Faubion had opened in 1986
and which had been struggling ever since. The Shakespeare team's plan
was to gut the interior and install a thrust-stage theater for their shows.
But in the midst of these plans they got an unexpected call from James
Reilly, then chief executive officer of the Metropolitan Pier and Exposition Authority, the municipal organization that owns and manages
both the McCormick Place convention center on the South Side and

Navy Pier, the patchwork complex that juts east into Lake Michigan from Grand Avenue and offers shops, restaurants, fast-food stands, boat rides, a carousel, a Ferris wheel, pushcarts, the Chicago Children's Museum, an IMAX movie theater, exhibition halls, the open-air Skyline Stage for pop concerts, and conservatory gardens.

Reilly, a man of some taste and intelligence, wanted a class-act attraction to place amid the commercial clutter of the Pier, and when plans for installing a new music and dance theater fell through, he turned to Shakespeare. Wary of the offer at first, and fearing that the Pier would be way out of the loop for their theater, Gaines and Henderson persuaded Reilly to fly over to England with them to attend a performance in the Royal Shakespeare Company's intimate thrust-stage Swan Theatre at Stratford-on-Avon so that he could see the kind of theater they wanted. Badly jet-lagged, Reilly steadfastly sat through *Cyrano de Bergerac* in the Swan, and on his return to Chicago, having been convinced that the Pier could accommodate CST's needs, he came up with an offer impossible to refuse. The Authority (McPier, for short) would put up $18.2 million in building and design fees, while CST contributed $13 million for construction fees, an endowment, and increased production costs.

One year later, on October 22, 1999, with a large new vertical outdoor sign announcing its presence, CST opened its handsome new six-story home with Gaines's staging of *Antony and Cleopatra*. The early reservations about the viability of Shakespeare on Navy Pier were quickly supplanted by astonishment at its immediate success. Its budget went from $3 million in its final (1998–99) season at the Page Center to $12.4 million for the 2004–5 season on the Pier, with a burgeoning subscription list of twenty-two thousand subscribers. In addition to the three main-stage productions, the theater offered shows in its two-hundred-seat, sixth-floor studio, one of which, director Gary Griffin's sublime miniature staging of the Stephen Sondheim–John Weidman musical *Pacific Overtures,* was restaged in 2003 by Griffin in London at the Donmar Warehouse, winning an Olivier Award as best musical production.

Further expanding its range with shrewd networking and on a scale that took on festival proportions, CST also took to showcasing work from abroad, bringing in and restaging productions that had originated at Shakespeare's Globe Theatre in London, the Stratford Festival of Canada, the Comédie-Française of Paris, and the Abbey Theatre of Dublin. Directors Peter Brook, Mark Rylance, Brian Bedford, and

Lawrence E. DiStasi, on stilts, as the hero of Lookingglass Theatre's *Metamorphosis*, adapted from the story by Franz Kafka, 2000

MICHAEL BROSILOW

Edward Hall all came in to praise the space. Bedford called it "a perfect jewel of a theater."

"Incredible," said Gaines, marveling at her powerhouse on the Pier. And she was right.

Back on mainland, and on prized real estate, another new theater space was created in, of all places, the former boiler room of the pumping station of the Chicago Water Works at 821 N. Michigan Avenue.

Built in 1869, the limestone pumping station and the crenelated Water Tower across the street on the west side of Michigan Avenue had survived the Great Fire of 1871 and were now Chicago landmarks. The Water Works still functioned as a pumping station for the city's water supply, but, in addition, it housed a small pizza-and-sandwich restaurant and a visitors' information center. When a low-end "see Chicago" tourist show was moved out, it also had an empty space that caught the attention of Lois Weisberg, commissioner of the Chicago Department of Cultural Affairs since 1989. Weisberg, a canny veteran of politics and the arts, had a history of involvement in Chicago theater. She had played theater games with Viola Spolin; she had taught theater at the annual summer Harand Camp in Beaver Dam, Wisconsin, which, under the guidance of the sisters Sulie and Pearl Harand, trained youngsters in music, dance, and drama; and in the 1950s she had organized the Shaw Society of Chicago, celebrating the work of George Bernard Shaw in its programs and productions. In her post as cultural commissioner, she set up a basic studio theater for use by small nonprofit groups in an interior space just off the 77 E. Randolph Street entrance to the Chicago Cultural Center, and across the street, at 66 E. Randolph Street, she had established in 2000 a ninety-nine-seat black box theater in the city-sponsored Gallery 37 Center for the Arts, a home for arts education for high school students.

A shrewd promoter and a consummate absorber and dispenser of good ideas, she believed that the Water Tower Water Works was a fine spot for a theater in the cushy shopping-restaurant-hotel area of North Michigan Avenue. And the group that seemed a likely choice for the place was the aspiring, exceptional Lookingglass Theatre, an innovative not-for-profit troupe without a permanent home but with sterling Chicago credentials and all the marks of a classic Chicago theater success story.

The troupe, organized in 1988, took its name from a 1987 production of director Andre Gregory's version of *Alice through the Lookingglass*, which they had created while they were students at Northwestern University and subsequently had taken to the Edinburgh Festival. There were eight founding members. David Catlin, one of them, says, "We were attracted to the strong physicality and presentational styles of the Cirque du Soleil and Pilobolus dance group. That's the kind of daring theater we wanted to be."

Like many young Chicago theater artists before and after them, they lived a precarious existence. They moved from space to space, doing double duty as carpenters, designers, and electricians as they set up their performance areas. For a time, they created a bustling little cultural center called Edge of the Lookingglass in a storefront at 62 E. Thirteenth Street. (The Smashing Pumpkins played there early in the rock group's history.) They ate microwaved burritos from a nearby Amoco service station, and they survived, according to company member Philip R. Smith, "through the power of brute force and stupidity." David Kersnar, a founding member, "seemed to float up in a cloud of blue smoke," Catlin says, referring to a short-circuit accident that occurred while Kersnar was working on an electric wiring hookup. Realizing that their high-ceilinged space had poor acoustics, they hired an "acoustician" whose solution was to spray a dense foam into the rafters. This didn't improve the acoustics much, and it caused a stinging in the eyes for actors and audiences alike.

Their early shows were barely attended. Mary Zimmerman, a few years ahead of them as a graduate student when they were all at Northwestern, joined the troupe and in 1990 reproduced the four-and-a-half-hour version of *The Odyssey* she had first directed at N.U. "We were really shaken up by it," Catlin says, but at many a performance, the fourteen actors onstage outnumbered the people in the audience. "On a good night," Catlin recalls, "our stage manager would tell us that there was a customer for every actor in the cast."

But they went on. They made their first strong mark on the theater scene in 1990 with an imaginative and stirring adaptation of Upton Sinclair's 1906 novel *The Jungle*, directed by founding member David Schwimmer. It was indeed a daring project, with actors hung by their heels to represent the animal carcasses in the hellish stockyards.

Presented in the large, open warehouse space of Chicago Filmmakers at 1229 W. Belmont Avenue, the production had a grand, epic sweep in its staging, unusual for such a young director.

Schwimmer, who early on longed for the main chance, soon left for Los Angeles, where his pursuit of film and television work led to fame and riches for his acting in the TV series *Friends*. The glamour of his career gave Lookingglass a touch of the alluring star quality that Steppenwolf has enjoyed, and, for his part, Schwimmer steadfastly supported the home team with generous financial contributions and, in 1998, with an acting turn, taking the title role in an adaptation of Fyodor Dostoyevsky's *The Idiot*.

Zimmerman, meanwhile, became the company's star director, her talent certified by a MacArthur Foundation "genius" grant. She came

Joe Sikora as a white suburban boy tryng vainly to do the urban hip-hop thing in *Race: How Blacks and Whites Think and Feel about the American Obsession*, premiere production at the new Lookingglass Theatre, June 2003
MICHAEL BROSILOW

from a family of academics, her mother being a specialist in the works of George Sand and an avid reader of Marcel Proust. At Northwestern, Zimmerman had studied under Frank Galati, who, in turn, had studied under Robert Breen, an early advocate of "chamber theater," a form in which works of literature that had not been originally meant for the theater were adapted for the stage. Much of Zimmerman's work reflected these literary and scholarly influences, but to them she added her special gift for creating stunning stage pictures. In her 2000 *Eleven Rooms of Proust,* mounted in a series of different spaces in an empty North Side warehouse, for example, she staged scenes from the author's monumental *Remembrance of Things Past* that were nothing short of ravishing in their use of sculpted space and brilliant color.

Scene from director Mary Zimmerman's fairy-tale
fantasy *The Secret in the Wings*, 2003
MICHAEL BROSILOW

She gave Lookingglass a box-office boost in 1992 with her lush, mystical adaptation of *The Arabian Nights*, and in 1998 she produced a great success with her serenely beautiful staging (around a clear blue wading pool) of Ovid's *Metamorphoses*. Extended at length in Chicago at the Ivanhoe Theatre, it went on to score a big hit in New York and earned her the 2002 Tony Award as best director of a play.

Lookingglass's glory was not limited to producing a TV star and an award-laden director, however. In 1994 in the Goodman Theatre Studio, actor-writer Bruce Norris's *Up against It* captured the antic fun of the unproduced Beatles screenplay (by Joe Orton) on which it was based. In 2001, company member Heidi Stillman's smartly adapted version of *Hard Times* in the Ruth Page Center emerged as a production, partly set in a traveling circus, that stands favorable comparison with the best of Charles Dickens stage adaptations.

Allowing for an occasional flop (*Her Name Was Danger . . .* in 1999) among its mostly original works, Lookingglass also kept up a high average of smashingly staged plays (often with the considerable aid of scenic designer Daniel Ostling), and it remained true and faithful to its roots in works about such Chicago heroes as the novelist Nelson Algren and the architectural photographer and preservationist Richard Nickel. The premiere production on the open stage of the Water Works, on June 14, 2003, featured splendid ensemble work in a theatrically liberating adaptation by company members Schwimmer and Joy Gregory of *Race: How Blacks and Whites Think and Feel about the American Obsession,* by the venerable Chicago author Studs Terkel, the same man who had started his own career in the theater with the Chicago Repertory Group in the 1930s.

It cost $8 million to get Lookingglass into its new 250-seat theater (and a small studio), with $1.5 million each contributed by the state and city governments. Once ensconced, the company received a lease on the space, at a dollar a year for up to twenty years.

Of course, as the Noble Fool failure had demonstrated, a handsome new home and a prime central location do not guarantee success. Having moved into a fine new building, you must come up with fine new shows to fill it, and that requires a balance of aesthetics and economics that not every organization, regardless of its street address, can sustain from season to season.

Still, the downtown revival, moved along by government and private funds, brought a fresh, important luster to the city, a luster that Mayor Daley was eager to acknowledge. Speaking in an August 2000 ceremony in front of the Water Tower Works, he said, "Bringing Lookingglass, a company dedicated to creating groundbreaking theater, into our historic treasure, the Water Works, we are celebrating the strength of Chicago's past and the exciting possibilities for our future." Then, in a typical Chicago flourish, he added, "Lookingglass's downtown location will bolster Chicago's growing reputation as the new theater capital of the United States."

It was an exaggeration, and, at the same time, it was an acknowledgment of the importance of indigenous theater in the life of the city. In the small theaters that are the enduring source of youthful creativity, in the grand institutions that have evolved from those small beginnings, and in the reclamation of a prime downtown space as a base for a homegrown troupe such as Lookingglass, we had found and were duly celebrating a theater of our own.

Attending a party heralding the imminent opening of the Water Works space, and noting the anticipated arrival in 2005 of producer Tony DeSantis's 560-seat commercial theater in the nearby Water Tower Place complex, I blithely said to Mary Zimmerman, "Well, it looks like this year we're in for another renaissance."

"Oh, Richard," she said, with a knowing smile, "in Chicago, it's always a renaissance."

What began as a small cluster of youthful troupes has grown into a major industry of
resident theaters, each one reaching out for support and subscribers.

Chapter 22

"They've Become Institutions"

"Renaissance" is not a word to be tossed around casually, and, in truth, there were times when the people who soldiered on in the day-to-day work of theater in Chicago felt that "renaissance" was much too grand a term for what they were doing.

Robert Shook, whose career as a lighting designer began in the early 1970s, says, for example, "A lot of what we did was bad. We would hear talk about a 'renaissance' in Chicago, and we did have a certain pride of community, but we knew that for every good show we produced, there were four or five that were not so hot. I wondered when we would be found out; I was always worried that next year we would be has-beens."

Still, renaissance or not, the work went on, driven by the same kind of fierce energy that has amazed (and sometimes appalled) visitors to Chicago since the city's beginnings. The drive that brought the city and its theater life to a dizzy height of activity at the end of the nineteenth century, and the daring and determination that had fostered Hull House and the Little Theatre movement in the early part of the twentieth century, were still in the air in midcentury, when a new generation of theater artists took control of the city stages. Perhaps, as Gregory Mosher

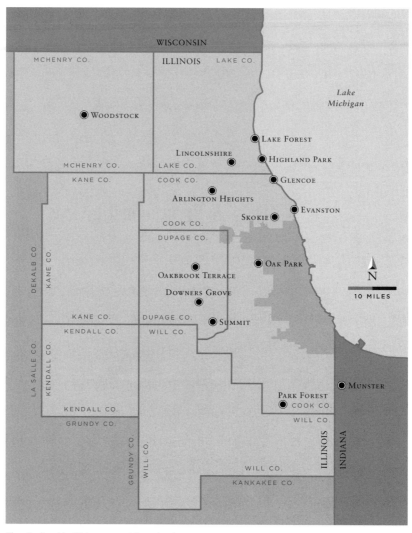

Theaterland in Chicago and its suburbs
STEVE RAVENSCRAFT

suggested, this energy spilled over from the protest movement of the late
1960s, but wherever it came from, it engendered a commitment to a theater community that is extraordinary.

Theater, being an integral part of community life, is bound to follow the fortunes of the city. The millions invested in restoration of Loop
theaters in the 1990s was made possible in great part by the boom of

the general economy. And the widespread trauma caused by the 9/11 terrorist attacks of 2001 was given as a possible reason for a lag in subscription sales from customers uncertain about committing to a schedule. But in Chicago, in good times and bad, the shows—of every quality—continue to appear and the new theaters do keep popping up. The boundaries of the community have moved out from a small circle centered on the city's North Side to a string of enterprising theaters extending from Apple Tree Theatre in north suburban Highland Park to the Illinois Theatre Center in south suburban Park Forest. The shows—of every quality—continue to appear.

The artistic menu of white middle-class realism has been diversified by a strong mix of African American groups: Chicago City Players, the eta Creative Arts Foundation, and the Black Ensemble and Congo Square theaters, among others. Under the leadership of director Henry

Dennis Zacek, Martha Lavey, and Robert Falls, artistic directors of Victory Gardens, Steppenwolf, and Goodman theaters, respectively, holding their Tony Awards for excellence in regional theater
COURTESY OF LEAGUE OF CHICAGO THEATRES

Godinez, projects such as the Goodman's Latino Theater Festival are stirring up interest in that important, neglected field; and fledgling groups, including the Silk Road Theatre Project, are devoting work to plays of Asian, Middle Eastern, and Mediterranean backgrounds.

The evolution of resident theater since 1960 is certainly not unique to Chicago. Nor is Chicago a utopia of pure-minded artistry. As elsewhere, the tour buses here spill out customers for such durable franchise entertainments as *Tony n' Tina's Wedding* at the low end and *Blue Man Group* at the high end. The long-run champion of Chicago shows, before its home, the old Blackstone Hotel, was closed down for building code violations, was *Shear Madness,* an audience interactive mystery comedy that was cutting-edge only in its campiness.

Yet through sheer size, in its wide variety and deep diversity, Chicago has become preeminent. It is a big city, bigger than Seattle or Minneapolis or Boston, or any other city with an indigenous theater scene of distinction, and because it's so big, it can contain more of everything, including theater.

And this scene continues to grow. In 1979, when the League of Chicago Theatres was founded as an advocacy organization for groups large and small, it had forty-three members. In 1990, the number grew to a hundred, and in 2004, its twenty-fifth anniversary, the League boasted 156 members.

In this time period, the Chicago theater community went through a world of changes. It rose from up-and-coming status to an almost mythical reputation as a center of creativity. It saw the rise and fall of scores of theaters and at the same time the near-miraculous ascension of some small, scrappy theaters into large, prestigious organizations.

As the years rolled out, actors who had started out as youngsters tipped into middle age, a fact that Lookingglass Theatre discovered in 2003 when its once-limber original ensemble of 1988 had to strain a little to deliver the athletic zest that had defined the troupe in its first, youthful stages.

Key theaters such as Wisdom Bridge and the Body Politic failed and vanished, while others zoomed into amazing success. Steppenwolf Theatre moved from a church basement to a state-of-the-art home of its own, and Chicago Shakespeare Theater's productions went from a pub's rooftop to an elegant courtyard theater on Navy Pier.

Virgil Johnson, whose work as a costume designer began with many of the early storefront operations, looks back in wonder at such cases. "They've become institutions," he says, "and that makes them very different in their agendas. They're not the same young, independent souls they once were. They have new responsibilities."

Institutionalization has brought greater resources, larger audiences, and increased national prestige to the major resident theaters of Chicago (and everywhere else, for that matter); but success has come at a price. Big budgets have meant big pressure to maintain the subscription base, the heavy-duty management structure, the deep-pockets board members, and the high-tech production values that are associated with top-rank organizations. Always seeking financial support, the theaters lust for big-time individual donors and corporate sponsors for both full seasons and specific productions and programs.

In the process, the dividing line between not-for-profit and commercial theaters has become increasingly blurred. Commercial producers look to the large resident theaters as a cheaper, less stressful haven (with a guaranteed audience of subscribers) for trying out their shows, while the not-for-profit theaters look to the big names attached to these projects as a way to boost attendance.

The large-scale productions that the major institutions present to Chicago audiences make up a key part of theater life in this big city. But the essential strength of theater here continues to lie in the spirit of the off-Loop groups who labor on, taking big risks in their small theaters, producing failures and triumphs alike, and receiving little reward for their pains.

Cookie Gluck, a costume designer, remembers talking to David Mamet about the future of their art when she and the playwright were both very young and just starting out in Chicago theater. As she recalls, Mamet said, "Who do you think will be remembered twenty-five years from now as the great creative forces of our theater? Not the ones who thought only about getting out and cashing in. We'll remember the people who lived in the garage, ate the dog food, and went on with the work because they loved it."

That may be a romantic notion, but it's a convincing argument when one looks at the community of talent that these small theaters have built.

Chicago is a city where theater is produced for the sake of producing theater. In the middle of the country, it has a theater scene removed from the immediate influence of Broadway and the movies. It does not have the high-stakes economy of New York, and it does not have the television- and film-driven business of Los Angeles. What it has is a theater community and people eager to work in that community.

Much of the population of this community receives its training from a generous spread of gifted individual teachers and from local schools, which every year turn out scores of theater majors ready to put their stamp on the scene. The teachers, from early pioneers like Neva Boyd and Viola Spolin to the later mentors Alvina Krause, Bella Itkin, Virgil Johnson, Frank Galati, Mary Ann Thebus, Sheldon Patinkin, and Byrne and Joyce Piven, have been important influences on Chicago performance. Northwestern, DePaul, and Loyola universities and Columbia College all have theater departments that not only train future artists but give valuable additional employment (and income) to theater professionals on their faculties. And although the University of Chicago has never had a theater training program, its alumni list boasts the considerable distinction of containing the core founding members of The Second City.

The flow of young talent from these schools directly into the theater community has been constant and immediate. To Charles Newell, who came to Chicago in 1994 as the new artistic director of Court Theatre at the University of Chicago, such a youth movement was astounding. After graduating from college, Newell says, "I grew up on the regional theater circuit. I worked at Hartford Stage, the Arena Stage in Washington, D.C., the Guthrie Theatre in Minneapolis. It was a mentoring process, where I could learn from the senior directors there. But what I saw in Chicago was very different. Here, the graduating classes would get out of school and then found a theater, right away. There was no waiting, no middle stage. Every year, they reinvented the wheel, jumping right in and making the same old mistakes, but with incredible energy."

This procession of instant entry has led to a heavily homegrown succession of leadership in Chicago. The artistic directors of the city's top three theaters—Robert Falls at Goodman, Martha Lavey at Steppenwolf, and Barbara Gaines at Chicago Shakespeare Theater—all started their careers in Chicago and worked their way up to their top positions in the 1980s and 1990s. It is the same on every level of work. John Morris, a prime architect of theater spaces, Steppenwolf and Lookingglass among them, got his start as a carpenter at Goodman Theatre. Shook, who got his first jobs as a lighting designer in tiny off-Loop theaters, later founded a firm that lights up monumental building façades and sculpture installations.

Program for the first season of the International Theatre Festival of Chicago

AUTHOR'S COLLECTION, USED BY PERMISSION OF *PLAYBILL*

The strength of the Chicago orientation and its dominance in every aspect of theater has its downside, as well. There's a danger of becoming insular, of not learning enough from the resources of the great world outside. The International Theatre Festival of Chicago, produced every two years from 1986 to 1994, was an intense, full-out attempt to stage productions from around the world in Chicago and to enlarge the theater horizons of the audiences and artists of the city. It presented large-scale presentations by the National Theatre of Great Britain, Kenneth Branagh's Renaissance Theatre Company, and the English Shakespeare Company, along with experimental work by Robert Wilson and Robert LePage and smaller, brilliant troupes from Lithuania, Greece, Mexico, Israel, Ireland, South Africa, and Spain. But it had to close down, according to Jane Nicholl Sahlins, its cofounder and executive director, in large part because of insufficient initial capitalization and the vexing lack of a yearly presence in the city. (In the beginning, there also was resistance from some Chicago theaters, who saw the festival as a competing force for funding and box-office dollars.)

There have since been efforts by other organizations—Performing Arts Chicago, the Museum of Contemporary Art, and the Chicago Humanities Festival—to continue the importation of international attractions to the city, and Chicago Shakespeare Theater wisely brought in outside directors, actors, and theater groups from abroad to complement its own distinctive Chicago style in performance. The rambling old Athenaeum Theatre, 2936 N. Southport Avenue, thanks to the persistent, year-by-year efforts of producer Fred Solari, has become a home for offices and small performance spaces of not-for-profit theaters, as well as the scene of an annual local dance festival in its nine-hundred-seat main-stage auditorium and an occasional theater import. And there have been some individual donors of significant impact, including Hope Abelson, a former Broadway producer and an abundant source of support for local theaters since the 1960s, and Merle Reskin, a former actress, who has given generously to several organizations. (The Blackstone Theatre at 60 E. Balbo Drive, was renamed the Merle Reskin Theatre in 1992, in honor of the funding her husband provided to preserve the theater and keep it as a performance space for the Theatre School of DePaul University.) But in Chicago, there is a lack of leadership in the essential, big-deal corporate financing and bold individual entrepreneurship that could set up an operation along the lines of the Brooklyn Academy of Music, bringing in national and international theater presentations of major importance (and major cost).

The talent drain continues. Broadway and Los Angeles are always lures for gifted artists who have grown up in Chicago. Maintaining a decent lifestyle is not easy on Chicago theater wages, and although youth and ambition can get an artist past the first few years of existence, "Sooner or later," as actress-director Amy Morton has succinctly put it, "you get tired of eating macaroni and cheese."

At the peak of his acclaimed work as a Chicago actor in the 1980s, Denis O'Hare said, "My head is beginning to hit the ceiling here." So he moved to New York, becoming a highly regarded, consistently employed actor there—and winner of the 2003 Tony Award for best featured actor in a play (*Take Me Out,* by Richard Greenberg).

Still, the migration has slowed down, and, despite the drain, the talent pool has deepened. When the Goodman Theatre in 2003 mounted the large and excellent Edward Albee Festival of plays and special events, it had the home-based resources to do so with an all-Chicago lineup of top-notch directors and actors.

In the old days, graduates would take off for the East or West Coast with barely a moment of work done in Chicago. Now, though the city is still a jumping-off place, it is also a home base. Promising juveniles have grown into respected character actors. Directors, designers, and actors have spent their whole careers in Chicago, buying houses, raising families, and founding theaters. Directors Galati and Zimmerman and actors Mike Nussbaum and John Mahoney, among others, have careers that lead them to other cities and bigger paychecks, but they prefer to make their homes in the Chicago area. And so do some of the older artists who, after years away, return to continue work in their home city. Howard Witt, an actor who had attended the Goodman School of Drama in the 1950s but had spent most of his career far from Chicago, came back to the city in 1993, enjoying a series of rich, ripe character roles that the community's theaters could offer him.

Curious about the tales of opportunities in Chicago, young theater people in the United States and abroad have migrated to the city, plunging into the stream of activity with the eagerness of those to the city born. They learn that the city's newspaper reviewers will pay attention to productions in the smallest theaters, and they discover that Chicago audiences, who love to see big stars on big stages, are nonetheless open to new work and new players. There may be less sophistication among the audiences, but there's less cynicism too.

There are strong, valid reasons for living and working in this city. Prominent among them is the ever-present feeling of "community" (a word you will hear often in Chicago). Along with the competition, there is a real familial sense of caring and sharing, which gives individuals a concern for and interest in what other artists are doing. Perhaps this comes, in part, from the Chicago tradition of improvisation, which demands trust and cooperation among actors working together toward the same ensemble goal.

Above all, there is a "commitment" to "the work" (two more terms often repeated in Chicago) which allows the aspiring theater artist to learn by doing. "I came back for the work," says Damon Kiely, artistic director of the American Theater Company. A Chicago boy, he had moved to the opportunities of New York, involving himself in the management of off-Broadway theaters there. But, he says, "In New York, it was all about waiting for the next big thing. I didn't want to wait around for that. I wanted to be part of an ensemble. I wanted to do the work, and Chicago lets you do the work."

Morton, a Chicago actress from the very start of her career, tells younger artists who are new to the scene, "You're not going to become famous here, and you're not going to become rich, so you might as well do good work. Hone your craft. You don't have anything to worry about except doing the work." Of course, there is always the hope of grabbing

BRETT NEVEU, PLAYWRIGHT:
"WE ALL SUPPORT EACH OTHER"

I was born in California, raised in Iowa, and studied theater at the University of Iowa in Iowa City, which is where I met my wife, Kristen, an artist. After graduation in 1992 we went to Minneapolis, and I worked with the Playwrights Center there. But playwrights I knew, like my friend Rebecca Gilman, kept telling me to come to Chicago. "You can get produced here," they said. "You'll get reviewed here." That sounded good, and we moved to Chicago.

Brett Neveu
FREDRIC STEIN

To earn a living, I worked at a lot of different places, including Uncle Fun, the novelty shop on Belmont Avenue. To get started in theater, I continued something I carried over from Iowa City. It was called the No Shame Theater. You just get up in front of an audience and do your act. I came on carrying my suitcase, took out my little boxes of props, and did basically an adult puppet show, with characters ranging from a bunny rabbit to a monkey on a stick. The shows were a combination of Dadaism, *The Muppet Show, Laugh-In,* and plain old potty-mouth antics. Then I started getting short plays produced at events like the Coyote Arts Festival, the Bailiwick Director's Festival, the Aardvark's Estrogen Fest, and Collaboraction Theater Company's Winter Sketchbook. In 1997, I joined Chicago Dramatists, a great place for playwrights to develop their work, and since then I've had a pretty steady run of plays presented in Chicago at the Aardvark, Factory Theatre, Stage Left, A Red Orchid, Terrapin, and American Theater Company. I've gotten commissions from Goodman and Steppenwolf, which is really unusual, to have both those big theaters asking you to write for them.

I love working in Chicago. This community gives you so much. In New York, it's "What do you want from me?" and in Los Angeles, it's all about money. But in Chicago, we're all on the same playing field. We all help each other, we all support each other, we all look out for each other. The end is to make good theater.

the brass ring. "Do I think about Broadway?" director Lou Contey asks, rhetorically. "Every day. But I want to get there on my own terms, with my own show. Meanwhile, there is the work in Chicago. I can find my voice here."

Broadway, meanwhile, is eager to sell its shiny wares to audiences in Chicago. Clear Channel and the Nederlander Organization, powerful New York–based firms, in the late 1990s between them gained control of the three large Loop commercial houses—the Shubert, Cadillac Palace, and Ford Center for the Performing Arts, Oriental Theatre— and imported virtually all the big touring shows to those houses for their "Broadway in Chicago" seasons, adding the Auditorium Theatre to their booking venues in 2003. They also used their theaters as testing grounds for Broadway-bound musicals, giving Chicago customers a first look at *Aida* (1998) and *The Producers* (2001) at the Cadillac Palace and *Sweet Smell of Success* and *Movin' Out* (both 2002) at the Shubert. (The not-for-profit Goodman also got into this game, acting as host for tryouts of *The Visit* in 1999 and *Bounce* in 2003, both musicals with blue-ribbon pedigrees that aimed—unsuccessfully, as it turned out—for New York productions.)

The big shows that do the big business in the big downtown houses are almost all New York enterprises. Some plays (*Glengarry Glen Ross*) and musicals (*Grease*) that started small in Chicago have returned home in touring productions. But Chicago's artistic and economic strength in the theater remains anchored in its small and midsize troupes. And if the fame and fortune of Broadway don't materialize in Chicago, then neither do its disastrous financial failures. It's possible to fail, and fail again, and still go on to score a success. One flop does not kill a career.

There are still plenty of low-rent storefronts that can be turned into theaters; and if those should happen to be in short supply, small Chicago troupes have shown that they can use such varied venues as restrooms, saloons, and even automobiles as performance spaces. As Zimmerman, who lives in Evanston and teaches at Northwestern, says, "We're in an ideal theater town, because, for one thing, it's significantly less expensive to produce here."

Sometimes, however, the desire to break away, to produce without stinting, to roll the dice in a daring gamble, is too great. Patricia Cox Hunckler, one of the earliest and savviest marketing experts to emerge

The cast of Steppenwolf Theatre's 1980 staging of Lanford Wilson's *Balm in Gilead*, lined up for a group portrait onstage in the old Jane Addams Center of Hull House, 3212 N. Broadway. In its gritty majesty, in its strength of ensemble playing, in its significant impact on the city's reputation as an arts center, it embodied the glory of work in the Chicago theater community.

LISA EBRIGHT, SPECIAL COLLECTIONS AND PRESERVATION DIVISION, CHICAGO PUBLIC LIBRARY

in the theater scene of the 1970s, cautions, "Small theaters get to the point where they want to rock out, to do something bigger. It's okay to take risks, but if you don't have the financial cushion to fall back on, you can go out of business very quickly."

In Chicago, the way to become big is to start small. You pay your dues; you learn your craft; you have your hits and your flops; you persevere. And sometimes, if you're good enough and smart enough and lucky enough, the audience finds you and supports your work, and you outgrow your small status and move on to greater challenges.

The theater artists of Chicago are ambitious, of course. They want a brighter career, a more generous lifestyle. But they are at their best when, in the great Chicago mode, they are focused on the work at hand and not the prospects ahead, however tempting those prospects might be.

The Goodman's 1998 production of *Death of a Salesman* was not intended as a Broadway show. It was created as another piece of work to be done in Chicago. Yet in one of those happy instances that keep people talking about an ongoing Chicago renaissance, the work became something wonderful, and it moved from the Goodman to a triumphant Broadway reception.

In the middle of a celebration for the show's arrival in New York in 1999, Bob Falls stood amid a crowd of hometown partygoers who had traveled to Manhattan for the event and, in a glorious bit of imagery, told them, "Well, here we are on Broadway. It's the icing on the cake.

"But always remember, Chicago is the cake."

SCORES OF PEOPLE GRACIOUSLY GAVE of their time and resources in order to make this book happen. Many of them contributed directly to the history through their memories and insights, which are recorded in the preceding pages. Many others worked, often in unexpected ways, to help shape the content and design of the final product. Throughout, amazingly generous goodwill and support for the work always came eagerly from old friends and new acquaintances alike. To all of them the author extends his deepest thanks.

A Theater of Our Own, for starters, stems from a four-part series of retrospective articles I wrote just before stepping down as chief critic of the *Chicago Tribune* in March 2002. Put together as "40 Years on the Aisle," the series appeared in the *Tribune*'s Sunday Arts section, beautifully designed and packaged under the guidance of the section's editor, Linda Bergstrom. Although very little of the wordage of the series has carried over, it made this book possible.

Susan Betz, editor of Northwestern University Press, saw the articles, asked me if I would like to turn them into a book, and sent me on my way, with irresistible encouragement and enthusiasm, into a project that ended up being much larger and far more exciting than I had ever envisioned. One of the pleasures of the two years of hard work and great fun that went into the book has been working with her and the N.U. Press staff.

As the manuscript moved along, it received additional attention from several friends: Margie Korshak, whose instincts for shepherding the book to publication and marketing were unfailingly accurate; Tim Samuelson, cultural historian of the Chicago Department of Cultural

Affairs; Stephen Kercher, assistant professor of history at the University of Wisconsin, Oshkosh; and Lois and Wayne Wille, whose editorial judgment and knowledge of Chicago history were invaluable.

The extensive research resources for the history include staff members of the Chicago Historical Society, Theatre Historical Society of America, and the Department of Special Collections of the University of Chicago Library, with special care given by Diana Haskell of the Newberry Library, Marj Halperin of the League of Chicago Theatres, and, above all, from Elizabeth Holland, Glenn E. Humphreys, and Constance Gordon of the Special Collections and Preservation Division of the Chicago Public Library. Press officers of individual theaters who inexhaustibly provided data are Cindy Bandle, Jay Kelly, Alida Szabo, Cathy Taylor, Beth Silverman, Noreen Heron, and William Massolia.

The illustrations, some of them rare and reprinted here for the first time in decades, came from many sources.

Among the institutions tapped for photos were: the New York Public Library for the Performing Arts, the University of Michigan at Ann Arbor Library, the Associated Press/World Wide Photos, and the *Chicago Tribune*, where Debra K. Bade, editor of News Research and Archive, and her staff members were models of courtesy and efficiency.

Individual photographers who freely dug into their archives are Jennifer Girard, Michael Brosilow, Lisa Ebright, and Donna Dunlap. Fred Stein, a colleague from my good old *Chicago Daily News* days, took several new, sharp pictures especially for the book, and Steve Ravenscraft helped set the scene by designing pinpoint locator maps.

Tracking down illustrations turned into something of a treasure hunt, with new riches regularly unearthed. Theater programs from the collections of Patricia Moore, Jay Marshall, Elayne LeTraunik, Joseph R. DuciBella, and Kip Kelley were a gold mine of information on the city's theater life, dating back to the 1890s. John H. Scharres, managing director of the Woodstock (Illinois) Opera House, loaned out the very rare photo of nineteen-year-old Orson Welles as Claudius in *Hamlet*. Gilbert Johns, an old and dear friend, took time out from a holiday in Paris to scour the Bibliothèque Nationale de France in order to find just the right photo of Sarah Bernhardt. And Lawrence DeVine, former theater critic of the *Detroit Free Press*, even came up with a promotional lapel button issued for the premiere of David Mamet's *Lone Canoe* at the Goodman Theatre in 1979.

Finally, a tip of the hat to Twyla Tharp, a choreographer blessed with a keen sense of theater, who unwittingly gave me the go-ahead for this book. I interviewed her in 2002 while she was preparing her production *Movin' Out* for its move from the Shubert Theatre in Chicago to Broadway, and near the end of our talk, she took over and asked me what I was up to. Well, I bumbled, I was thinking of doing a book on the history of theater in Chicago. "Do it," she said. "It's essential."

Now that I've done it, I realize that, as usual, she was right.

Adams, Rosemary K., ed. *A Wild Kind of Boldness: The Chicago History Reader.* Grand Rapids, Mich.: William B. Eerdmans, 1998.

Anderson, Margaret. *My Thirty Years' War: The Autobiography, Beginnings and Battles to 1930.* New York: Horizon Press, 1969.

Andreas, A. T. *History of Chicago, from the Earliest Period to the Present Time.* Chicago: A. T. Andreas, 1886.

Berkowitz, Gerald M. *New Broadways: Theatre across America: Approaching a New Millennium.* New York: Applause Books, 1997.

Brandt, Nat. *Chicago Death Trap: The Iroquois Theatre Fire of 1903.* Carbondale and Edwardsville, Ill.: Southern Illinois University Press, 2003.

Browne, Maurice. *Too Late to Lament.* Bloomington: Indiana University Press, 1956.

Coleman, Janet. *The Compass.* New York: Alfred A. Knopf, 1990.

Cutler, Irving. *The Jews of Chicago: From Shtetl to Suburb.* Champaign: University of Illinois Press, 1996.

Dedmon, Emmett. *Fabulous Chicago.* New York: Athenaeum, 1981.

Dennis, Charles H. *Eugene Field's Creative Years.* Garden City, N.Y.: Doubleday, Page, 1924.

Glover, Lyman B. *The Story of a Theatre.* Chicago: Lakeside Press, 1898.

Gold, Arthur, and Robert Fizdale. *The Divine Sarah: A Life of Sarah Bernhardt.* New York: Alfred A. Knopf, 1991.

Gross, Samuel Eberly. *The Merchant Prince of Cornville.* Cambridge, Mass.: University Press, 1896.

Guzman, Richard, and David Starkey, eds. *Smokestacks and Skyscrapers: An Anthology of Chicago Writing.* Chicago: Wild Onion Books, 1999.

Hatch, Anthony P. *Tinder Box: The Iroquois Theatre Disaster 1903.* Chicago: Academy Chicago, 2003.

Henderson, Mary. *Theater in America: 250 Years of Plays, Players and Productions.* New York: Harry N. Abrams, 1996.

Jefferson, Joseph. *The Autobiography of Joseph Jefferson.* Cambridge, Mass.: Belknap Press of Harvard University Press, 1964.

Kogan, Herman, and Rick Kogan. *Yesterday's Chicago.* Miami, Fla.: E. A. Seeman, 1976.

Kogan, Herman, and Lloyd Wendt. *Chicago: A Pictorial History.* New York: Bonanza Books, 1958.

Larkin, Colin. *The Virgin Encyclopedia of Stage and Film Musicals.* London: Virgin Books, 1999.

Lawrence, Jerome. *Actor: The Life and Times of Paul Muni.* New York: G. P. Putnam's Sons, 1974.

Leonard, Will. *Chicago Stagebill Yearbook 1947.* Chicago: Chicago Stagebill, 1947.

Lewis, Lloyd, and Henry Justin Smith. *Chicago: The History of Its Reputation.* New York: Harcourt, Brace, 1929.

Liebling, A. J. *Chicago: The Second City.* New York: Alfred A. Knopf, 1952.

Lowe, David Garrard. *Lost Chicago.* New York: Watson-Guptill, 2000.

McCabe, John. *George M. Cohan: The Man Who Owned Broadway.* Garden City, N.Y.: Doubleday, 1973.

McNulty, Elizabeth. *Chicago Then and Now.* San Diego: Thunder Bay Press, 2000.

Miller, Donald L. *City of the Century: The Epic of Chicago and the Making of America.* New York: Simon & Schuster, 1996.

Monroe, Harriet. *A Poet's Life: Seventy Years in a Changing World.* New York: Macmillan, 1938.

Morgan, Anna. *My Chicago.* Chicago: Ralph Fletcher Seymour, 1918.

Patinkin, Sheldon. *The Second City: Backstage at the World's Greatest Comedy Theater.* Naperville, Ill.: Sourcebooks, 2000.

Pierce, Bessie Louise. *A History of Chicago, Volume II, From Town to City, 1848–1872.* New York: Alfred A. Knopf, 1940.

Sahlins, Bernard. *Days and Nights at The Second City: A Memoir, with Notes on Staging Review Theatre*. Chicago: Ivan R. Dee, 2001.

Sandrow, Nahma. *Vagabond Stars: A World History of Yiddish Theater*. New York: Harper & Row, 1977.

Schwartz, Bonnie Nelson, ed. *Voices from the Federal Theatre*. Madison: University of Wisconsin Press, 2003.

Seller, Maxine Schwartz, ed. *Ethnic Theatre in the United States*. Westport, Conn.: Greenwood Press, 1983.

Sills, Paul. *Paul Sills' Story Theater: Four Shows*. New York: Applause Books, 2000.

Smith, Alson J. *Chicago's Left Bank*. Chicago: Henry Regnery, 1953.

Spolin, Viola. *Improvisation for the Theater*. Evanston, Ill.: Northwestern University Press, 1999.

Sweet, Jeffrey. *Something Wonderful Right Away*. New York: Limelight Editions, 1987.

Thompson, Slason. *Eugene Field: A Study in Heredity and Contradictions*. New York: Charles Scribner's Sons, 1901.

Thomson, David. *Rosebud: The Story of Orson Welles*. New York: Alfred A. Knopf, 1996.

Viskochil, Larry A. *Chicago at the Turn of the Century in Photographs: 122 Historic Views from the Collections of the Chicago Historical Society*. New York: Dover Press, 1984.

Woll, Allen. *Black Musical Theatre: From Coontown to Dreamgirls*. Baton Rouge: Louisiana State University Press, 1989.

Ford Center for the Performing Arts, 42, 269, 293; crowd at, *268;* location, *266*
Ford Motor Company, 269
Foreman, Richard, 216
Fornes, Maria Irene, 146
Forrest, Edwin, 9
Fortress (sci-fi thriller), 173
Forty-five Minutes from Broadway (Cohan), 42
Forum Theatre, 136, 172
Fosse, Bob, 72
Fosser, William, 145
Four Plays of Today (Aldis), 62
Fox, Raymond, 196
Foy, Eddie, *36,* 36
Frank's Wild Years (Waits), 226
Franz, Dennis, *163, 167,* 196
Franz, Elizabeth, *262,* 262–63
Fredman, Beatrice, 125, 126
Freedom of the City, The (Friel), 30, 179
Free Street Theater, 147–49, 190; performance at, *148*
Friedkin, William, 208
Friedman, Marla, 126
Friedman, Richard, 214
Friel, Brian, 179, 199, 200
Friends (TV series), 279
Fritzel's restaurant, 92
Frogs, The (musical), 244; scene from, *244*
From the Second City (revue), 30, 113
Front Page, The (Hecht and MacArthur), 72
"Funeral," scene from, *113*

Gabor, André, 109
Gaines, Barbara, *202, 236, 237,* 273–75, 277, 288
Galati, Frank, 135, 136, 196, 279; as actor, *199,* 202; as director, 212, 218, 227, 230, 261, 290, (at Goodman) 255–57, *259,* 288
Galileo (Brecht), xi, 256; program, *250*
Gallery 37 Center for the Arts, 277
Galloway, Paul, 207
Galsworthy, John, 44, 48, 49
Game Show, The (Gordon), 161–62
Gamester, The (Regnard), 237; scene from, *236*
Garfield, John, 193
Garland, Hamlin, 59
Garrick Theatre, 21–23, *22, 23,* 55, 265
Garson, Barbara, 136
Gay and lesbian theater, 241–42
Geer, Will, 95
Gehry, Frank, 272
Gelber, Jack, 125, 129
Genet, Jean, 120
German audiences, 55
Gerstenberg, Alice, 62

Getting Out (Norman), 207, 226; playbill, *194*
Ghetto (Sobol), 245–46; scene from, *245*
Ghosts (Ibsen), 53
Gibby's Majestic Grill, 92
Gide, André, 109
Gielgud, John, 64
Gilbert, Lou, *121*
Gilman, Rebecca, 186, 260, 261, 292
Gilpin, Charles, 56
Gilroy, Frank D., 127
Gladiator (Logan), 244
Glass Menagerie, The (Williams), 225–26; review of, 90–91; scene from, *225*
Gleason, Frederick Grant, 21
Glengarry Glen Ross, 30, 183–86, 232, 253, 293; scenes from, *184, 185*
Glickman's Palace Theatre, 54; handbill, *54*
Globe Theater, 19
Gluck, Cookie, 165, 287
Godinez, Henry, 257, 285–86
God of Isaac, The (Sherman), cast of, *202*
God's Man in Texas (Rambo), scene from, *213*
Goldberg, Arthur, 81
Golden Boy (Odets), 83
Goldman, Daniel, 109
Goldman, "Red Emma," 64
Goldsmith, Oliver, 48
Golman, Daniel, 137, 138
Goodman, Benny, 46
Goodman, Kenneth Sawyer, 67–68, *68*
Goodman School of Drama, 76, 79, 291; created (1931), 72; faculty, 94; graduates, 75, 94–95, 108, 138, 145, 147, 206
Goodman Theatre, 193, 258; directors, 147–48, 206, 211, 213, 216, 251, 257, 259–61, 285; entrance to old, *71;* founded, 67–68, 251; location, *266,* 271–72; new (1998), 23; old company, 78; performances at, xi, 138, 183, 186, 202, 244, 249, 252–54, 260–63, 290, 295; playbills, *66, 194, 250;* Stage 2, 179, 180, 182, 222, 251, 253; turns professional (1969), 178–79, 251; tryouts at, *293*
Goodman Theatre Studio, 184, 216, 253, 280
Good Night Ladies, 88
Goodrich, Grant, 3
Gordon, Carolyn Purdy, xv, 162, *163,* 164, 165, 176, *177,* 178
Gordon, David, 167
Gordon, Max, 76, 106
Gordon, Stuart, 117, 189, 201; and Organic Theater, 151,

159, 161–74, *163, 172, 178,* 265
Gordon-Clark, Susan, *170*
Grace Hayward Stock Company, 51
Graham, Jory, 133, 134
Grand Opera House, 20, 29
Grant, Ulysses S., 17
Granville-Barker, Harley, 63, 150
Grapes of Wrath, The (Steinbeck), 30, 230; playbill, *218;* scene from, *231*
Grapey, Marc, 244, *246,* 246
Grease (musical), 30, 152, 154–57, 220, 235, 293; Burger Palace Boys of, *155;* playbill, *144;* scene from, *156*
Great Chicago Fire. *See* Chicago
Great Depression, 72–73, 74, 75–76, 89, 267
Great Northern Theatre, 33, 77, 79, 83, 92
Green, Paul, 66, 82, 251
Greenberg, Richard, 290
Greene, Bob, 207
Gregory, André, 278
Gregory, Lady Augusta, 49, 60
Gregory, Chester II, 241
Gregory, Joy, 280
Griffin, Gary, xvii, 139, 238, 245, 274, 275
Griller (Bogosian), 257, 262
Grizzard, George, 147
Grooms, Red, 217
Gross, Alan, 159, 186, 203
Gross, Samuel Eberly, 29, 31–32
Grotesques (Head), 63; scene from, *62*
Group Creativity Projects, 108
Group Theatre (New York), 82, 83, 193
Guare, John, 217, 252
Guerra, Tom, 141
Guinan, Francis, 226
Guthrie, Lee, 261
Guthrie, Tyrone, 91–92
Guthrie Theatre (Minneapolis), 91, 121, 148

Hagen, Uta, 92
Hailey, Oliver, 199
Hair (musical), 100, 122
Hairspray playbill, *264*
Halberstam, Michael, *237,* 237–38
Hall, Edward, 277
Hall, Kyle, 241
Halpern, Charna, 248
Halpern, Dina, 54
Hamilton, Allen, 262
Hamlet (Shakespeare), 7, 13, 24, 64, 78, *78,* 91, 210, 211
Hammond, Percy, 60, 70
Hampton, Christopher, 226
Hannah and Martin (Fodor), xvii
Hansbury, Lorraine, 91

RICHARD CHRISTIANSEN HAS BEEN an arts journalist for more than forty years, covering theater, dance, film, and the visual arts in Chicago, the nation, and abroad. He began his career in 1956 as a reporter at the City News Bureau of Chicago and moved to the *Chicago Daily News* a year later. In 1978, he joined the *Chicago Tribune* as its critic at large and moved on to become the arts and entertainment editor and, subsequently, chief critic and senior writer, a post he held until his retirement in 2002.